CHILDREN AND ADULTS WITH ATTENTION DEFICIT DISORDERS

ADD and Adolescence: Strategies for Success from CH.A.D.D.

CH.A.D.D.®

Graphic Design by: Filar Design Group, Ltd.
Editorial and Publication Management by: Rosenberg Communications, Inc.

Queries regarding rights and permissions should be addressed to:
CH.A.D.D.
499 N.W. 70th Avenue, Suite 101
Plantation, Florida 33317
phone   954.587.3700
e-mail   http://www.chadd.org/

Printed in the United States of America

Library of Congress Catalog Card Number: 96-71611

ISBN 0-9634875-1-5

Table of Contents

Table of Contents, continued

Introduction

When a group of dedicated and concerned parents and professionals founded Children With Attention Deficit Disorders (CH.A.D.D.) in 1987, the organization's focus was on children. In 1993, responding to a growing need for support and information for adults who have ADD, we changed our name to Children and Adults With Attention Deficit Disorders. Today, we are hearing more and more about a new area of concern: ADD and adolescence. On a regular basis, our members are telling us: "My child is growing up. My child is now a teenager and what worked before doesn't seem to be working now."

CH.A.D.D.'s mission is to better the lives of individuals with ADD and of those who care for them. When we learn from our members that individuals living with ADD and their family members are facing new challenges, one of the most important ways that we try to respond is by providing scientifically-based, cutting-edge information.

Through letters, phone calls, and e-mail messages, CH.A.D.D.'s members have been asking for our help, letting us know that, as their children are growing up, they and their now-teenaged children are confronting new challenges. *ADD and Adolescence: Strategies for Success from CH.A.D.D.* is dedicated to helping teenagers with ADD and their parents address these challenges by providing strategies and tips for:

- managing the increased workload of high school and juggling the varying expectations of different teachers;
- building strong and constructive relationships with peers;
- handling, in a productive fashion, the natural parent-child tensions that come with adolescence; and
- dealing with the many other challenges that confront all teenagers.

In this collection of articles, some of which have appeared in CH.A.D.D. publications or been presented at CH.A.D.D. conferences, and some of which are being published for the first time, parents and educators will find valuable suggestions, information, and strategies for helping teenagers with ADD succeed. You will recognize the writers; they are among the nation's leading experts from the fields of education, psychology, and medicine. You will also find several poignant and insightful first-person stories.

We want to thank everyone who made this book possible, including the individual authors, members of CH.A.D.D.'s Professional Advisory Board, those who contributed introductions to each chapter, and CH.A.D.D.'s National Office Staff. We also want to thank our members, who regularly reach out to us, letting us know how we can continue to be of help.

If you are a teenager who has ADD, we hope that you will be able to apply the skills discussed in this book in your life and that you find a compassionate and sympathetic "voice" in the pages that follow. If you are a parent, educator, or clinician, we hope that this volume, by increasing your understanding of ADD and adolescence, and by providing concrete suggestions, will make a difference in the life of a teenager that you know who has ADD.

CH.A.D.D. National Board of Directors

Foreword

Russell A. Barkley, Ph.D.
University of Massachusetts Medical Center
Worcester, Massachusetts

One of the least-studied age groups of individuals with ADD is that of adolescence. While some information has become available from the handful of follow-up studies tracking hyperactive children into adolescence and adulthood, such research has given us but a glimpse of the myriad difficulties and issues that children with ADD and their families face as the children enter this important phase of physical and psychological development. New theoretical developments in the understanding of ADD suggest that, by this stage of development, children who do not have ADD will have developed the lion's share of their eventual self-control, although even this will continue to progress into their early thirties. Adolescents who do not have this disorder will, by now, have developed a more advanced sense of time, the past, and the future and will use this sense more in the control of their own behavior as they move through the teenage years. Greater self-awareness and more advanced emotional self-regulation will be progressing during this phase. So will the capacity for self-motivation that comes to supplant the need for frequent environmental rewards and other consequences used to motivate children without ADD to persist at important life-tasks, such as school work and other goal-directed activities. Normal teens will be increasingly able to adhere to rules, instructions, and even morals as they move through adolescence and into young adulthood. However, the research that exists on adolescents with ADD implies that they may be lagging behind their peers in these critical abilities that serve self-regulation, time management, goal-directed behavior, and social development. Thus, families and adolescents with ADD will be in need of much guidance and support as they negotiate this important developmental stage.

So I was most pleased to learn of the preparation of this book and honored to be asked to prepare the Foreword. This publication undoubtedly will help to further address the relative dearth of information available to clinicians and parents on this developmental phase of children with ADD. And what a publication it is, filled with a diversity of national experts discussing various topics related to ADD and its management. Here the reader will find not only new and valuable information on the nature of ADD at this developmental stage and how best to approach its diagnosis, but also on the possible comorbid conditions that will be seen with it in many cases. I was pleased to see some attention given to gender issues, which I personally believe to be under-studied in individuals with ADD, especially at this developmental stage. There is also much here about the management of teens with ADD, including advice on school management, parent and teen counseling, and psychopharmacological treatment. Even more commendable is the section on advocacy and the privileges and protections afforded those with ADD under current laws and regulations; this will prove increasingly critical for those with ADD as they enter adulthood. And clinicians and families will be delighted to finally see some sound guidance on preparing the adolescent with ADD for college and even the workplace. Bravo!

CH.A.D.D. is to be congratulated for bringing together this wide range of experts on so diverse a set of topics focused upon adolescence and ADD. The reader will not be disappointed and will find here a rich resource of knowledge and advice about the many important issues facing the adolescent with ADD and their families and educators.

CHAPTER 1

DIAGNOSIS AND TREATMENT

An Introduction by Michael Gordon, Ph.D.

SUNY Health Science Center at Syracuse
Professor, Department of Psychiatry
Director, ADHD Program

Myths die hard. No matter how much data exist to prove their inaccuracy, they find a way to linger. The myth that AD/HD recedes with the onset of adolescence is among the hardiest. Despite all the research evidence to the contrary, it still holds sway with many educators, administrators, and practitioners. You know the consequence: youngsters who desperately require services are too often denied them.

Why hasn't it been painfully obvious that AD/HD symptoms persist beyond puberty? Part of the answer lies in the natural history of the disorder. The most observable symptoms, overactivity and physical impulsiveness, diminish over time. The AD/HD adolescent will be less likely to bolt from his seat and zip about the classroom. He probably has also developed enough self-control to refrain from jumping on kitchen cabinets or from dashing into traffic.

What remains are symptoms which, while highly disruptive, are far more subtle to detect. They make themselves known through poor report cards, unsatisfactory relationships with peers and family, and hundreds of hasty decisions that interfere with successful adjustment.

Another reason why the disorder is often discounted in adolescence relates to another sturdy myth: That all teenagers are oppositional, poorly controlled, underachieving, and generally deranged. Because adults typically see adolescents as disturbed anyhow, it's not always easy for them to spot what truly represents abnormal behavior. Bona fide symptoms of a disorder are too quickly attributed to the purported ravages of adolescent turmoil. If they aren't dismissed as symptoms of adolescence, they are often misconstrued as a byproduct of poor character, family disturbance, or rampant irresponsibility.

While the myth that AD/HD evaporates upon adolescence still endures, its influence is on the wane. As you will read in the following articles, some progress has been made in documenting the nature of the disorder during the teen years. Also, emerging is a sense of how best to help adolescents compensate for their disorder.

But diagnosis and treatment of AD/HD in teens is tricky business because the deficits associated with AD/HD are often embedded within a constellation of other learning and psychiatric problems. They also have a habit of masquerading in the guise of other disorders. For example, a youngster's antisocial behavior may well be fueled by an underlying impulsive style. But it's the delinquent behavior that is easiest to identify. And, finally, because the disorder itself is defined by a point along a dimension of impairment, room always exists for a degree of arbitrariness.

Despite the challenges inherent in identifying and treating adolescents with AD/HD, several factors ease the burden. The early onset and consistent presentation of the disorder mean that youngsters who are referred for the first time in adolescence, if they truly suffer from the disorder, will arrive with a track record of impairment. Individuals who have AD/HD show signs of the disorder early and, certainly by adolescence, evidence of a disrupted life. For those children who were identified as young children, the chances are high that their AD/HD characteristics will remain in force to the extent that the diagnosis will still likely be justified.

The treatment of adolescents who have AD/HD is also aided by developmental advances in the ability to understand concepts and to express concerns and ques-tions. While some of those verbal expressions might well be of the "There's nothing wrong with me, leave me alone!" category, at least the teenager finds it easier to voice objections and communicate around issues related to having the disorder.

With any luck, the myth of the disappearing disorder will continue its decline and empirically-based information will fill the void. But as awareness grows about the persistence of the disorder, we must also be vigilant that criteria remain tight and that treatments offered are based on science and not testimonials. What none of us wants to see is the replacement of one myth by others.

Assessment of Attention Deficit Disorders: A Team Approach

by Harvey C. Parker, Ph.D.

The primary characteristics of Attention Deficit/Hyperactivity Disorder are not difficult to spot in a classroom. However, not all children who are inattentive, impulsive, or overactive have ADD. These same symptoms can be the result of other factors, such as frustration with difficult schoolwork, lack of motivation, emotional concerns, or other medical conditions. A comprehensive assessment by a team of professionals who work in conjunction with the parents and the child can usually help determine whether problems are the result of ADD or other factors. In the United States, as in several other countries, members of an assessment team usually include physicians, psychologists, social workers, and school personnel, such as teachers, guidance counselors, or learning specialists. Each member plays an important role in providing input into the assessment process.

THE PHYSICIAN'S ROLE

The family physician is generally familiar with the child's medical history and has some knowledge of the child through previous treatment contact. A careful review of the child's medical history may alert the doctor to health problems that may be responsible for the display of ADD symptoms. Routine physical examinations of children with ADD are essential in ruling out the possibility of a medical illness that may be causing ADD-like symptoms. Although no specific laboratory test is available to diagnose ADD, the physician may want to conduct certain tests to determine the overall health of the child. Tests such as chromosome studies, electroencephalograms (EEGs), magnetic resonance imaging (MRI), or computerized axial tomograms (CT scans) may be conducted, but are not used routinely to evaluate ADD.

Child and adolescent psychiatrists and pediatric neurologists, trained in the assessment and treatment of such neurobiological disorders as ADD, often play an important part in identifying the disorder and other conditions that may produce symptoms similar to those shown in individuals with ADD, such as learning disabilities, Tourette Syndrome, pervasive developmental disorder, obsessive compulsive disorder, anxiety disorder, depression, or bipolar disorder.

THE PSYCHOLOGIST'S ROLE

The clinical or school psychologist serves an important function on the assessment team. This individual administers and interprets psychological and educational tests of cognition, perception, and language development (such as intelligence, attention span, visual-motor skills, memory, impulsivity) as well as tests of achievement and social/emotional adjustment. Results of such tests can provide important clues as to whether a child's difficulties are related to having ADD and/or other problems with learning, behavior, or emotional adjustment.

Psychologists and other mental health professionals often integrate data collected from parents and teachers who complete behavior rating scales about their child. Such scales offer quantifiable, descriptive information about the child, thus providing a way to compare the child's behavior to that of other children of the same sex and age. Most of the rating scales used to assess ADD provide standardized scores on a number of factors, usually related to attention span, self-control, learning ability, hyperactivity, aggression, social behavior, anxiety, etc. Some of the more popular rating scales used in the assessment of ADD are:

- Conners Teacher Rating Scale (CTRS) and Conners Parent Rating Scale (CPRS)
- ADD-H: Comprehensive Teacher Rating Scale (ACTeRS)
- AD/HD Rating Scale
- Child Attention Profile
- Child Behavior Checklist (CBCL)
- Home Situations Questionnaire
- School Situations Questionnaire
- Academic Performance Rating Scale (APRS)

THE SCHOOL'S ROLE

Assessments for ADD should always include information about the student's current and past classroom performance, academic skill strengths and weaknesses, attention span, and other social, emotional, or behavioral characteristics. Such information can be gathered through teacher interviews, review of cumulative records, analysis of test scores, and direct observation of the student in class. The student's adjustment in class should relate to aspects of the instructional environment, namely the curriculum in which the student is working; teacher expectations for the class and for the individual student; methods of instruction employed by the teacher; incentives for work completion; methods of teacher feedback to students; and comparative performance of other students in the class.

THE PARENTS' ROLE

The child's parents are also important members of the assessment team. Parents have a unique perspective on their child's previous development and current adjustment, as they have witnessed the child in a variety of situations over a number of years. Information from parents is usually acquired by interview or through questionnaires, of which the focus is usually on obtaining overall family history, current family structure and functioning, and on documenting important events from the child's medical, developmental, social, and academic history relevant to the assessment of ADD.

THE CHILD'S ROLE

An interview with the child offers the clinician an opportunity to observe the child's behavior and can yield valuable information as to the child's social and emotional adjustment, feelings about his or her self and others, and attitudes about school and other aspects of life. However, even children with ADD often behave well during such interviews. Therefore, observations of the child's behavior, level of activity, attentiveness, or compliance made during the interview sessions should not be taken as completely true of the child in other settings. Developmentally appropriate behavior in a one-on-one setting does not diminish the likelihood of the child having ADD.

THE TEAM'S ROLE AFTER THE ASSESSMENT

Ideally, after all the data has been collected, members of the assessment team should collaborate to discuss their findings. Integrating the information collected should lead to a thorough understanding of the child's physical, academic, behavioral, and emotional strengths and weaknesses. If a diagnosis of ADD (and/or other conditions) is established, treatment planning should be done in all areas where interventions are recommended. The physician may discuss appropriate medical interventions with the child and parents. The psychologist or other mental health professional may discuss counseling, behavior modification, or social and organizational skills training options. The school may set up classroom interventions to accommodate the child's areas of need in school or may provide special education or related services. Once the initial assessment is completed and appropriate treatment is instituted, there should be routine follow-up by members of the assessment and treatment teams to determine how the child is progressing. ADD, being a chronic condition, will often require long-term care and monitoring on a regular basis. Clearly, parents play a key role in encouraging members of the assessment and treatment teams to work together consistently for the best interests of the child. Coordination of all this, whether it be by a parent or a professional, is no easy task, but the outcome is usually well worth the effort.

*This article first appeared in the
Summer/Fall 1995 CH.A.D.D.er Box.*

Harvey Parker, Ph.D. is a clinical psychologist in Plantation, Florida. He is a co-founder of CH.A.D.D. and served as CH.A.D.D.'s National Executive Director for four years. Having been in practice for over twenty years, Dr. Parker has developed a special interest in working with children with ADD and their parents. He draws upon his experience as a former teacher and psychologist to apply educational and behavioral principles to the treatment of ADD in children. He is the author of numerous books, chapters, and articles on ADD.

The Many Faces of ADD: Comorbidity

by Thomas E. Brown, Ph.D.

Attention deficit disorders have many different faces. They come in two basic types, but over 50 percent of persons diagnosed with either type also have another psychiatric disorder which may mask or complicate their ADD. If these additional disorders are not recognized, effective treatment of children, adolescents, or adults with ADD may be severely compromised.

Some individuals with ADD are quiet, almost lethargic people who are rather "spacey" and tend to move cautiously in their dealings with tasks or persons. These individuals have an ADD without much hyperactivity, "predominantly inattentive type" as classified in DSM-IV. Others with ADD are "hyper" high energy people who tend to move impulsively, talk excessively, are easily bored and often try to do several things at one time. This is the ADD with hyperactivity; it is classified as "combined type" in DSM-IV if at least six inattentive symptoms are also present and as "predominantly hyperactive-impulsive type" if they are not (American Psychiatric Association, 1994).

There appear to be some common cognitive problems underlying ADD of both basic types (Biederman, 1993; Brown, in press, a,b,c). Getting organized, understanding directions, starting work, sustaining attention, staying on-task, finishing a task, and remembering things tend to be much more difficult for persons with ADD than for most individuals without ADD.

A majority of persons with either basic type of ADD also experience emotional, cognitive, or behavioral difficulties that are not on the ADD symptom lists. Over 50 percent of those diagnosed with ADD also meet diagnostic criteria for one or more additional psychiatric disorders (Halperin, Newcorn & Sharma, 1991). Depressive disorders, learning disorders, anxiety disorders, substance abuse, aggression and behavior disorders, and sleep disorders, have all been reported to occur in persons with ADD significantly more often than in people without ADD (Biederman, 1991b; Wilens, 1994). Those whose ADD is combined with such disorders may experience greater difficulty in school, work, mood, and social relationships; they may also need different or additional treatments.

The medical term for two or more disorders occurring in a person concurrently, e.g., ADD and depression, is "comorbid." When particular disorders are frequently comorbid with each other, important questions are raised about how the two disorders may be related. Does "A" cause or render one vulnerable to "B?" Or vice-versa? Or are "A" and "B" really both components or consequences of another disorder? Calling disorders comorbid is simply to recognize that they show up at the same time; it doesn't explain why this happens.

CAUSES OF COMORBIDITY

One primary reason for high rates of comorbidity between ADD and various other psychiatric disorders may be genetic. Biederman and colleagues (1991a) demonstrated that close biological relatives of children with ADD are far more likely to have ADD, major depressive disorder, multiple anxiety disorders, conduct disorder, anti-social personality disorder, and/or substance abuse than are relatives of children without ADD. All of these disorders tend to run in families and may be inherited in various combinations by some, though not all, family members.

Other causes of comorbidity may be environmental. For example, a child with combined type ADD may grow up in a community where he is likely to be exposed to gang activity and substance abuse. These environmental factors may substantially increase the likelihood of that child developing a conduct disorder along with the ADD.

Comorbidity may also be a reaction to living with ADD. From their earliest years, many people with ADD experience intense and sustained frustration in their efforts to learn, to work, and to get along with other people. Often, they suffer ongoing criticism from teachers, parents, siblings, and peers. Years of chronic, sustained frustration and criticism, especially if the ADD has not been diagnosed and the individual feels, "It's all my fault," may produce dysthymia — a chronic, low-grade depression, comorbid to the ADD. Other disorders may similarly develop reactively.

ADD & Disruptive Behavior Disorders

Some comorbid combinations tend to occur more frequently with one type of ADD than with another. ADD of the combined type is more often comorbid with disruptive behavior disorders. One of these is oppositional defiant disorder (ODD) where a child is hostile and negativistic, chronically arguing and defying parents and other authorities. When a child with ADD is severely oppositional, that child may meet ODD diagnostic criteria and need treatment for both ODD and ADD.

About 35 percent of those with ODD also demonstrate the more severe behavior problems classified as conduct disorder (CD); these may include truancy, physical cruelty to animals or people, and criminal activities. Children whose ADD is comorbid with just ODD are likely to get into trouble in school and community, but they do not carry the same high risk for poor long-term adult outcomes as do those with comorbid CD (Barkley, 1990).

ADD & Anxiety and/or Mood Disorders

Mood disorders include dysthymia (low grade chronic depression), major depressive disorder (immobilizing depression) and bi-polar disorders (alternating manic and depressive episodes). Anxiety disorders include panic disorder (brief episodes of immobilizing terror), social or specific phobias (intense fear of social situations or of other specific objects or situations), obsessive-compulsive disorder (chronic inability to get rid of disturbing thoughts [obsessions] or repetitive behaviors [compulsions] which one feels compelled to do to reduce anxiety), and generalized anxiety disorder (chronically excessive anxiety and worry).

Although anxiety and mood disorders appear more frequently in ADD without hyperactivity, either or both may appear in combined type ADD. Jensen (1993) recently reported on a group of 47 school-aged children diagnosed as having AD/HD (using *DSM III-R*) where 49 percent also received diagnoses of either depression alone (n=10), anxiety disorder alone (n=5), or both depression and anxiety (n=8).

ADD & Learning/Communication Disorders

The combination of ADD with learning disorders and/or communication disorders can be seriously disabling. Learning disorders are present when achievement in reading, math, or written expression is significantly below that expected for age, IQ, and schooling. Communication disorders impair the ability to understand others' communications and/or to use language to express oneself, or impair the ability to make expected sounds of speech.

Cantwell and Baker (1991) reported that in a sample of 600 children with impairments of speech and/or language, 30 percent had comorbid ADD, while in a matched group who also had learning disorders, 63 percent had comorbid ADD. Persons with ADD who are impaired in their ability to communicate with others or whose ability to read, write, and/or do arithmetic is compromised are at significant risk for academic underachievement *and* for problems in social interaction and fragile self-esteem.

Although children with comorbid ADD and learning disorders are at high risk, they often do not receive complete treatment. Children diagnosed with learning and/or communication disorders are often placed in special education programs without being assessed and treated for comorbid ADD. Appropriate treatment of ADD symptoms in those with learning or communication disorders may increase the effectiveness of educational remediation programs and enhance the students' capacity for adaptive social interactions

ADD & Sleep/Awakening Disorders

Although not yet widely studied, the comorbid combination of ADD with disorders of sleep and/or awakening is often the focus of complaints by children and adults — their chronic insomnia exacerbates their ADD symptoms by depriving them of needed rest and/or severe difficulties in awakening make them chronically late for school or work. Reports from parents also highlight the stress and disruptive effects of these disorders upon families of children with ADD. Another comorbid problem reported by some with non-hyperactive ADD is excessive daytime sleepiness; this may appear as borderline narcolepsy. Unfortunately, little is currently known about what causes the apparently high incidence of sleep disorder comorbidities with ADD. However, some authors, including Wilens and colleagues (1994), and this author (Brown,c, in press) have recently begun to report on pharmacological treatments that may help to alleviate the disruptive impact of sleep disorders on persons with ADD.

ADD & Substance Abuse

One of the most complex comorbid combinations with ADD is substance abuse. Longitudinal studies indicate that among persons with ADD who do not have conduct disorder (CD), the incidence of substance abuse is no higher than in the general population. However, for those with ADD and comorbid CD, risk of substance abuse is greatly increased; among adults diagnosed as substance abusers, over 70 percent are estimated to have ADD (Wilens, in press). This overlap raises the question as to whether persons who have ADD and are recovering from addiction might increase their chances of abstinence if their ADD is pharmacologically treated. There are certainly risks in treating recovering persons with medications for ADD, but there are also risks in not treating ADD in recovering persons.

Other Disorders Comorbid With ADD

ADD can also be comorbid with Tourettes Syndrome (where multiple motor and vocal tics are present), with borderline personality disorder (characterized by a pervasive pattern of unstable moods, fluid self-image, and intensely conflicted interpersonal relationships), and with a variety of "atypical" developmental disorders, e.g. Asperger's syndrome and pervasive developmental disorder (where a person demonstrates repetitive, stereotyped patterns of interests or behaviors and a severely impaired ability for reciprocal social interaction). Often these other comorbidities are ignored by "heirarchical diagnosis" in which it is assumed that the "more severe" diagnosis subsumes the ADD and therefore no direct treatment for the ADD is warranted. Further research is needed to determine when and how it may be useful to treat symptoms of ADD directly when they are comorbid with these other disorders.

Implications for Assessment & Treatment

Much is still unknown about comorbid relationships between ADD and other disorders. It is not yet clear where the boundaries should be drawn to delineate between the cognitive problems included in ADD and those classified as learning disorders. Many disagree about how much depressed mood comes with ADD and when it should be clinically classified as depression. For now, it may be sufficient to recognize that some persons with ADD fully meet diagnostic criteria for one or more other psychiatric disorders, while others may not fully meet criteria for another disorder but may have many comorbid symptoms that significantly impact their ADD.

Clearly, accurate diagnosis — including questions of comorbidity — should take place prior to treatment planning. Given the high rates of comorbidity with ADD, no evaluation for ADD should be considered complete until adequate screening for possible comorbidities has been done. And if ongoing treatment of ADD seems ineffective, the possibility of unrecognized comorbid problems should be considered. Research-based guidelines for assessment and treatment of ADD comorbidities are still very exploratory and tentative, though some integrated reports are beginning to appear (Biederman, 1993; Jensen, 1993; Brown, in press, c).

Whether or not full criteria for a comorbid psychiatric diagnosis are met, comorbid symptoms should be taken into account in planning treatment. Sometimes this involves avoiding usual treatments; for example, persons whose ADD is accompanied by significant anxiety symptoms may become more anxious on the usual stimulant treatment for ADD. They may need a different medication or combined medications may be needed — an individual with comorbid anxiety, mood, or behavior disorder may need mood stabilizing medications (e.g. antidepressants) along with stimulants for ADD (Gammon and Brown, 1993). Or additional interventions may be needed. A person with ADD and substance abuse may benefit from concurrent twelve-step programs and medications for ADD.

Gradually, findings about comorbidities with ADD may lead not only to more effective treatments, but also to increased understanding of the subtle and interactive complexities of the human mind.

This article first appeared in the Fall 1994 ATTENTION!

Thomas E. Brown, Ph.D. is a clinical psychologist who maintains a private practice in Hamden, Connecticut where he specializes in treatment of high-IQ adolescents and adults with ADD. Dr. Brown is a clinical supervisor in the Psychology Department at Yale University and has presented papers, workshops, and symposia on ADD at national meetings of various organizations.

REFERENCES

American Psychiatric Association (1994) *Diagnostic & Statistical Manual of Mental Disorders, Fourth Edition.* Washington, D.C.: American Psychiatric Association.

Barkley, R. A., Fischer, M., Edelbrock, C. S., & Smallish, L. (1990). The Adolescent Outcome of Hyperactive Children Diagnosed by Research Criteria: An 8-Year Prospective Follow-up Study. *Journal of American Academy of Child & Adolescent Psychiatry*, 29(4), 546-557.

Biederman, J., Faraone, S. V., & Lapey, K. (1991a). Cormorbidity of Diagnosis in Attention-Deficit Disorder. In G. Weiss (Eds.), *Attention-Deficit Hyperactivity Disorder* (pp. 335-360). Philadelphia: W. B. Saunders.

Biederman, J., Faraone, S. V., Spencer, T., Wilens, T., Norman, D., Lapey, K. A., Mick, E., Lehman, B. K., & Doyle, A. (1993). Patterns of Psychiatric Comorbidity, Cognition, and Psychosocial Functioning in Adults With Attention Deficit Disorder. *American Journal of Psychiatry*, 150(12), 1792-1798.

Biederman, J., Newcorn, J., & Sprich, S. (1991b). Comorbidity of attention deficit hyperactivity disorder with conduct, depressive, anxiety and other disorders. *American Journal of Psychiatry*, 148(5), 564-577.

Brown, T. E. (in press,a) *Brown Attention Deficit Disorder Scales.* San Antonio, TX.: The Psychological Corporation.

Brown, T. E. (in press,b). Differential Diagnosis of ADD vs. ADHD in Adults. In K. G. Nadeau (Eds.), *A Comprehensive Guide to Attention Deficit Disorder in Adults* New York: Brunner/Mazel.

Brown, T. E. (Ed.). (in press,c). *Attention Deficit Disorders and Comorbidities in Children, Adolescents and Adults.* Washington, D.C.: American Psychiatric Press.

Cantwell, D. P., & Baker, L. (1991). Association Between Attention Deficit-Hyperactivity Disorder and Learning Disorders. *Journal of Learning Disabilities*, 24(2), 88-95.

Gammon, G. D., & Brown, T. E. (1993). Fluoxetine and Methylphenidate in Combination for Treatment of Attention Deficit Disorder and Comorbid Depressive Disorder. *Journal of Child & Adolescent Psychopharmacology*, 3(1), 1-10.

Halperin, J. M., Newcorn, J. H., & Sharma, V. (1991). Ritalin: Diagnostic Cormobidity and Attentional Measures. In L. L. Greenhill & B. B. Osman (Eds.), *Ritalin: Theory and Patient Management* (pp. 15-24). New York: Mary Ann Liebert, Inc.

Jensen, P. S., Shervette, R. E., Xenakis, S. N., & Richters, J. (1993). Anxiety and depressive disorders in attention deficit disorder with hyperactivity: new findings. *American Journal of Psychiatry*, 150(8), 1203-1209.

Wilens, T. E., Biederman, J., & Spencer, T. (1994). Clonidine for Sleep Disturbances Associated with Attention-Deficit Hyperactivity Disorder. *Journal of American Academy of Child & Adolescent Psychiatry*, 33(3), 424-426.

Wilens, T. E., Spencer, T. J., & Biederman, J. (in press). ADHD and Psychoactive Substance Abuse Disorders. In T. E. Brown (Eds.), *Attention Deficit Disorders and Comorbidities in Children, Adolescents and Adults*, Washington, D.C.: American Psychiatric Press.

Thomas. Brown, Ph.D. has an independent practice of clinical psychology in Hamden, CT. He is a Clinical Supervisor at the Yale Psychological Services Clinic in the Department of Psychology, Yale University. He is the editor of Attention Deficit Disorders and Comorbidities in Children, Adolescents, and Adults *(American Psychiatric Press) and the author of the* Brown Attention Deficit Disorders Scales (BADDS).

ADD in Females:
From Childhood to Adulthood

by Kathleen Nadeau, Ph.D.

The majority of writing and research on ADD has traditionally focused on males, who were believed to make up 80 percent of all those with ADD. Today, more and more females are being identified, especially now that we are more aware of the non-hyperactive subtype of ADD. Girls and women with ADD face a variety of issues that are gender specific. This article will highlight some of those differences, and will explore some of the unique struggles faced by females with ADD.

CHILDHOOD ISSUES FOR GIRLS WITH ADD

Let's start with the recollections of childhood and adolescence by two women with ADD: Marie and Lauren. Marie is an introverted, "primarily inattentive" thirty-four-year-old woman with ADD, who has struggled with anxiety and depression in addition to ADD, both in childhood and in adulthood:

"The thing I remember the most was always getting my feelings hurt. I was a lot happier when I played with just one friend. When someone teased me I never knew how to defend myself. I really tried in school, but I hated it when the teacher called on me. Half the time I didn't even know what the question was. Sometimes I would get stomach aches and beg my mother to let me stay home from school."

These recollections are very different from those of a typical elementary school-age boy with AD/HD. Marie was hyper-sensitive to criticism, had difficulty with the rapid give-and-take of group interactions, and felt socially "out of it," except in the company of her one best friend. She was a compliant girl whose greatest desire was to conform to teacher expectations and not to draw attention to herself. Her distractibility created agony because of teacher disapproval and the resulting embarrassment in front of her peers.

On the other hand, Lauren's "hyperactive-impulsive" ADD patterns are more similar to those seen in many boys with AD/HD. Now twenty-seven, she recalls being stubborn, angry, defiant and rebellious, and physically hyperactive. She was also hypersocial:

"I can remember in grade school that everything felt frantic. I had a fight with my mom almost every morning. At school I was always jumping around, talking, and passing notes. Some of my teachers liked me, but some of them — the really strict ones — didn't like me. And I hated them. I argued a lot and lost my temper. I cried really easily too, and some of the mean kids in the class liked to tease me and make me cry."

Although we see the argumentativeness and defiance in Lauren, which we see more often in boys who have AD/HD, we also see that, like many girls with ADD she was hyper-social and hyper-emotional. Life for Lauren, as for some other girls with ADD, was an emotional roller coaster. She was very disorganized, and had very low tolerance for stress.

ADOLESCENT GIRLS WITH ADD

Let's take a look at Marie and Lauren's recollections of adolescence. Life for each of them seemed to become even more difficult. Adolescence is difficult enough as it is — when ADD is added to the mix, problems are amplified and stresses are intensified.

"High school just overwhelmed me. None of my teachers knew me because I never spoke up in class. Exams terrified me. I hated to study and write papers. They were really hard for me and I put them off until the last minute. I didn't date at all in high school. People didn't dislike me, but I bet if I went back to a class reunion that no one would remember who I was. I was pretty emotional, and it got ten times worse just before my period."

— Marie

"I was totally out of control in high school. I was smart, but a terrible student. I guess I worked on being a 'party animal' to make up for all the things I wasn't good at. At home I was angry, totally rebellious. I snuck out of the house after my parents went to sleep at night. I lied all the time. My parents tried to control me or punish me, but nothing worked. I couldn't sleep at night,

and was exhausted all day in school. Things were bad most of the time, but when I had PMS I really lost it. School meant nothing to me."

— Lauren

Marie and Lauren presented very different pictures during their teenage years. Marie was shy, withdrawn, a daydreamer who was disorganized and felt overwhelmed. Lauren was hyperactive, hyper-emotional, and lived her life in a high stimulation, high risk mode. The differences in Marie's and Lauren's behaviors are obvious, but what do they have in common?

(1) Severe pre-menstrual syndrome.
In teenage years, the neurochemical problems caused by ADD are greatly compounded by hormonal fluctuations. These combined dysregulated systems can result in tremendous mood swings, hyper-irritability, and emotional over-reaction.

(2) Tremendous concern with peer acceptance.
Girls with ADD seem to suffer more as a result of peer problems than do boys with ADD. Although Lauren had many friends, her emotionality repeatedly got in the way. Marie, by contrast, felt overwhelmed and withdrew, and felt most comfortable in the company of one close friend. Both, however, had a strong sense of "being different" from their peers.

(3) Among impulsive-hyperactive girls, a sense of shame.
Adolescent boys who are impulsive and hyperactive may be viewed as simply "sowing their oats." They may even gain peer approval as they rebel against authority, or as a result of their hard drinking, fast driving, or sexually-active lifestyle. Girls, however, tend to receive much more negative feedback from parents, teachers, and peers when they behave in such a manner. Later, as young women, they often join the chorus of accusation and outrage, blaming themselves and feeling a strong sense of shame for their earlier behavior.

Raising Girls with ADD — Some Helpful Approaches

Just like adolescent boys with ADD, these girls need structure and guidelines at home. While males with ADD may behave in a very angry and rebellious fashion, for many girls, their life is an emotional roller coaster. They may withdraw and become depressed if they feel overwhelmed and socially rejected at school. Highly hyperactive-impulsive girls may engage in constant, dramatic screaming battles at home, where it feels much safer to release their fears and frustrations. Helping them to re-establish emotional equilibrium, especially in relation to hormonal fluctuations, is critical. For girls, more so than for many boys, home needs to become a place to calm down and to refuel emotionally. All too often, however, parents are drawn into tumultuous battles, rather than providing a much needed calming influence. How can you help as a parent?

(1) Teach your daughters to establish a "quiet zone" in their lives.
Whether shy and withdrawn, or hyper and impulsive, girls with ADD often feel emotionally overwhelmed. They need to learn stress management techniques from an early age, and to understand that they need emotional "time out" to regroup after an upset.

(2) Try to minimize corrections and criticism.
Too often, parents — with the best of intentions — shower girls who have ADD with corrections and criticisms. "Don't let them hurt your feelings like that." "You'd forget your head if it wasn't attached to your shoulders." "How do you expect to go to college with grades like that?" "If you just relaxed, dressed a little better..." These girls, whether loud and rebellious, or shy and retiring, typically suffer from low self-esteem. Home is not only an important place to refuel, it is where confidence — so frequently eroded during the day at school — must be rebuilt.

(3) Help them look for ways to excel.
Girls with ADD typically feel that they are "not good at anything." Their distractibility, impulsivity, and disorganization often result in mediocre grades. Likewise, they often don't have the persistence, the "stick-to-it-iveness," to develop skills and talents like many of their friends. Helping girls with ADD find a skill or ability, and then praising and recognizing them for it are terrific positive boosts. Often, the life of an adolescent girl with ADD reaches a positive turning-point when she is lucky enough to find an activity that can raise her self-esteem.

(4) Seek medical treatment if PMS is severe.
PMS is something that many females with ADD may need to carefully manage throughout their lives. If PMS is severe in adolescence it should be taken seriously, and managed carefully. Sometimes severe PMS is managed through the use of anti-depressants with the dosage level being varied according to the menstrual cycle.

Special Issues Faced by Women with ADD

The same themes of social and physiological differences between males and females with ADD continue to play themselves out as adolescent girls become women with jobs, marriages, and families.

For a woman with ADD, her most painful challenge may be created by her own overwhelming sense of inadequacy at fulfilling the roles she feels that her family and society expect her to play. Both on the job and at home, women are often placed in the role of caretaker. While men with ADD are advised to build a support system around themselves, not only do few women have access to such a support system, society had traditionally expected women to *be* the support system.

The emergence of "dual career couples" has intensified the struggles for women with ADD. Over the past two decades, more and more women have been required to fulfill not only the more traditional roles of wife and mother, but also to function efficiently and tirelessly as they juggle the demands of a full time career. Divorce is also hitting women with ADD harder than their peers who do not have ADD. Divorce rates are close to fifty percent among all marriages in the United States; divorce becomes even more likely when ADD is added to the list of marital stressors. Following divorce, it continues to be predominantly mothers who act as primary parent for children. By adding ADD to the huge burden of single-parenting, the result is often chronic exhaustion and emotional depletion.

The hormonal fluctuations that commence at puberty continue to play a strong role in the lives of women with ADD. The problems they experience due to ADD are greatly exacerbated by their monthly hormonal fluctuations. Some women report that the stresses of parenting their children — who may have ADD — while attempting to struggle with their own ADD, reaches crisis proportions on a monthly basis as they go through their premenstrual phase, often lasting as long as a week.

Although the number of older women yet identified with ADD is small, it seems quite reasonable to assume that the hormonal changes associated with menopause would be expected to, once again, exacerbate ADD symptoms of emotional reactivity.

If You Are a Woman with ADD, What Can You Do To Manage Your Life Better?

Here's a list of twelve actions (and attitude changes) that could help make your life more manageable and, therefore, less stressful:

(1) Give yourself a break!
     Often the biggest struggle is an internal one. Societal expectations have been deeply ingrained in many women. Even if a loving husband said, "Don't worry about it," women would place demands upon themselves. Breaking out of a mold that doesn't fit can take time and effort. Working with a therapist who really understands issues related to ADD may help shed the impossible expectations that you have of yourself.

(2) Educate your husband about ADD and how it affects you.
     Your husband may feel anger and resentment about an ill-kept house or badly-behaved children,

assuming that you "just don't care." He needs to appreciate the full brunt of ADD's impact upon you. Get him on your side; strategize how to make your life at home more "ADD-accommodating" and "ADD-friendly."

(3) It's only spilled milk!
     Try to create an "ADD-friendly" environment in your home. If you can approach your ADD and that of your children with acceptance and good humor, explosions will decrease and you'll save more energy for the positive side of things.

(4) Simplify your life.
     You are probably over-booked and chances are your children are, too. Look for ways to reduce commitments so that you're not always pressed for time and hurried.

(5) Choose supportive friends.
     So many women describe friends or neighbors who make them feel terrible by comparison — whose houses are immaculate, whose children are always clean, neat, and well-behaved. Don't put yourself in situations that will send you back to impossible expectations and negative comparisons.

(6) Build a support group for yourself.
     One woman with ADD related that housework was such drudgery for her that she often couldn't bring herself to do it. One of her techniques, however, was to invite a friend, who shared similar tendencies, to keep her company while she completed some particularly odious task.

(7) Build in "time-outs" daily.
     Time-outs are essential when you have ADD and are raising children. It's easy to not find time for time-outs, though, because they require planning. Make them routine so that you don't have to keep planning and juggling. For example, ask your husband to commit to two blocks of time each weekend when he will take the kids away from the house without you. Arrange for a regular baby-sitter several times a week.

(8) Don't place yourself in burn-out.
     One mother with ADD, who is doing a great job of parenting her two children who also have ADD, is able to recognize her limitations. With two such challenging children she arranges for a month-long, summer sleep-away camp each summer. She also arranges for brief visits, one at a time, to grandparents. This allows her to spend time with each son without him having to compete with his brother.

(9) Eliminate and delegate.
     Look at things that you require of yourself at home. Can some of these things be eliminated?

Can you afford to hire someone to do some of them?

(10) Learn child behavior management techniques.

On the outside looking in, it may be easy for other parents to judge you if your children misbehave. What any parent of a child with ADD knows is that they don't respond to the usual admonishments and limits the way other children do. You have a super-challenging job. Get the best training you can find. There are excellent books on behavior management techniques for children with ADD.

(11) Get help for PMS or Menopausal Symptoms.

They are likely to be more severe in women with ADD than they may be in other women. Managing the destabilizing effect of your hormonal fluctuations is a critical part of managing your ADD.

(12) Focus more on the things you love.

There are many aspects of keeping a house and raising children that are rewarding and creative. Look for positive experiences to share with your children.

Women with ADD need to understand and accept themselves. They need to quit blaming themselves for not meeting the expected demands of two of life's most "ADD-unfriendly " jobs: that of housewife and mother. They also need the understanding and acceptance of their husbands, their families, and friends. These are women who are struggling valiantly against demands that are difficult, if not impossible, to meet. Instead of measuring success in terms of clean dishes and folded laundry, women with ADD must learn to celebrate their gifts — their warmth, their creativity, their humor, their sensitivity, and their spirit — and to look for others who can appreciate the best in them as well.

This article first appeared in the
Spring 1996 ATTENTION!

This article is adapted from Adventures in Fast Forward, *by Kathleen G. Nadeau, a book on life, love and work for adults with ADD, published by Brunner/Mazel, 1996.*

Kathleen G. Nadeau, Ph.D. is Director of Chesapeake Psychological Services of Maryland, a private clinic that specializes in diagnosing and treating adolescents and adults with ADD. She is the editor of A Comprehensive Guide to Attention Deficit Disorder in Adults: Research, Diagnosis, and Treatment, *the first guide for professionals on adults with ADD and is the author of several books on ADD.*

Current Trends in the Medication Management of Attention Deficit Disorder

by James J. McGough, M.D. and Dennis P. Cantwell, M.D.

Medication is the single-most frequently used intervention in the treatment of Attention Deficit Disorder. Evidence for the usefulness of medication in the management of ADD is so strong that clinicians should consider its potential for benefit in any individual given the diagnosis. This article reviews current knowledge and trends in medication therapy for the management of ADD.

Research over the past fifty years has increasingly revealed ADD to be a biologically-based brain disorder. Evidence suggests that ADD may result from a genetic predisposition, although environmental factors can contribute to expression of symptoms. ADD is much like other medical conditions such as high blood pressure or diabetes. Patients with high blood pressure or diabetes often use medication together with lifestyle changes for control of symptoms. Similarly, medication can be an essential part of therapy for ADD, particularly when combined with appropriate changes at home, school, and/or work.

Several types of medication are currently used in the treatment of ADD. These are (1) psychostimulant medications, (2) certain antidepressant medications, and (3) other psychotropic drugs used in certain specific cases. Each of these types of medication will be reviewed below.

STIMULANT MEDICATIONS

Physicians have used stimulant medications for treatment of behavioral difficulties in children since the 1930s. Stimulant medications improve attention span and decrease disruptive behaviors in 70 to 80 percent of children with ADD. More research has been done to assess the effects of stimulants on children with ADD than any other medication for any other childhood disorder. In over fifty years of use, stimulants have been given to hundreds of thousands of children with no evidence of significant harm or long-term risk.

Stimulant medications currently on the market include methylphenidate (Ritalin), d-amphetamine (Dexedrine), and pemoline (Cylert). Each of these med-

ications generally works equally well. An individual who fails to respond to one stimulant occasionally will do well with another. Methylphenidate is prescribed to approximately 90 percent of children who take medicine for ADD. D-amphetamine is less expensive than methylphenidate, but is not always available. Standard methylphenidate and d-amphetamine provide benefit for about four hours, and are usually given before and at lunch time. The positive effects of these medications are noticeable within forty-five minutes after the appropriate dose is given. Longer acting forms of methylphenidate and d-amphetamine are available if a student is uncomfortable taking medication at school. The long-acting forms may be somewhat less effective. Pemoline is given once a day and is effective for eight to nine hours. Pemoline is effective within two days after beginning an appropriate dose.

In rare cases, patients can become tolerant to the beneficial effects of stimulant medication. More frequently, increasing body weight with age requires an increase in absolute medication dosage. It is therefore important to have continued monitoring of medication. Patients often require adjustments in medication dose, or changes in type of medication, to assure on-going benefit.

SIDE EFFECTS

Any medication can cause side effects. Physicians, parents, and patients with ADD must do a "cost-benefit analysis" and determine if the risks of taking a stimulant medication outweigh the potential benefits. It is important to remember that refusing to treat ADD also carries significant risk for development of school failure, poor self-esteem, substance abuse, and anti-social behaviors.

The most common side effects of stimulants are sleep problems and appetite loss. Some patients also suffer increased restlessness, headaches, stomach aches, or weight loss. These side effects usually go away after several weeks or with dose adjustment.

Physicians were once concerned that long-term use of stimulants in young children would lead to decreases in overall height. Long-term follow-up studies show this is generally not true. A more significant concern is the development of motor tics or Tourette's Syndrome. Approximately 1 percent of children treated with stimulants develop tics. Stimulants may bring out tics in individuals predisposed to them. Tics often resolve after stimulants are discontinued, but they can occur indefinitely. In the past it was general practice to stop stimulant medication if tics occurred. At present some clinicians will continue the stimulant if it provides clear benefit and manage the tics as a simple side effect of the medication.

RISKS OF ADDICTION

Parents and some clinicians may have concerns that children will become dependent on stimulant medications. A second concern is that stimulants will be sold on the street as drugs of abuse.

There is no available evidence suggesting a risk of addiction with these medications. It is evident that without treatment 30 percent of children with ADD go on to develop significant substance abuse difficulties. Some physicians prescribe pemoline, which has no recreational potential, in patients they deem at risk for abusing medication.

ANTIDEPRESSANT MEDICATIONS

Between 60 and 80 percent of individuals with ADD will respond to certain antidepressant medications. Physicians may choose an antidepressant medication when a patient has significant depression or anxiety in addition to ADD. Antidepressants are also used when an individual can not take a stimulant. Antidepressants have a longer period of action than stimulants and may be useful when medication effects are required over the entire day.

The most commonly used antidepressants for ADD are imipramine (Tofranil), nortriptyline (Pamelor), and desipramine (Norpramin). Although it takes three to four weeks for antidepressants to be effective for depression, relief from ADD is immediate with an adequate dose. ADD symptoms sometimes improve with antidepressant doses lower than required to treat depression.

Typical side effects of these antidepressants are similar to over-the-counter cold remedies. These include dry mouth, constipation, and drowsiness. Antidepressants have caused irregular heart beats in some very rare cases. Physicians insure drug safety by monitoring EKGs and medication blood levels. Unlike stimulants, antidepressants cannot be discontinued on a short-term basis. Patients can develop a flu-like syndrome if they miss medication doses, although they are at no risk for serious harm.

OTHER MEDICATIONS

Other psychiatric medications have use in certain specific cases for the management of ADD. Monoamine oxidase inhibitors (MAOIs) are a class of antidepressant that has been useful in children and adults with ADD. Use of MAOIs require dietary restrictions which are often not practical with younger patients. Several antipsychotic medications, notably thioridazine (Mellaril), chlorpromazine (Thorazine), and haloperidol (Haldol), are useful when patients show severe, unmanageable aggression or impulsivity. Antipsychotic medications have been shown to be superior to stimulants in some patients with ADD and low IQ.

PROPER ASSESSMENT

Clinicians must carefully assess the presence of ADD and related disorders prior to initiation of medication therapy. Unruly school behavior is not sufficient reason to initiate medication therapy. Information should be obtained from as many sources as possible, including parents, teachers, and the patient. A physical examination, hearing test, and laboratory studies may reveal other general medical conditions. Educational testing may be necessary to assess the presence of associated learning disabilities.

INDICATIONS FOR MEDICATION

A diagnosis of ADD is not an automatic indication for drug therapy. In mild cases, modifications in family and classroom structure may be sufficient to control symptoms. Medication should be considered in all severe cases, particularly if a child is at risk for expulsion from school. Physicians often refrain from using medication in children younger than age four. Medications for ADD are expensive, but are much lower in cost than psychosocial interventions. Some families are extremely reluctant to use medication and should not be coerced into using it. A patient should not be given medication if the family is unwilling to comply with a physician's plan for monitoring its effects.

The potential for benefit from medication should be considered in any patient with ADD. It is a mistake to ignore this potential benefit and attribute a child's behavioral difficulties to "emotional difficulties" or problems in the child's environment. Parental conflicts, school disruptions, and peer rejections often improve dramatically once a child is placed on medication.

ASSESSMENT OF MEDICATION RESPONSE

Rating scales have been designed to help clinicians assess ADD in a variety of settings. The most commonly used scales include Conners Rating Scales, Child Behavior Checklists, AcTers, SNAP-IV, and others.

Scores on these scales are compared before and after a patient begins treatment. This provides a more objective way to assess if treatment is working.

Continuous Performance Tests, or CPTs, are computerized tests used to measure response to treatment. CPTs take between nine and twenty minutes to complete. Some clinicians determine optimum medication dose based on results from these tests. Other cognitive studies, such as the PAL and MEM tests, offer additional information on drug response to that provided by the CPT. It is a mistake, however, to diagnose ADD solely on the basis of these measures. Clinical information from parents and teacher rating scales remain the best indication of medication response.

TERMINATION OF TREATMENT

Many clinicians attempt to take patients off medication at least once a year. These medication holidays are useful to assess continued efficacy and need for pharmacotherapy. Medication treats ADD only while the individual is taking it. Many children and adolescents choose to stop medication during junior high or high school. Studies now demonstrate that a majority of individuals with ADD continue to have impairment throughout their lives. Medication helps many adult patients experience considerable improvement. Older adolescents and adults with ADD need to determine the circumstances when medication provides benefit. Medication regimens can then be designed to help older patients optimize their functioning.

FUTURE RESEARCH

Much research is currently underway to improve medication therapies for ADD. Several newer antidepressants, including buproprion (Wellbutrin) and fluoxetine (Prozac), have shown considerable promise in several treatment studies. A new stimulant medication, Adderall, has recently been approved. It remains to be seen if Adderall will provide some advantage over other medication choices. Recognition of ADD in adults has led to much ongoing work aimed at tailoring treatment strategies for adult needs.

Comprehensive treatment of ADD requires the integration of multiple interventions designed to address physical, psychological, educational, vocational, and social needs of patients. A comprehensive, five year study is currently underway to determine the optimal combination of therapies necessary for effective treatment of ADD. Medication will undoubtedly remain a standard component in the management of patients with this disorder.

This article first appeared in the Winter 1995 ATTENTION!

James J. McGough, M.D. is Assistant Clinical Professor of Psychiatry at the UCLA School of Medicine, Los Angeles, California. Much of his clinical and research work focuses on children, adolescents, and adults with ADD.

Dennis P. Cantwell, M.D. is the Joseph Campbell Professor of Child Psychiatry at the UCLA Neuropsychiatric Institute, Los Angeles, California. He was named the first recipient of the Elaine Schlosser Lewis Award for Research on Attention Deficit Disorders in recognition of his significant contributions and lifetime body of work in ADD.

Medication Usage Trends for ADD

by Daniel J. Safer, M.D.

Although Benzadrine (dl amphetamine) was first reported as a treatment for behavior problems in overactive youths in the mid-1930s and methylphenidate (Ritalin) in the early 1960s, treatment for behavior problems in youths consisted mainly of psychotherapy, at least until the mid-1960s. This was viewed as appropriate since it was generally assumed that childhood behavioral difficulties were exclusively caused by deviant emotional responses to a disordered upbringing. Following the entry of Thorazine, Tofranil, and Librium into the pharmaceutical market in the 1950s to treat adult emotional disorders, psychiatric medication treatment for adults rapidly expanded. An acceptance of pharmacotherapy for children's psychiatric disorders followed, but far more slowly. There was a broad-based and substantial reluctance then to treating maladjusted elementary school students with medications. In 1970, this became a national concern when an Omaha newspaper erroneously reported that 5-10 percent of the area's students were being treated with stimulant medication. A congressional inquiry followed, and public apprehension soon decreased after a positive report from a federally-appointed blue ribbon panel was issued in 1971.

Changes in the Indications for Medication Treatment for ADD and the Medications Utilized

In the 1970s, stimulant medication was prescribed primarily for "hyperkinetic" (hyperactive) youths. Only about 7 percent of those treated with stimulants then had an attentional/learning problem without a notable degree of restlessness. By the late 1980s, the proportion of these non-hyperactive, inattentive youths who were using stimulant medication tripled. There was also an increasing trend to use stimulant medication to treat aggressive/conduct disordered behavior with or without associated ADD.

In the early 1970s, around one-fifth of all children with ADD who used medication were receiving some type of sedative or tranquilizer such as Mellaril and Benadryl. At that time, as many youths with ADD were receiving dextroamphetamine as were receiving methylphenidate. However, by the 1980s, the sedative-tranquilizer share of medications used to treat ADD dropped to 3 percent of the total, and methylphenidate accelerated to capture 90 percent of this market, with dextroamphetamine and pemoline (Cylert) splitting most of the remainder.

CHURCH OF SCIENTOLOGY ANTI-METHYLPHENIDATE CAMPAIGN, 1986-1990

An anti-methylphenidate media blitz in association with numerous lawsuits was begun in 1986 as the outgrowth of an anti-psychiatry campaign. In many cities, it was successful in frightening parents about medication side effects and professionals about possible litigation. It was not until 1990 that the anti-methylphenidate campaign faded when the campaigners shifted their focus to Prozac.

THE 1990s

Following the anti-methylphenidate campaign, stimulant treatment resumed its steady expansion. To keep pace, the Drug Enforcement Administration (DEA) increased production quotas for methylphenidate. Surprisingly, the quotas increased five-fold between 1990 and 1995.

An increase in the prescription rate of methylphenidate in the 1990s can be ascribed to a number of factors. These include: (1) prolongation of stimulant treatment for students into their secondary school years; (2) increased use of methylphenidate by girls with ADD; (3) increased use of stimulant treatment for adults with ADD and adult depression; (4) increased use of methylphenidate for non-hyperactive youths with inattentiveness and learning disabilities; (5) increased parental comfort with the safety of stimulant treatment for youths and a heightened appreciation of its therapeutic impact; and (6) increase in the youth population.

THE RECENT EXPANSION OF METHYLPHENIDATE TREATMENT FOR ADD

The five-fold increase in the DEA production quotas for methylphenidate in the 1990s accurately reflects an increase in the use of the medication, but to a somewhat misleading degree. Federal production quotas are bureaucratically arrived at estimates that often vary from year to year. For example, the national production quotas for amphetamines (primarily dextroamphetamine) were 417, 168, 628, and 238 Kg in 1990 through 1993 respectively. Such fluctuations have been somewhat less for methylphenidate.

A more accurate assessment of increases in the use of methylphenidate in the U.S. can be obtained from recent research, most of which has not yet been published. A significant national physician audit noted a doubling of youths with ADD (ages five-seventeen) treated by physicians from 1990 through 1994. A Maryland Medicaid database analysis revealed a 76 percent increase in methylphenidate prescriptions between 1991 and 1993. DEA's ARCOS database figures indicated a 97 percent increase from 1989 to 1993 in bulk methylphenidate sales to U.S. pharmaceutical distributors. In Baltimore County, MD, the number of students on medication for ADD increased an average of about 20 percent per year from 1991 to 1995. Thus, based upon relatively current research findings, an overall increase of 100-150 percent from 1990 to 1995 in the prescription rate of methylphenidate for the treatment of ADD appears to have occurred.

STIMULANT TREATMENT FOR ADD IN 1994-95

In the late 1980s, around 700,000 youths with ADD were being treated with stimulant medication in the U.S., so that a 2 to 2.5 fold increase in use suggests the treatment of around 1.6 million youths in 1994 to 1995. Since there are 38 million youths ages five through fourteen and 53 million youths ages five through eighteen (in 1994), then an estimated 3 to 4.2 percent of U.S. youths (depending upon the age range selected) are receiving stimulant treatment for ADD. This medication treatment estimate indicates that around one-half of the 6 to 7 percent of youths ages five through twelve, of whom research has identified as having ADD, are receiving stimulant treatment in the U.S. at this time.

The average 3.6 percent estimate of U.S. youths on stimulants for ADD is close to the 2.9 percent figure for Baltimore County students (ages five through eighteen) in 1993, and the 3.7 percent figure for Maryland Medicaid youths (ages five through fourteen) treated with methylphenidate in 1993. If corrected for age, it is also not substantially different from the finding that 1.1 percent of Michigan youths (ages zero through nineteen) received methylphenidate in early 1992. It does, however, contrast with the finding that 1.1 percent of the five to fourteen-year-old enrollees at the NW Kaiser Permanente HMO were being treated with methylphenidate in 1991.

The 3.6 percent youth estimate on stimulants does not take into account the fact that approximately 20 percent of youths who use stimulants are not hyperactive, but have learning and attentional problems. Such youths were not indicated as having AD/HD under DSM-III in the mid-1980s when epidemiological studies identified AD/HD at 6 to 7 percent. In addition, the 3.6 percent composite estimate for stimulant treatment obscures the fact that around half of the total number of youths with ADD who use stimulants are ages seven through ten, when medication usage rates are proportionately higher.

MEDICATION RATE VARIATIONS IN RELATION TO GENDER, RACE, AND FAMILY INCOME

School aged boys are placed on stimulants more often than girls, at a 4:1 ratio in the primary grades and at a 5:1 ratio in middle school. African-American youths

TRENDS IN STIMULANT TREATMENT

1937	First report of stimulant treatment (Benzadrine) for youths with behavior problems.
1954	Methylphenidate (Ritalin) enters the pharmaceutical stimulant market.
1964	Early studies by Conners and Eisenberg at the Johns Hopkins Hospital spread the word about therapeutic effects of stimulants in hyperactive children.
1970s	Dextroamphetamine (Dexadrine) and methylphenidate are the major stimulant medications used to treat hyperkinetic children. Stimulants are used primarily for overactive elementary school youths with serious behavior and academic problems residing in economically advantaged areas.
1974	Pemoline (Cylert) enters the pharmaceutical stimulant market.
1980s	Methylphenidate substantially takes over the stimulant treatment market. More youths with ADD are kept on stimulants into their secondary school years. More girls with ADD are placed on stimulants.
1986-1990	An anti-methylphenidate media and lawsuit campaign results in the declining use of stimulants for ADD.
1990-1995	Use of methylphenidate doubles after the anti-methylphenidate campaign fades. Use of stimulant treatment in middle schools nearly equals the elementary school rate. Around 20 percent of stimulants are given to non-hyperactive youths with attentional and learning problems.
1993-1995	Stimulant use increases for adults with ADD and for some conduct disordered youths.

tend to use medication for ADD at a somewhat lower rate than their Caucasian counterparts, and rural youths are prescribed stimulants less often than urban youths.

PRESCRIBING TRENDS

Stimulants are infrequently prescribed outside of North America. This is largely because of legal barriers imposed by most governments to limit their availability.

CONCLUSION

The prominent increase in the use of stimulant treatment over the last thirty years in the U.S. primarily reflects its measurable symptomatic benefit for the great majority of youths with ADD. At least 90 percent of parents whose children are receiving stimulant treatment for ADD report that the medication is useful.

However, the doubling of methylphenidate in the 1990s and the widening range of its treatment applications (e.g., adults with ADD, learning-disordered and conduct-disordered youths, borderline cases of ADD) has led some to question if stimulants are now being "overused." This question can be answered from the symptomatic perspective by careful research. In the 1970s and 1980s, around 75 percent of hyperactive youths clearly benefited from stimulants in controlled clinical trials and about the same percentage of youths receiving stimulants in naturalistic school studies showed distinct and measurable improvements. In 1995, additional assessments of diagnostic subgroups and school populations could easily determine if the symptomatic results of stimulant treatment remain as satisfactory. Beyond the symptomatic perspective are broader research questions beyond the scope of this report.

*This article first appeared in the
Fall 1995 ATTENTION!*

Daniel J. Safer, M.D. is an Associate Professor (part-time) with the Division of Child Psychiatry at the Johns Hopkins University School of Medicine in Baltimore. He is the co-author of "Hyperactive Children: Diagnosis and Treatment," and has written forty-eight articles and two books.

CHAPTER 2

EDUCATION

An Introduction by Sandra Reif

Resource Specialist, San Diego Public School System

Author of *How to Reach and Teach*

ADD/ADHD Children (Simon and Schuster)

What do our children need to meet the educational challenges of the middle and high school years? What are some of the issues that parents and educators must address to help our adolescents with ADD succeed in school?

All too often at this age, we hear our children talk about school as "boring," and they don't see the connection between what is being taught in school and their own lives. Instruction at this level must be meaningful, challenging, and relevant — eliciting active participation and student involvement. It is critical that we motivate our adolescent students, engaging their interest and tapping into their strengths. We must provide opportunities in every classroom that allow students to learn to work together cooperatively, communicate effectively, and develop strong academic and study skills. The curriculum and schedule needs to provide options, variety, choices, and balance.

We must not tolerate mediocrity in the classroom or teachers who go "through the motions" without extending themselves, or adapting and developing the skills to meet the needs of their students. We owe it to our children to provide them with an optimal education, which means teachers who:

- motivate and inspire their students to be the best that they can be;
- are good role models who are firm, fair, and clearly in charge;
- are positive and enthusiastic;
- enjoy teaching and communicate that they are interested in and care about their students;
- encourage and welcome close communication between home and school; and

- maintain positive and high expectations along with support to those students in need to allow them to achieve success.

Adolescents have a strong sense of justice and fair play. Protection of their image and being treated with respect are of utmost importance. They need to feel "safe and comfortable" in the classroom environment (knowing they will be treated with dignity and not deliberately criticized or embarrassed in front of their peers). Students need structured, positive classrooms that are welcoming and inclusive. They also must have the chance to voice their feelings, concerns, and ideas.

It often happens that, when we have children with maturing bodies who look "grown up," we place unrealistic expectations upon them. Adolescents have a very critical need for structure, and frequent monitoring both at home and school (even as they complain and resist). There is a greater need for guidance and open channels of communication than ever before. This is especially true due to the power of peer influence and outside pressures that our children are exposed to every day. Close communication between parents and teachers is also necessary. In middle school and high school this becomes much more difficult with several different teachers, a myriad of projects and assignments due, and varying expectations. It is helpful when there is an adult at school willing to be a "case manager" (officially or unofficially), someone who will be able to monitor progress, advise, and intervene in school situations.

These are the years when it is very difficult for parents and teachers to find that proper balance: how to teach our children to assume responsibility for their own learning and behavioral choices and how to intervene as we guide and support them to success. Parental involvement in our adolescents' education is critical. A strong partnership between the home and school must be forged. Some skills and issues take on even greater significance as children move up in the grades such as: building organization and study skills, time management, coping with the high demands and many transitions, learning how to negotiate the system, and use compensatory strategies. The authors of the following articles share expert advice and many practical and proactive strategies for parents and teachers that address these issues, as well as other important tips for school success.

(Editor's Note: A special addition to this chapter is the September 16, 1991 U.S. Department of Education Policy Memorandum, which details how schools are to serve children with ADD. This policy memorandum, which has the force of law, specified for the first time that children with ADD may be eligible for special education and related services solely on the basis of having ADD. Parents are urged to copy the policy memorandum and, as needed, share it with educators.)

A School-Based Consultation Program for Service Delivery to Middle School Students with Attention Deficit/Hyperactivity Disorder

by Edward S. Shapiro, George J. DuPaul, Kathy L. Bradley, and Linnea T. Bailey

A school-based consultation program for providing services to middle school students with attention deficit/hyperactivity disorder (AD/HD) is described. Services were offered at three levels: inservice training, on-site consultation, and advanced training with follow-up consultation. The program began by providing core knowledge about AD/HD and effective intervention skills when working with adolescents. Following the inservice, the program providers used a behavioral consultation framework to offer participating school districts fifteen days of individualized consultative services within a sixty-day period. Advanced knowledge and follow-up consultation were made available after the consultation process was completed. Results indicated that, across a total of fifty-seven participating school districts, 2,928 different personnel had contact with project activities. Although school districts varied as to the types of project services they accessed, most districts chose to use general inservice programs focused on knowledge dissemination to general and special education teachers, as well as consultation concerning individual students. Outcomes of the project suggested that the model was successful in substantially increasing knowledge and services to middle school students with AD/HD. Implications for future implementation and expansion of the model are discussed.

Over the past decade, substantial attention has been devoted to achieving a better understanding of attention deficit/hyperactivity disorder (AD/HD) in children. AD/HD is a disruptive behavior disorder composed of developmentally inappropriate levels of inattention, impulsivity, and overactivity (American Psychiatric Association, 1994). Literally thousands of published studies examining etiology, development, assessment, and intervention for children with AD/HD have made it clear that this disorder continues to have an impact on the lives of children throughout their adult years (Barkley, 1990; Weiss & Hechtman, 1993).

Despite the substantial effort devoted to researching this disorder, the primary focus of study has been on the course of AD/HD in elementary-age children. The limited research examining AD/HD in middle and junior high school-age students has tended to show that 70 to 80 percent of individuals with AD/HD continue to display these same symptoms (albeit with diminished intensity) into adolescence and that 30 to 50 percent of children with AD/HD are impaired by their symptoms as adults (Barkley, 1990). It has also been reported that adolescents with AD/HD often display higher levels of criminal activity, elevated levels of conduct disorders, higher rates of suspension, and greater risk of school dropout (e.g., Barkley, Fischer, Edelbrock, & Smallfish, 1990).

Increased demands of the instructional setting in middle schools, such as having multiple teachers, changing classes every forty-five minutes, using a locker to store needed materials, and being required in certain classes to take notes, force all children to develop sound organizational skills. Unfortunately, children with AD/HD often have significant deficits in this area (Barkley, 1990); DuPaul & Stoner, 1994). Additionally, teachers begin to have heightened expectations for independence, placing substantial responsibility on their students for completing assignments and other routine academic requirements. Students with AD/HD usually also have significant deficiencies in these areas. Beyond these problems in academic skills, adolescents with AD/HD typically display social deficits that have an impact on their performance (Landau & Moore, 1991). These students often lack friends, get into significant difficulties with authorities, and are not well liked by their peers.

Adolescents with AD/HD are most likely to receive treatment through medical and/or clinical-based practitioners (Barkley, 1990). Although such services are effective and necessary, given the myriad difficulties students with this disorder encounter in educational settings, it is necessary to supplement clinic-based treatment with intervention delivery in the schools (DuPaul & Stoner, 1994; Power, Atkins, Osbourne & Blum, 1994). A collaborative team approach, headed by the school psychologist as case manager, has been advocated (DuPaul & Stoner, 1994; Pfiffner & Barkley, 1990; Power et al., 1994; Teeter, 1991). To have an impact on the school-based treatment of adolescents with AD/HD requires that teachers and other school professionals have a substantial knowledge concerning how best to accommodate and work with these students. Although school-based programs have many advantages, one of the greatest limitations in their implementation, especially at the middle and junior high school level, is the lack of knowledge and skills regarding AD/HD among teachers and other school professionals (Reid, Vasa, Maag, & Wright, 1994). The acquisition of this knowledge is a critical prerequisite for any effective school-based consultation program.

Among the variety of consultation models that have been proposed for working with school personnel (see Dougherty, 1995; Zins, Kratochwill, & Elliot, 1993 for reviews), the behavioral consultation model appears to have the most potential for effectively working with students with AD/HD, given the documented success of contingency management interventions with this population (see Fiore, Becker, & Nero, 1993 for a review). However, at least two aspects of the implementation of this model need to be modified in servicing students with this disorder. First, school personnel must be provided with information about the characteristics of children with AD/HD, effective methods for identifying students, and procedures for school-based intervention. This is particularly important for those professionals (e.g., school psychologist, special educator) who are likely to be serving as consultants with general education teachers. Second, few consultants have a mandate or the time to provide direct services to students. Typically, consultant services are provided indirectly through general education teachers who, in turn, work directly with students. Direct involvement by a consultant with students with AD/HD at particular stages of the consultation, however, can offer teachers and other school personnel opportunities to observe firsthand how to assess and/or intervene with students.

Providing services to students with AD/HD may require an approach to consultation that combines consultative procedures directed at system and teacher levels. At a system level, the consultant would be responsible for (a) ascertaining the extent of need in the school district, including the types of behavioral and learning problems experienced by students with AD/HD and faced by teachers; (b) establishing the inservice training needs of the district and school personnel; (c) determining the system impediments to change; and (d) meeting those identified inservice training needs. At a teacher or support staff level, the consultant would be responsible for conducting behavior management training sessions, coordinating weekly sessions to develop and monitor classroom management plans, and providing emotional support for teachers.

The purpose of the present article is to describe a program for providing consultative services to school personnel working with young adolescents with AD/HD. The program consisted of three levels of service delivery:

- establishing core knowledge across participants (Level 1);
- providing on-site consultative services for district generated specific needs (Level 2), and
- follow-up consultation with advanced training (Level 3) to sustain program implementation.

THE PROGRAM

In recognition of the need for increased expertise among school personnel in working with students with AD/HD, the Lehigh University-Consulting Center for Adolescents with Attention Deficit Disorders (LU-CCAADD) was established through a grant from the U.S. Department of Education. The project's primary objective was to design a school-based behavioral consultation model for educational personnel working with young adolescents with AD/HD at the middle school and junior high school levels (defined as fifth through ninth grades). The aim was to increase staff members' core knowledge of AD/HD and intervention skills. The program emphasized collaboration among students, teachers, related school personnel, parents, and consultants. All services were provided within general education settings and focused upon the social and educational needs and accommodations necessary for students with AD/HD. Also included was consultation at both individual student and system levels.

As noted above, LU-CCAADD provided services at three levels (illustrated in Figure 1). The first level involved providing a common knowledge base about AD/HD in adolescents as well as an understanding of effective intervention strategies to key school personnel who would participate in the project. Once this knowledge base was established, LU-CCAADD provided participating districts with on-site consultative services tailored to the identified needs of the individual districts (Level 2). The third level comprised advanced knowledge dissemination and follow-up consultation.

An important assumption underlying the program was that each district would bring a differing set of needs to the consultation process. Some districts self-identified their needs as wide-scale knowledge acquisition across the teaching and professional staff. Others required problem solving for specific individual cases. Still other districts saw themselves as requiring more system-level consultation concerning policy and procedures. As a result, one objective of LU-CCAADD became carefully matching types of consultative services to each district's needs.

Level 1: Inservice Training

A 2-day inservice training program that focused on core knowledge about adolescents with AD/HD was given. The inservice program also covered school-based assessment/identification of AD/HD as well as five intervention strategies found to be effective in working with young adolescents with AD/HD:

(1) School-based self-management strategies;
(2) School-based behavior management skills for teachers;
(3) Home-based behavior management for parents;
(4) Medication monitoring and pharmacological interventions; and
(5) Social skills and problem solving training.

Inservices were held over two consecutive days and were repeated three times during the school year for different groups. The same materials were used in each of the inservice presentations throughout the duration of the project. This training was designed as an introduction and overview for each area and served as a foundation for Level 2 services. All districts wishing to participate in Level 2 services were required to send at least one representative (maximum of three) to the Level 1 training. Each district was reimbursed by LU-CCAAD to offset costs for sending staff members to the inservice program.

Level 2: On-site Consultation

This level of service involved providing consultative services to districts on site by having LU-CCAADD send a trained staff member (in this case, a doctoral student) to the participating site. LU-CCAADD staff provided consultative services through a contractual agreement over a period of sixty days, of which fifteen days (two hours per day) were on-site. At the initial meeting with the consultant, the district identified its priorities for the consultative period from a list of service options developed by LU-CCAADD (see Table 1). Districts were permitted to use the list of service options in creative ways to meet their needs. For example, some districts used the Level 2 services to develop district policies on the identification and treatment of students with AD/HD. Others used Level 2 services to develop a district plan

---

LEVEL 1
INSERVICE TRAINING
Assessment of AD/HD
School-based Intervention
Parent Training
Collaboration with Community Professionals
Peer Relationship Interventions

LEVEL 2
ON-SITE CONSULTATION
Identification of Students
Individual Student Treatment
Additional Inservice
Communication with MD's
Parent Training
Peer Relationship Intervention

LEVEL 3
ADVANCED KNOWLEDGE DISSEMINATION AND FOLLOW-UP CONSULTATION
Follow-Up Assessment
Additional On-Site Consultation
Advanced Training in AD/HD

FIGURE 1. Consultation center program outline.

for communicating with physicians about students placed on medication.

On-site consultation represented the most significant and intensive part of the program. The first step in Level 2 services was to hold an action plan meeting with attendees designated by the school district. The purpose was to establish and delineate the services that would best meet the needs of this district, determine the specific schedule on which services would be delivered, assign responsibilities to district personnel for liaison and follow-through with the project consultant, and establish the assessment objectives and outcome measures to be used. Each district was also informed that it would receive a Consumer Satisfaction Survey (CSS) immediately following termination of services, as well as a request for follow-up data three months after services ended. Following the action-plan meeting, consultative services were then delivered according to the agreed-upon schedule.

Level 3: Advanced Knowledge Dissemination and Follow-Up Consultation

Services at Level 3 included advanced training in AD/HD, wide-scale dissemination of the training program, and follow-up assessment and consultation to participating districts. In order to provide opportunities to disseminate knowledge and expertise to a national, broad-based audience, LU-CCAAD offered one-week summer institutes focused on effective assessment and intervention for adolescents with AD/HD. Experts in the field of AD/HD came to Lehigh University and offered full-day presentations on topics such as psychopharmacology, social skills, cognitive interventions, school-based treatment, and family treatments. Those districts that participated in Level 2 services during the academic year were able to send one representative each to the institute at no charge.

Level 3 services also included a wide-scale dissemination plan where a step-by-step description of the program was given to school districts and educational service agencies interested in establishing consultation centers for students with AD/HD both in Pennsylvania and nationally. As part of this effort, a training manual and corresponding video were developed and distributed to all state departments of education (see Note).

Participating districts were given the opportunity of additional consultative services through telephone contact with project staff. Occasional on-site visits were also provided on an as-needed basis, with LU-CCAAD remaining as a frequent source of potential information for districts that had participated in the project.

TABLE 1

Menu of Services Offered by LU-CCAADD

Develop individual student intervention programs

Provide direct inservice

Assist building-level teams

Establish methods of identifying and monitoring students with ADD

Assist in communicating and interacting with physicians

Assist in implementing:
 Parent training
 Social skills training
 Cognitive social problem-solving training
 Self-management
 Evaluation of existing programs
 Assessments for social behavior problems

PARTICIPATING SCHOOL DISTRICT CASE STUDY

To more effectively illustrate what kind of participation occurred during the project, a chronology of service delivery for one school district following Level 1 is discussed next. The district elected to concentrate their efforts toward

(1) Building a strong knowledge base among the staff about AD/HD in adolescents;

(2) Creating practical classroom interventions for these students;

(3) Developing a district-wide procedure and policy manual for working with students with AD/HD.

This school district consisted of 3,701 students and was located in a suburb of a small city. The district's ethnic makeup was primarily White (96.5%) and was middle to upper-middle class, with 10 percent of the students receiving free or reduced lunch.

Table 2 shows the chronology of service delivery across the district's period of participation. The Level 1 inservice was attended by the district's coordinator of special education/psychological services, a guidance counselor, and a learning support (resource room) teacher. These individuals served as the primary team with whom the project consultant worked during the consultation process.

At the action plan meeting, the district identified three objectives that they wanted to accomplish during the consultation process:

(1) To create a policy regarding how the district planned to conduct assessments and provide services to students with AD/HD. Included in this policy would be a consideration of legal issues and the development of service plans under Section 504 of the Rehabilitation Act for students with AD/HD who were found not to be eligible for special education.

(2) To get specific assistance in designing effective classroom intervention strategies for teachers who work with students with AD/HD. To develop this capacity, the district wanted to create a specialized building-level team that would contain one member from each grade-level team to serve as a consultative resource.

(3) To obtain assistance in developing interventions for a specific seventh-grade student who had presented significant challenges to the school staff.

At the action plan meeting, it was decided first that a large-group inservice would be provided to the entire middle school staff. At that meeting, volunteers were to be sought who would function as part of an in-school team whose members would meet with the project consultant on a regular basis to receive training in effective strategies for working with adolescents with AD/HD. The project consultant would work directly with the coordinator of special education/psychological services in formulating the district policy. Finally, the consultant would meet with the seventh-grade-level team to facilitate the design of a specific intervention strategy.

At the school-wide two-hour inservice to all middle school staff, LU-CCAADD briefly reviewed the characteristics of AD/HD and how these problems are manifested in adolescents. They then discussed strategies designed to prevent behavior problems in students with AD/HD (e.g., teaching note-taking skills, keeping an extra set of texts at home, allowing tape recording of lectures); home-school communication programs (such as the use of daily behavior report cards); self-management; social skills training; and a response cost raffle. At this inservice, a number of teachers volunteered to be part of the building AD/HD team.

Following this inservice, the project consultant began meeting with the seventh-grade-level team to help design an effective strategy for a student who was refusing to follow directions, frequently disturbing classmates, refusing to complete required work, and engaging in other off-task behaviors. The team chose to design and implement the self-management program that was presented as part of the inservice. This intervention, an adaptation of the procedure described by Rhode, Morgan, and Young (1983); Smith, Young, Nelson, and West (1992); and Smith, Young, West, Morgan, and Rhode (1988), aims to teach students to systematically judge the quality of their own behavior against that expected by their teachers. Implementation of the intervention was monitored through a series of grade-level meetings attended by the project consultant, as indicated on Table 2. At one other grade-level meeting (5/31/94), a second student was discussed and a decision was made to implement a daily report card program for this student also. Again, the consultant helped to facilitate the design and implementation of the intervention. The development of the district policy manual was coordinated in meetings between the project consultant and the school district's coordinator for special education/psychological services. Over the course of these meetings, district guidelines were designed and circulated to all parents. Included in the policy guidelines were the processes by which students with AD/HD could be offered assistance. This included services available through the Instructional Support Team (a state mandated pre-referral intervention team) as an identified special education student under the category "other health impaired" and under Section 504 of the Rehabilitation Act. Information about the local Children and Adults with Attention Deficit Disorder (CH.A.D.D.) chapter was also provided. Procedures for assessment and effective intervention strategies were delineated. The policy was accepted by the district administration and distributed to all parents.

At the end of the school year, it was decided to repeat the two-day inservice but present it to the entire school district. A total of forty-seven staff members attended, of whom forty-two were teachers. The building-level AD/HD team and the project consultant held a final meeting to set goals for the following year.

The project consultant provided a total of 19.75 hours of time during a sixty day consultation period (slightly more than the contracted fifteen hours). Follow-up data were collected three months after the consultation ended. The original team who attended the Level 1 inservice were sent a brief survey on which they were asked collectively the following questions:

(1) Were the interactions that had been developed through the Level 2 consultation still being implemented with the same students?

(2) Had these interventions been implemented with additional students?

(3) Were the interventions developed through the consultation process added to the IEPs of any students?

(4) Were staff in the district seeking additional training?

(5) Was the district using the training provided to them through the project to train their own staff?

TABLE 2

Chronology for a Participating School District

DATES (1994)	SERVICES PROVIDED
3/14, 3/15	Level 1 inservice
4/6	Action plan meeting
4/20	Faculty inservice
4/22	Meeting to facilitate development of district policy and procedure for students with AD/HD
5/11	Grade-level team meeting to review target student's problem
516	Grade-level team meeting to develop self-management plan for target student
5/20	Meeting with parents of targeted student to present self-management plan
5/31	Grade-level team meetings
6/2	Meeting with building-level AD/HD team to establish team's role and purpose
6/3	Observations of specific students throughout the day
6/14	Faculty inservice
6/15	Faculty inservice
6/20	Meeting with building-level AD/HD team to set goals for next year

(6) What other resources did the district believe it still needed to address the needs of students with AD/HD?

The district's response to the survey indicated that the district had continued to use the interventions with these same students, also had used the interventions with many other cases (number not specified), and had not added interventions to the IEPs of any students. District staff were seeking additional training as individuals, but the building-level AD/HD team had continued to provide services at the middle school. District personnel continued to feel they needed more training on effective strategies.

At Level 3 the district sent the entire district team to all four days of the summer institute and paid the costs not covered by the project. Follow-up consultation via telephone was offered to the district twice in regard to questions about the implementation of the self-management intervention.

GENERAL PROGRAM OUTCOMES

Across the entire three years of the project, a total of 169 school personnel from 57 school districts attended Level 1 inservices. Attendees included general education teachers, special education teachers, school psychologists, guidance counselors, supervisors of special education, pupil personnel directors, principals, and school nurses. Prior to and immediately following each Level 1 inservice, the AD/HD Knowledge Test (Anastropoulos, Shelton, & DuPaul, 1992), a twenty-two-item multiple choice test asking questions about etiology, assessment, and intervention strategies, was administered. Using a total percentage accuracy score on the test, project professionals found an average improvement across project participants of 18 percent, from a mean of 75 percent at pretest to a mean of 93 percent at posttest. A t test for correlated samples indicated that this difference was statistically significant ($T = 17.21$, $p < .01$).

Consultation for individual cases was provided directly to approximately 169 students across the 57 districts. However, indirect effects on students not directly targeted through the on-site project consultation were also evident. Across the 57 districts, these same intervention strategies were implemented with an additional group of 592 students. Thus, one important and encouraging outcome of the program was that direct consultation with school staff on specific cases resulted in a "spread of effect" to others in need. Between September 1992 and January 1995, the project had direct contact with 2,436 school-based personnel and 492 parents across the 57 school districts.

Districts varied substantially in the types of services requested. The two most frequently used were inservices to faculty (91% of districts served) and consultation about an individual student (75% of districts served). Other frequently selected services included assisting in setting up parent training programs (33% of districts served), helping to establish district policies on AD/HD (26% of districts served), and assisting in the development of building-level AD/HD teams (28%).

The request for completion of a ten-item Consumer Satisfaction Survey was obtained from fifty-one (89%) of the participating districts. Results showed very high levels of satisfaction across all items. The mean satisfaction scores across these districts for each question are presented in Table 3.

A follow-up survey consisting of five questions was sent to all participating districts three months after consultation ended. Data were obtained from forty-three of the districts that had participated in Level 1 and 2 services. Response rates were less than expected due to the absence of individual contact persons from some districts.

The first question asked the districts to indicate if the interventions designed for specific students during the consultation process were being continued with those same students. Results showed that twenty-four (71%) of the thirty-four districts that had implemented an intervention for a specific case through the Level 2 consultative service continued using that intervention with the targeted students at follow-up. An examination of comments received from these districts suggested that, in almost all cases where intervention was discontinued, extenuating circumstances had arisen (e.g., student had moved).

The second question asked whether districts had adapted their new interventions to other students not specifically targeted during the Level 2 consultation services. Of the forty-three districts responding, twenty-six indicated they had started interventions with other students. Included among these were five districts that had discontinued the intervention with the originally targeted student and two districts that had chosen not to implement an intervention for any specific student during Level 2 services.

The third question asked if the intervention strategies learned through the consultation program were added to the IEPs of students with AD/HD who had also been previously classified as in need of special education. Responding districts indicated that a total of 146 students had specific additions to their IEPs related to behavior management programs learned through the consultation services.

The final two questions asked if districts were seeking additional training about AD/HD. A total of 68 percent of the districts indicated that staff were seeking additional training in AD/HD. It was noted that in some districts resistance to the view that AD/HD is a medically related disability was evident. On the other hand, one district noted that an inservice was scheduled for all K through Grade 8 staff as a result of participation in the project.

The week-long summer institutes were well attended, averaging 70 persons per day in 1993 and 90 per day in 1994 and 1995. Of the districts eligible to send a representative to the institutes, fifty-two (91%) had someone attend at least one of the four days. A total of forty-two (74%) had someone in attendance from their district on all four days.

DISCUSSION AND CONCLUSIONS

The overall outcomes of the program were very successful in improving the knowledge base of middle school personnel in working with adolescents with AD/HD. Inservice programs were selected as a means of service delivery by over 90 percent of the districts. Assistance in designing interventions for individual students was provided for over 75 percent of the districts. Additionally, at a ratio of greater than three to one, school districts reported that strategies learned through the consultative process had been used with other students for whom no specific consultation was provided from the program consultant. Feedback from the districts indicated that they had high levels of satisfaction with the consultation services that they received and that substantial improvement was evident in the school personnel's knowledge of AD/HD.

Despite the very positive outcomes of this program, certain limitations of the implementation and findings must be acknowledged. Although the program was implemented across a fairly wide geographical region within eastern Pennsylvania and western New Jersey, the outcomes may be related to the particular part of the country in which the program was put in place. Implementation in a more urban or more rural area may result in changes in the program that were not considered under its current development. In particular, the application of the program in school districts with large numbers of culturally and linguistically diverse students needs to be examined. Replication of the program in different locations and types of school districts would offer a clearer understanding of potential influences that geographical region and ethnic diversity might play.

Another limitation of the program involves the very nature of many school-based programs. The presence of school district strikes, scheduling conflicts, and other projects in the schools may have limited the integrity with which the program was implemented in some sites. Likewise, the problems experienced with obtaining follow-up data from some of the initial project participants may have limited the conclusions we could draw about program outcomes. Future research should carefully examine the relationships between these types of school-based issues and effective program outcomes.

A third limitation was the lack of data obtained on student outcomes. Although the primary objective of the program was acquisition of knowledge about AD/HD in adolescents by school staff, the "bottom line" for any consultation program must be its ultimate impact on the quality of educational programs for children. Those persons conducting future replications of the program may want to obtain more specific data on the impact of interventions put in place for individual students.

The outcomes of the consultation process were not always successful. Although it was difficult to provide empirical and quantitative evidence for failure, certain qualitative aspects of the consultation process appeared to be related to successful outcomes. Anecdotal reports suggested that the strongest predictors of success were administrative support, the availability of a district-based contact person, the attendance of a school district observer during meetings, the recruitment of motivated teachers with whom to work, and the selection of appro-

TABLE 3

Mean Scores Across Districts on the Consumer Satisfaction Survey

ITEM	MEAN SCORE
1. Services consistent with description?	2.95
2. Consultees satisfied with training in interventions?	2.70
3. Materials readily available?	2.92
4. Opportunity for communication and feedback?	2.91
5. Services provided in cost and time efficient manner?	2.84
6. District personnel satisfied with services of LU-CCAADD?	
7. Any benefit associated with district's involvement?	2.28
8. Any harm associated with district's involvement?	1.00
9. Measurable gains in social skills behaviors behaviors of students?	2.08
10. Improvements in understanding of AD/HD and behavioral alternatives	2.73

Note. Response scale: 1 = *never*, 2 = *sometimes*, 3 = *always*. N = 51.

priate students when developing an intervention. These same issues have been repeated throughout the school reform literature as critical components to effective school reform (e.g., Bacharach, 1990; Knoff, 1995; Knoff & Batsche, 1995; Lennox, Hyman, & Hughes, 1988). Efforts to document more empirically the critical variables to an effective consultative program such as ours clearly are needed.

Finally, the LU-CCAADD program involved a link to university faculty who shared high levels of expertise in AD/HD. Some questions may be raised whether such a linkage is necessary for success. Although the program has been described and nationally disseminated in such a way that the university link is unnecessary, empirical evaluation of this program without the university tie has yet to be demonstrated.

Although results from the three years of our project indicate that a school-based consultation program can result in effective service delivery for staff working with young adolescents with AD/HD, many issues remain to be explored. Among these, the degree to which other agencies can enact this program without federal grant support needs to be determined. One possibility is that such services could be regionalized through forming multidisciplinary "AD/HD consultant teams" within intermediate education units. Work has begun with several groups around the country who have shown interest in implementing the LU-CCAADD program in this manner. Second, the applicability of this program to students at the elementary and high school levels has yet to be explored. There is no reason to believe, however, that it cannot easily be translated upward or downward to school personnel working at these levels. Finally, as school personnel gain greater expertise in assisting students with AD/HD, the consultation program must evolve to meet more complex needs. The challenge is for educational and clinical professionals to collaborate more effectively to promote success for individuals with AD/HD across home, school, and community settings.

Despite the challenges in providing services to students with AD/HD, the program described here offers a potential mechanism for enhancing school-based services to adolescents with AD/HD. Consistent with the suggested framework for consultation described by Pfiffner and Barkley (1990) and Teeter (1991), the present program has demonstrated substantial improvements in the knowledge base of a large number of school-based professionals, as well as parents of students with AD/HD. Continued efforts to evaluate effective school-based services to students with AD/HD clearly are needed.

Reprinted with permission of Journal of Emotional and Behavioral Disorders, *4(2), 73-81 (1996) by PRO-ED., Inc.*

Edward S. Shapiro, Ph.D. is a professor and coordinator of the School Psychology Program at Lehigh University in Bethlehem, Pennsylvania and is the editor of School Psychology Review.

George J. DuPaul, Ph.D. is an associate professor, School Psychology Program, at Lehigh University and an associate editor of School Psychology Review.

Kathy L. Bradley, Ed.S. is a doctoral student in school psychology at Lehigh University.

Linnea Bailey, M.Ed. is a doctoral student in counseling psychology at Lehigh University.

Author's Note

This project was made possible by a grant from the U.S. Department of Education, Office of Special Education Services, Division of Personnel Preparation (Grant No. H029K20455). The opinions expressed in this article do not represent the views of the Department of Education.

The project manual and videotape describing the model's implementation are available from the first author for $35.00.

References

American Psychiatric Association. (1994). *Diagnostic and statistical manual of mental disorders-IV* (4th ed.). Washington, DC: Author.

Anastopoulos, A.D., Shelton, T.L., & DuPaul, G.J. (1992). *Test of AD/HD knowledge.* Unpublished manuscript, University of Massachusetts Medical Center, Worcester, MA.

Bacharach, S.B. (1990). *Education reform: Making sense of it all.* Boston: Allyn & Bacon.

Barkley, R.A. (Ed.). (1990). *Attention-deficit hypercitivity disorder: A handbook for diagnosis and treatment.* New York: Guilford.

Barkley, R.A., Fishcer, J., Edelbrock, C., & Smallish, M. (1990). The adolescent outcome of hyperactive children diagnosed by research criteria: An eight year follow-up study. *Journal of the American Academy of Child and Adolescent Psychiatry, 29,* 546-557.

Dougherty, A.M. (1995) *Consultation: Practice and perspectives in school and community settings* (2nd ed.). Pacific Grove, CA: Brooks/Cole.

DuPaul, G.J. & Stoner, G. (1994). *AD/HD in the schools: Assessment and intervention strategies.* New York: Guilford.

Fiore, T.A., Becker, E.A., & Nero, R.C. (1993). Educational interventions for students with attention deficit disorder. *Exceptional Children, 69,* 163-173.

Knoff, H.M. (1995). Best practices in facilitating school-based organizational change and strategic planning. In A. Thomas & J. Grimes (Eds.), *Best practices in school psychology, Volume III* (pp. 239-252). Washington, DC: National Assocation of School Psychologists.

Knoff, H.M. & Batsche, G.M. (1995). Profect ACHIEVE: A school reform process for at-risk and underachiving students. *School Psychology Review, 24,* 579-603.

Landau, S. & Moore, L. (1991). Social skill deficits in children with attention deficit hyperactivity disorder. *School Psychology Review, 20,* 235-251.

Lennox, N., Hyman, I.A., & Hughes, C.A. (1988). Institutionalization of a consultation-based service delivery system. In JU.L. Graden, J.E. Zins, & M.J. Curtis (Eds.), *Althernative educational delivery systems: Enhancing instructional optionals for all students* (pp. 71-89(. Washington, DC: National Association of School Psychologists.

Pfiffner, L.J. & Barkley, R.A. (1990). Educational placement and classroom management. In R.A. Barkley (Ed.), *Attention-deficit hyperactivity disorder: A handbook for diagnosis and treatment* (pp. 489-539). New York: Guilford.

Power, T.J., Atkins, M.S., Osbourne, M.L., & Blum, N.J. (1994). The school psychologist as manager of programming for AD/HD. *School Psychology Review, 23*, 279-291.

Reid, R., Vasa, S.F., Maag, J.W., & Wright, G. (1994). An analysis of teachres' perceptions of attention deficit hyperactivity disorder. *The Journal of Research and Development in Education, 27*, 195-202.

Rhode, G., Morgan, D.P., & Young, K.R. (1983). Generalization and maintenance of treatment gains of behaviorally handicapped students from resource rooms to regular classrooms using self-evaluation procedures. *Journal of Applied Behavior Analysis, 16*, 171-188.

Smith, D.J., Young, K.R., Nelson, J.R., & West, R.P. (1992). The effect of a self-management procedure on the classroom academic behavior of students with mid handicaps. *School Psychology Review, 21*, 59-72.

Smith, D.J., Young, K.R., West., R.P., Morgan, D.P., & Rhode, G. (1988). Reducing the disruptive behavior of junior high students: A classroom self-management procedure. *Behavioral Disorders, 13, 231-239.*

Teeter, P.A. (1991). Attention deficit hyperactivity disorder: A pscchoeducational paradigm. School Psychology Review, 20, 266-280.

Weiss, G. & Hechtman, L.T. (1993). Hyperactive children grown up (2nd ed.). New York: Guilford.

Zins, J.E., Kratochwill, T.R., & Elliott, S.N. (1993). Handbook of consultation services for children: Applications in educational and clinical settings. San Francisco: Jossey-Bass.

Adolescents with ADD: The Transition From Childhood to Adulthood

Why Educators and Parents Must Provide Educational Care to Bridge the Gap

Prepared by the Adolescent Sub-Committee of CH.A.D.D.'s Public and Professional Education Committee, October, 1995. Special thanks to the adolescent committees of the South Hills Pittsburgh and Northern Virginia chapters.

As your child becomes an adolescent, school problems may emerge or intensify. Progress toward independence may lag behind peers, and your teen's self-esteem may be in jeopardy.

Teachers in secondary schools expect students to demonstrate increased responsibility and independence. Adolescents with attention deficit disorders want to meet these expectations and may have fared relatively well in elementary school. However, the larger secondary school environment with its increased academic work load, social challenges, and greater demands for self-sufficiency and organizational skills is often overwhelming to these students and places them at a distinct disadvantage. This high risk environment can result in both a decline in grades and escalating behavior problems.

As educators and parents, we must recognize that developmental problems may appear at any age. In his book, *Educational Care* (1994), Dr. Melvin Levine states, "We are never really 'out of the woods.' As a child's brain develops, some functions may start to lag at any point.... Schools need to have systems in place for the timely detection and proper identification of these problems at any point during a child's education. It is common to screen very young children for educational readiness. In reality, issues of readiness extend well beyond kindergarten. For example, the readiness of twelve year olds for adolescence or of seventeen year olds for young adulthood should be a matter of prime concern for communities.... If we neglect the later on-set (problems), we will misinterpret and mismanage many children. Communities must invest in prevention throughout the years of childhood."

Fortunately, with the support of both parents and educators, appropriate accommodations, the identification of and building upon student strengths, and the development of self-advocacy skills, these teens can indeed achieve success in school and learn the skills necessary to become competent, responsible adults.

It is the challenge of parents and educators to forge an alliance to enhance each adolescent's educational outcomes by providing ongoing support and individualized "educational care".

(Note: ADD refers to all forms of attention deficit disorders in this article.)

SUPPORTING THE STRUGGLING TEEN IN SCHOOL

Parents have the ability to sense when their teen is having difficulty in school. They usually ask, "How can I know for sure?", "What can I do to assure s/he has the best environment for learning?", "How can I get everyone to pull in the same direction?" This information sheet has been designed to give you insights on managing these concerns.

You can usually be assured there is a situation requiring attention when you:

observe or hear your teen's:
- complaints about boredom
- disorganization
- tardiness
- failing to finish classwork
- excessive talking and/or note passing
- inconsistent performance
- easy distractibility and frustration
- low self-esteem
- careless errors in schoolwork

- difficulty following directions
- dislike for school and/or desire to drop out of school
- increased number of "sick" days.

hear from a teacher, your teen:
- must take more responsibility
- owes me twelve homework assignments
- needs to try harder
- rushes through classroom work
- could do it if s/he wanted to
- is constantly out of his/her seat, blurting out answers, and disrupting class
- doesn't seem to care
- is never prepared for class
- is bright, but not working up to potential.

notice
- an increase in call/notices from the school
- a drop in grades
- an increase in behavior problems
- a suggestion by the school that lower track classes be taken despite teen's good ability
- attendance problems such as truancy for the entire day or just certain classes
- social problems and/or changes in peer group
- mood changes with increased sadness, anger, or low self-esteem.

The comments and observations mentioned above are not exhaustive, but are based on common situations experienced by other parents. If any of these seem familiar, you should begin immediate action to acquire appropriate support for your teen within the school system.

Assistance for your child can be acquired at the school through several similar but different processes: (1) written, agreed-upon interventions, (2) interventions available under Section 504 of the Rehabilitation Act of 1973, or (3) interventions under the Individuals with Disabilities Education Act (IDEA).

The purpose of this article is not to provide a step-by-step approach to developing and implementing an Individualized Education Program (IEP) under the IDEA or a plan under Section 504. Rather, our purpose is to provide a general guide as to how to 1) approach the school problems of the teen with ADD, 2) involve the teen in the process, and 3) interact with the school system to problem solve (which may be informal or through specified procedures under the IDEA and/or Section 504). For information concerning procedures under the IDEA and Section 504, you may refer to the CH.A.D.D. Educators Manual.

The process for obtaining assistance is comprised of the following steps which will be discussed in detail in this document:

- Request a meeting to review concerns
- Prepare written information for the meeting
- Initiate teen's participation
- Attend scheduled meeting(s)
- Identify team to evaluate teen's struggles
- Prepare the plan of interventions
- Implement the interventions
- Monitor the effectiveness of the interventions
- Review and update the interventions as identified by monitoring the results

As you progress through these steps, keep in mind the teen's interests, abilities, and aptitudes. Please note there may be subtle variations in state law and local school district policies.

Movement from one grade or school to another can cause anxiety in the teen. Anxiety can be minimized by selecting teachers who are flexible and willing to work with the teen's special needs. This is usually addressed by requesting "hand scheduling" of classes instead of computerized scheduling. Depending on the local school system, the timing of this varies. One area may allow scheduling in the spring where others may entertain it just before school starts. You will want to consider:

- Order sequencing of classes (academically challenging classes may be handled better by some teens in the morning or by alternating challenging classes with less rigorous ones)
- Matching teaching styles of teachers with teen's learning style
- Taking one or two classes in the summer to reduce the workload during the regular academic year (consider only if summer school is offered or if the teen does not require a long summer break)
- The teen's medication administration schedule (less rigorous classes can be scheduled when lower medication levels can be tolerated)

If the teen is going to be attending a new school, schedule an orientation with a peer mentor, older student who has ADD, or the guidance counselor. If the student has his class schedule, walking from classroom to classroom in the order of the schedule will help the student orient himself to the building(s). The teen should meet with teachers just before school starts or early in the school year to discuss his/her needed accommodations. Parents should be sure the teachers have been advised of the need for accommodations.

Similarly, the parent(s) should schedule a meeting with the teen's teachers and guidance counselor to review progress and revise interventions which are not working. There is no better plan for success than good communication and a working partnership between parents and the school.

Additionally, the high school junior or senior should include planning for post high school options, college or vocational training. Schools are mandated by (IDEA) to prepare by age sixteen, an Individualized Transition Plan (ITP) for students in special education. If the teen is considering college, s/he can apply for non-standard SAT/ACT testing which allows extended time. The ADD disability must be documented but s/he does not have to be a special education student. The Office for Vocational Rehabilitation (OVR) can be a resource for either vocational training or assistance in college. Your teen's guidance counselor can schedule a meeting with the OVR to determine your teen's eligibility for these services.

Request a Meeting to Review Concerns

A request for assistance can be initiated by either a parent or an educator, and it can be done through a verbal or written request to the school. The preferred way is to prepare a written request to the school and keep a copy of it in your files since it provides documentation that may be useful in the future. The written request may be sent to either the principal, the guidance counselor, or other school official. Check with your teen's school principal before a written request is sent to identify the correct person and eliminate any delay resulting from sending it to the wrong person. Describe in the request your concerns and request a meeting to convene at mutually agreed upon time.

Prepare Written Information for the Meeting

As a parent, it is very important for you to have reviewed information about your child and prepared written materials for the meeting. Many parents find it helpful to keep all school records, medical reports, copies of school correspondence in a three-ring binder. The following items should assist you in your preparations:

- Locate and review your child's academic history using report cards. Look for a downward trend in the grades as you compared recent to earlier ones.
- Collect samples of your teen's work to concretely document concerns.
- Have available copies of any behavioral notices you received. Check with the school's attendance office if you do not have them available.
- Assemble all medical and/or psychological reports, diagnoses, and medication information.
- Prepare a detailed list of your concerns in order of priority along with suggestions for each one on how they can be handled.
- Prepare a packet of ADD information related to your child, i.e., if your teen has ADD without hyperactivity, an article explaining it would be most appropriate. Include articles about ADD such as medication treatment, behavior management, and information on accommodations. Have copies available for each participant.

Initiate Teen's Participation

How do parents and educators teach adolescents to take on the responsibilities of becoming their own advocates? First, parents and educators, then the teen, must develop an understanding of the student's strengths, learning problems, and needed accommodations. Second, parents must model through their own actions, and later through role playing, how to be a successful advocate. After modeling, it is essential that the responsibility be relinquished to the adolescent as s/he needs to gain a sense of control and ownership for a successful outcome. This will become very important when the student is faced with these issues in post-secondary education and in the workplace while, at the same time, increasing their confidence and independence.

There are some adolescents, especially those with extreme shyness, who may be uncomfortable or resistant about participating in a meeting. Their reluctance should be respected, but even these teens can begin learning how to be their own self-advocates by: (1) having discussions with their guidance counselor, (2) putting in writing their ideas for the meeting, (3) attending part of the school meeting. Hopefully, through success, they will begin to gain insight into how valuable self-advocacy can be, and they will play a more assertive role.

Finally, gaining the teen's agreement on the accommodations proposed at the meeting is very important as it allows the student to take "ownership", and it increases the chances of success. Once all choices have been made, the issues and the accommodations should be documented along with the expected outcome of each one.

Attend Scheduled Meeting(s)

You, the parent, should attend each meeting to offer information and knowledge of your teen. Depending on the local school system, there may be one meeting or multiple meetings to determine a course of action for your teen. The goal of the meeting(s) is to acquire assistance for your adolescent and to develop a plan and partnership toward that end. A key issue in any meeting affecting your child is to keep your composure and emotions intact. Seek to work with the school system in a cooperative manner. A confrontational approach at the outset may be counterproductive. If you as a parent feel insecure or uncomfortable and would like to have someone assist you in your efforts, consider acquiring the services of an educational advocate. An advocate can speak on behalf of both you and your child, and without the strain of being emotionally involved. Parents have the right to invite anyone they wish to attend the meeting with them.

Identify Team to Evaluate Teen's Struggles

Usually, the purpose of the first meeting is for all parties to agree and define what problems exist and to identify a course of action to deal with them. The information you collected or documented will be quite helpful in substantiating the fact that a problem exists. School personnel will offer their perspectives as well. When all agree there is enough evidence, you can expect a team to be formed for evaluating the issues needing assistance. The team generally will include your teen's teacher(s), guidance counselor, parent(s), school administrators, and your teen (if s/he wishes to participate). The teen's doctor or psychologist may also contribute information for the team's consideration if they are unable to participate in the meeting. In the event you are not invited to be part of the team, you should initiate a request to participate. Meeting dates and times should be agreeable to the members and should be scheduled far enough in advance for you to be able to attend.

Prepare the Plan of Interventions

The evaluation team will identify the adolescent's strengths, issues, and concerns. As the evaluation progresses, they are likely to separate issues that are seen throughout most of the classes and those which are specific to a certain class. Each teacher should be asked to provide input related to his/her class. One method to collect this information is to use the Classroom Performance Survey (see included addendum). After all teacher input is received, the information identified can be analyzed. If there are many issues to consider, the team will prioritized them, dealing with the more prevalent issues first. The issues can then be matched to those identified on the Adolescent Accommodations listing (see included addendum) to find suggested strategies that may assist the teen. As the team begins to examine what accommodations can be used to address an issue, the teen's learning style should also be considered. Two or three accommodations for each issue should result. One of the team members will be appointed the liaison and will coordinate home/school communication and monitor progress. The name of the appointed person and the associated responsibilities should be included in the written plan. Review dates should be established at agreed upon intervals to identify what's working and what's not. This, too, should become part of the documented plan.

At this point, the teen's input is necessary. The guidance counselor may be the best person to review the team's suggested interventions and the Adolescent Accommodations. The teen should identify which ones are felt to be the most helpful. Gaining the teen's agreement on the accommodations allows him/her to have some "ownership" and increases the chances of success. Once all choices have been made, the issues and the accommodation(s) should be documented along with expected outcome of each one.

Implement the Interventions

Parents will provide assistance in implementing the accommodation(s) affecting the home component and the affected teachers will provide the same in the school environment. Teachers who were not part of the evaluation team should be invited to review and comment on the accommodations prior to implementation. Input from the teachers will encourage their "ownership" and investment in a successful outcome. The liaison should provide all teachers with a copy of the plan when it will commence. The student may require coaching if his/her participation becomes too lax or non-existent.

Monitor the Effectiveness of the Interventions

The appointed liaison will collect the information which is needed for determining effectiveness of the designated interventions. The collection of information is done at predetermined intervals previously identified by the evaluation team. Each of the respective parties is responsible for their record keeping and/or work samples to substantiate progress or identify an area of concern.

Review and Update the Interventions as Identified by Monitoring the Results

Current results should be compared to what was occurring prior to the introduction of the accommodations. Be aware that what works one day/week/quarter/semester/academic year may not continue to work. Reviews will provide insight to issues before they become bigger. When an accommodation is not working, it should be modified or replaced with a different one as quickly as possible. The review process should continue throughout the academic year and should continue from one grade level to another. It allows ongoing participation of the partnership of individuals concerned about the teen.

Positive reinforcement should be given to the teen for his/her efforts. They can be made by the evaluation team, the team liaison, or the teen's guidance counselor. Parents can take this opportunity to provide positive feedback to the professionals who have assisted in the plan. The collaborative efforts and spirit of the parents, school, and teen will provide an environment with the likelihood for success.

Success will not be realized by all students. For some, there can be issues of serious academic, behavioral, substance abuse, and/or juvenile justice involvement. Any situation that has escalated to this level has no short term solutions. Cooperation of many agencies over an extended period of time is necessary to assist the teen in helping himself/herself understand the issue(s) and what must be done to improve it. Some jurisdictions have school/community agencies established to assist with these issues. Family or individual counseling or therapy may be a useful adjunct for these circumstances. Many teens are able to turn a negative situation around and eventually find success.

Conclusion

Teamwork is a process that requires time and effort — results are not always visible overnight. There are no quick fixes to some of these complex issues. Continued interest and participation of teachers, administrators, parent(s) and the student will provide the needed environment for success. It is possible for an ADD teen to attain success as well as an improved self-image during middle and high school. It is sincerely hoped these guidelines will provide you a platform for helping your teen find success and confidence.

CLASSROOM PERFORMANCE SURVEY

Teacher: _____   Subject: _____

Period: _____   Student's Name: _____   Date: _____

Purpose: (1) To identify student's strengths and areas of concern in the classroom.
            (2) To collect data about student's academic performance, participation and behavior.

		ALWAYS		SOMETIMES		NEVER
1.	Brings necessary materials to class	1	2	3	4	5
2.	Completes class assignments	1	2	3	4	5
3.	Completes homework on time	1	2	3	4	5
4.	Records assignments consistently	1	2	3	4	5
5.	Turns in completed work	1	2	3	4	5
6.	Completes long term assignments	1	2	3	4	5
7.	Attends to instructions in class	1	2	3	4	5
8.	Arrives to class on time	1	2	3	4	5
9.	Cooperates/participates in class	1	2	3	4	5
10.	Demonstrates skill in reading assigned texts and materials	1	2	3	4	5
11.	Demonstrates adequate spelling and writing skills in work	1	2	3	4	5
12.	Takes notes in class to study	1	2	3	4	5
13.	Performs satisfactorily on tests	1	2	3	4	5
14.	Completes assigned work with accurate computation/detail	1	2	3	4	5
15.	Completed assignments are legible	1	2	3	4	5
16.	Relates positively to teacher(s)	1	2	3	4	5
17.	Demonstrates respect for property	1	2	3	4	5
18.	Relates positively to peers	1	2	3	4	5
19.	Communicates own needs or asks questions	1	2	3	4	5
20.	Accepts assistance when needed or offered	1	2	3	4	5

Please add any additional skills, behaviors or concern which you feel impact on this students classroom performance and achievement (If you are using specific interventions, please indicate):

_____

_____

_____

_____

Return this form to: _____   before _____

Thank you for sharing your observations and concerns!!!

ADOLESCENT ACCOMMODATIONS

Children with attention deficit disorders face unique academic and behavioral challenges in the classroom. With today's understanding and deepening insight into this disorder, teens can now achieve success and personal fulfillment in school when proper adjustments and accommodations are made. The educational objective does not have to change. The path to the goal, however, must be planned to match the learning style of the individual student.

We know that although ADD affects many adolescents, no two are exactly alike. We must take into consideration the strengths, weaknesses, interests, and unique characteristics of each student in order to design the proper accommodations and teach the appropriate compensating skills. Additionally the dynamics between teacher and student, level of interest in the subject material, the student's particular learning weaknesses, and the qualities associated with the disorder must be understood before a learning program can be tailored for the individual student.

With a greater awareness and understanding of the unique hurdles facing adolescents with ADD, we are now able to modify learning programs which will not only enable these student to achieve success but also encourage self-advocacy in the education process. The chart below offers strategies to deal with many of the issues, teens with ADD face.

Accommodations Compiled by CH.A.D.D. of Northern Virginia's Parents and Professionals. November, 1994

Revised by the Adolescent Sub-Committee of CH.A.D.D.'s Public and Professional Education Committee. October, 1995

ADDITIONAL RESOURCES

CH.A.D.D. Educators Manual, 1992
School Strategies for ADD Teens by Kathleen Nadeau, Ellen Dixon, and Susan Biggs. Available by mail from Chesapeake Psychological Publications, 5041 A & B Backlick Road, Annandale, VA 22003, (703) 642-6697
Making the Grade: An Adolescent's Struggle with ADD by Roberta N. Parker
Winning the Homework War by Kathleen M. Anesko and Frederic M. Levine
Keeping A Head in School by Melvin Levine
Homework Without Tears by Lee Canter and Lee Hausner
Educational Care by Melvin Levine
ADD & the Law by Peter and Patricia Latham
Secondary Education and Beyond, Learning Disabilities Association, 1995

ISSUE	STRATEGY
	Organization
Does not record assignments consistently or completely	(1) Structured outline/overhead
	(2) Use a calendar or planner
	(3) Announce and post assignments on blackboard in the same location
	(4) Allow time at beginning of class to copy down assignments rather than the end. Include preparation items not just written assignments, i.e., study for quiz/test, read pages/chapters, make yourself a review sheet
	(5) Teacher sign-off in assignment book (student must take to teacher in the later grades)
	(6) Reward or incentive for writing down assignments (by parents)
	(7) Read assignment into tape recorder
	(8) Training on use of automated "homework" hotline (post codes near telephone)
Does not bring necessary materials home	(1) Second set of books at home (Purchased from publisher or provided by school)
	(2) Place checklist of what needs to be brought home on which day on the inside of the locker
	(3) Color code book covers, workbooks, & notebooks
	(4) Use pocket folder to carry worksheets and other assignment information

continued on next page

ISSUE	STRATEGY
Does not complete homework assignments on time	(1) Request flexibility on late work turned in and receive credit (2) Names & phone numbers of several good students in each class (study mates) (3) Provide long range assignments in writing (4) Mail home assignments for next several weeks (Parents provide stamped, self-addressed envelopes) (5) Obtain teacher's school phone number and free period (6) Develop a written contract with student and provide choices for student (7) Obtain copy of class syllabus to find out what is expected of student (8) Evaluate effectiveness of medication (9) Periodic progress reports (10) Track grades—gives immediate feedback of class progress
Does not turn in completed work	(1) Routinely collect by asking child at the beginning of class for completed work (2) Use pocket folder to hold completed assignments (3) Prepare backpack at night instead of the morning (4) Have teacher call parent if 3 assignments are missing
Does not come to class prepared	(1) Zippered pouch for pencils, erasers, calculators, etc. (2) Pack backpack immediately after homework is completed (3) Add homemade shelves to locker to provide easier access to materials & better visibility (4) Color code book covers, workbooks, & notebooks (5) Designate a "point of contact" individual who can coordinate communication and support for teen
Difficulty with long term projects	(1) Ask teacher to break into to smaller, manageable components with intermediate deadlines (consider for entire class) (2) Ask teacher for details of project in writing (3) Teach use of "month-at-a-glance" calendar to track long-term assignment

Attention

ISSUE	STRATEGY
Does not attend to given instructions	(1) Encourage student to ask questions when information is not understood (2) Schedule class earlier in school day (3) Evaluate effectiveness of medication (4) Preferential seating (front & center or away from distractions) (5) Simplify/repeat complex directions (6) Provide both oral and written instructions (7) Use proximity or cueing method when giving directions
Does not complete class assignments	(1) Location of child in classroom (preferential seating) (2) Ineffective level of medication (3) Require high quality work while reducing quantity of work

Social Skills

ISSUE	STRATEGY
Does not communicate needs	(1) Ask student one question a day that student is capable of answering (2) Involve student in all types of parent/teacher meetings (3) Schedule self-advocacy training and meetings with teachers

continued on next page

ISSUE	STRATEGY
Difficulty relating to teachers, administrators, or other people in authority	(1) Rehearse at home how to ask questions and when to ask them (2) If child has tendency to be inappropriate, alert teachers before problems arise (3) Provide conflict resolution training
Difficulty relating to peers	(1) Team projects — Have teacher pair students instead of letting students choose (2) After school "clubs" and activities (3) Social exposure through activities outside of school
Rejects needed assistance	(1) Peer tutor or a non-parent tutor (2) Develop rapport with outside person who is "on their side" (3) Problem solve with student offering the student choices in how to resolve

Behavior

Arrives late or skips class/school	(1) Seek out root cause for behavior (2) If tired, consider earlier bedtime (3) If depressed, get appropriate treatment (4) Carry on conversations after arriving in the classroom instead of in the hallway (5) Pupil contract with parents (6) Mediation/problem solving discussions/training
Disrupts class/Acts out	(1) Effective medication level (2) Seat away from friends (3) Doesn't know behavior is unacceptable — develop method to make student aware (private cue/signal) (4) Instruct teen in self-management techniques (5) Post clear rules in classrooms (6) Develop positive behavior support plan (7) Utilize conflict management techniques (8) Analyze behavior to determine what triggers it and its results (9) Establish "chill out" location and signal to utilize it
Difficulty in remaining seated	(1) Allow legitimate movement by allowing student to move around (special project, errands, going to restroom, erasing board)

Transitions
(Class to Class/Grade to Grade)

Difficulty in managing changes in routine	(1) Prepare student for changes in normal routine (2) Provide consistent behavior expectation in all settings (3) Develop behavior support plan (4) Alert ancillary staff (secretaries, bus drivers, cafeteria staff) and inform of behavior plan (5) Ensure communication between current and previous teachers to share strategies (6) Arrange for student to meet with new teacher(s), tour new school (7) Schedule IEP meeting (for special education students) to develop or update Individual Transition Plan (ITP)

continued on next page

ISSUE	STRATEGY

Self-Esteem

Seems unhappy; complains of boredom; express dislike for school; may talk about dropping out of school

(1) Identify and build on strength and interests
(2) Provide frequent praise and recognition of success
(3) "Engineer" opportunities for academic and social success
(4) Assign student to be peer teacher or assist with younger students
(5) Recognize problems resulting from skill deficits vs. noncompliance
(6) Praise in public; reprimand in private
(7) Look for sign of stress; provide encouragement or reduce work load
(8) Mark correct responses on tests/assignments, not errors
(9) Do not permit humiliation, teasing, scapegoating by peers
(10) Convene IEP or Section 504 team to revise plan

Other

Scheduling of classes (hand scheduling)

(1) Schedule academic classes when the student is most alert
(2) Consider interspersing academic classes and electives
(3) Request teachers having attributes that match student's style of learning
(4) Select teachers that are very structured in their teaching methods
(5) Consider medication administration schedule

Poor handwriting

(1) Allow printing instead of cursive
(2) Accept typewritten material (keyboarding or word processor)
(3) Use of a note taker
(4) Tape record, especially review sessions with prior teacher approval
(5) Reduced or shortened assignments (odd or even problems or one paragraph instead of three)
(6) All extra time to copy assignments, complete tests, worksheets, etc.

Poor note taking skills

(1) Use outlines or diagrams
(2) Use notetakers
(3) Obtain copy of teacher's notes
(4) Portable computer
(5) Copy of another student's notes
(6) Tape record to fill in holes in notes
(7) Tape record review sessions with teacher approval

Poor test taking skills

(1) Allow extra time
(2) Test in a quiet place
(3) Read test out loud
(4) Dictate answers to a scribe
(5) Change format of test (multiple choice, true/false, essay, fill in the blank) — use format easiest for student
(6) Provide testing breaks
(7) Get test/answer sheet back for review
(8) Extra credit for correcting errors
(9) Allow choice of how to present knowledge of information
(10) Write answers directly on test instead of "scantron" answer sheet

continued on next page

ISSUE	STRATEGY
Poor spelling skills	(1) Use Franklin Spellers (headphone if speller talks) or other spell check tools (2) Spelling errors to be overlooked on some assignments where spelling is not the major point of concern
Poor math skills	(1) Use of calculator, especially with converting fractions to decimals (2) Use graph paper or turn notebook paper sideways to assist with alignment of numbers (3) Limit amount of problems to be completed (4) Scribe copies problem from book to paper
Poor reading/comprehension skills	(1) Use previewing strategies, such as identifying highlighted words, reviewing section headings, and reviewing end of section/chapter questions to identify what is important (2) Use "Cliff Notes" when appropriate to gain an understanding of subject matter prior to reading the complete document (3) Use books on tape to assist in comprehension (4) Make copies of text pages and underline, use highlighters, or write in margins to emphasize important information (5) Provide list of items to be found while completing reading assignments
Self advocacy	(1) Set up meeting with teacher(s), guidance counselor, and student (2) Have student complete a self advocacy worksheet
Study skills	(1) Homework time each day (2) Tutors (3) Teach organization, study, and time management skills

Helping Your High School/College Student Keep Academically Fit

by Harvey C. Parker, Ph.D.

Just as regular exercise and healthy eating keep the body physically fit, developing good study habits can keep a student academically fit. Parents who have children in high school or college have probably noticed that they are faced with increased school work, which usually requires more reading, more writing, and more planning and organization for short- and long-term assignments. What can help a child facing an elevated work load? Often, good study habits can mean the difference between success and failure. Students who have developed techniques to organize their time, study more efficiently, and effectively prepare for tests generally have a better chance to improve their grades in school. Following are several strategies for students who need help managing their school work.

TIME MANAGEMENT STRATEGIES

If you find yourself in a time crunch with too much to do and too little time to do it in, or if you find that you procrastinate and waste time, you may want to try some time management strategies to help you budget your time more effectively.

Successful time management requires a system for short- and long-term planning that will help you budget time in the upcoming days, weeks, and even months. To start, make a list of activities that require significant amounts of your time. Most students find that their time is taken up with five types of activities: class attendance; studying and homework; personal responsibilities; job responsibilities; and recreational activities.

The next step is to get an appointment book that shows "a week at a glance." First, mark off all the time during the week when you will be attending class. Second, fill in your work schedule if you have a job. Decide on a time each day that you can devote to studying and block off those times. Also, allot some additional time for personal chores and fill in some time each day for recreation. Third, write down important dates in your appointment book, such as dates when assignments are due, appointments, and social and family

activities. Get into the habit of carrying your appointment book with you and write notes down frequently. The more you use your appointment book, the more you will come to rely on it. Check the entries in your appointment book each morning before you start the day, at least once during the day, and again each night before the day's end.

Another way to manage time effectively is to use "to do" lists to set your goals and priorities for the week and for each day. Start each week by writing down five things that you would like to accomplish for that week. It could be organizing your desk, cleaning your car, working on a research paper, etc. These items will be your main goals for the week.

Next, you should make a "to do" list for each day. Your list should be prioritized with the most important objectives emphasized in some way (highlighted, underlined). These items are the ones you will make a priority to complete that day. Your list might look something like the following:

(1) Study for math test.

(2) Go to library — do research for English report.

(3) Pick up paper at bookstore.

(4) Get haircut this afternoon.

(5) Be at dentist's office by 4:30.

Anything not done by the end of the day should be placed on the next day's list. At the end of the week, grade yourself on how well you accomplished your five main goals for the week and how well you accomplished those items on your day-to-day "to do" list.

STUDY TIPS

Another important step in keeping up with schoolwork is to adopt effective study habits. Make a commitment to study regularly and stick to it. Set up routines for studying that take into consideration when to study, where to study, and with whom to study. You may want to experiment with various times and environments until you identify which one is best for you. For example, some students are "morning people" and prefer to study early in the day, while others find that they study best in the evenings. Get into the habit of forming a study routine at the times best suited for you.

In addition to considering the time of day that you study best, you should also think about the environment in which to study. Some students concentrate best in areas absolutely free from distractions; some need "white noise," such as quiet music that screens out other distractions; and others like more activity around them, or find they study best with the radio or the television on. Some students with ADD report that a quiet room free of all distractions does not necessarily represent the best environment when it comes to studying. What's important is that your study place feels right to you.

Another factor to consider is whether you study better alone or with a study group. For some subjects, you may be better going it alone, whereas for other subjects, getting together with friends or classmates can truly help. Group studying can be especially good when there is a good deal of work to wade through or if you find the work particularly difficult and may have questions. Not only do study partners have the advantage of having someone to rely on to answer questions or explain assignments, they also can often make studying more interesting and enjoyable.

NOTE-TAKING STRATEGIES IN CLASS

Since it is impossible to remember exactly what teachers say in class, note-taking is extremely important. Although an attentive listener may be able to recall main ideas of a lecture for a few days, most details are forgotten fairly quickly, if not immediately. In addition to ensuring that you have a permanent record of information presented in class, the process of note-taking may also enhance alertness, memory, and learning. If you have ADD, note-taking can actually help you stay alert in class. You are less likely to daydream if you're focusing on what your teacher is saying. Even if you don't need notes in a class, writing down important points can actually help you pay attention better. In addition, because you activate different senses and modalities (kinesthetic, motor, internal speech) when you take notes, you may also stimulate memory functions and thus be able to recall information better. Following are some tips for effective note-taking:

(1) Keep notes well organized.
Notes for a particular subject should be kept in one section of a notebook with pages numbered and dated.

(2) Recognize important information.
When taking notes it is helpful to be able to distinguish important from unimportant information so you can avoid having to write down everything

the teacher says. Often, an instructor will give you clues as to what is important by changing voice volume, repeating information, giving one or more examples to illustrate and emphasize a point, or indicating something that will be on an exam.

(3) Use outlines or mind mapping.
Some people prefer to take notes in outline form because it presents information in a clear and concise manner. To use this format, you would start by writing down main ideas, which are then divided into sub-ideas and details. Making a mind map is another good way to take notes. Mind mapping is less formal than outlining and is a more personal way of representing ideas. You would write down the main idea first and draw a circle around it, then draw branches from the circle to reflect sub-ideas and smaller branches from sub-ideas to represent details.

(4) Identify unfamiliar vocabulary.
Any new vocabulary or terminology that you are not familiar with should be underlined and defined to increase your understanding of the subject.

(5) Review notes prior to class.
Before each class, you should review your notes from the previous day and preview any reading material.

(6) Ask permission to tape record classes.
If you are unable to focus attention enough to take notes or if you are unable to keep up with the instructor while taking notes, ask permission to tape record lectures so you can listen to them again. Try not to do this too much, though, because it takes time to listen to lengthy lectures.

(7) Take notes from reading materials.
Taking notes from your textbooks and other reading material is important as it will save you time when studying for an exam or writing a paper. Using note cards is one way to keep track of important information taken from your reading materials. You should include the source of each set of notes and a brief summary of the information read on each card and label cards by topic.

TEST PREPARATION STRATEGIES

One of the unfortunate characteristics of the human mind is that our memory tends to decay over time so material that has to be remembered well needs to be studied and re-studied if it is to be retained in memory. Memory traces become stronger with each repetition. Therefore, it makes sense that the more you review material in a course, the more easily you will remember information at examination time. It also makes sense that our minds remember information we understand better than information that is remembered by rote. It is important that you not only review notes, but also that you think about their meaning and try to integrate the information in some meaningful way rather than to simply memorize it.

A popular method for studying is the SQ3R method. SQ3R stands for Survey, Question, Read, Recite, and Review. This method suggests that you:

- Survey the sections to be studied in your text by looking over the main headings and the subheadings in those sections;
- Make up questions about the information surveyed;
- Read sections entirely;
- Recite the information out loud, if possible;
- Review your work.

During the survey step of the SQ3R method, you should skim through the sections to be studied in order to get an overview of the material. Next, take one portion of your reading and from the heading or subheading, formulate one or two questions about the material. Then, read those sections entirely and answer the questions you've made up. Recite the answers to your questions out loud along with other important points to be remembered in that section of your reading. After going through the entire section, review the information you covered and write down key words or phrases in margins or on note cards, or highlight with a marker.

USE MOVEMENT, STIMULATION, AND CONVERSATION TO STAY ALERT WHILE STUDYING

Based on the premise that an active mind will stay more alert than a passive mind, you should try to make the process of studying as active as possible. Instead of simply reading to study, combine reading and underlining, writing in margins of your book (if allowed), using highlighters to emphasize important information, and reciting information out loud. All these activities can help your mind stay active and alert during the studying process. You should also take as many breaks as possible. Breaks can be more beneficial than marathon study sessions. These strategies may be especially important for people with ADD since they have a tendency to be less alert and may benefit from stimulation during the tedious process of studying.

Developing good habits for time management, note-taking, and test preparation are the foundation upon which we can build our future learning. Using the above strategies may make learning easier, more enjoyable, and more effective — especially for students with ADD.

This article first appeared in the
Spring 1996 ATTENTION!

Harvey Parker, Ph.D. is a clinical psychologist in Plantation, Florida. He is a co-founder of CH.A.D.D. and served as CH.A.D.D.'s National Executive Director for four years. Having been in practice for over twenty years, Dr. Parker has developed a special interest in working with children with ADD and their parents. He draws upon his experience as a former teacher and psychologist to apply educational and behavioral principles to the treatment of ADD in children. He is the author of numerous books, chapters, and articles on ADD.

Planning for a Successful School Year

by Clare B. Jones, Ph.D.

Planning is like a good road map; it leads us in the right direction, keeps us on course along the way, and helps us reach our destination. The desired destination in our child's journey throughout the school year is success. In order to realize this success, however, we must plan ahead. When should we start? There's no better time than right now. Remember *"developing the plan is actually laying out the sequence of events that have to occur for you to achieve your goal."* (George L. Morrisey) Following are some steps you and your child should take in order to get prepared for the upcoming school year.

Schedule a Meeting With Your Child's Teacher(s)

Before the school year begins, arrange a meeting with your child's teacher or teaching team to review your child's strengths and challenges. If your child is eligible, present your 504 Plan with accommodations. Ask specific questions of teachers regarding their routines. Pleasantly request information about: (a) when homework is given; (b) where the teacher writes homework assignments; (c) how assignments are returned; and (d); if advance notice is given for tests or assignments. Then, suggest a *backup* plan for you and the teacher or teaching team to use in case your child experiences difficulties. For instance, your backup plan may consider the following areas:

- identification of an organized student whom your child could call if he forgets to write down a homework assignment;
- issuing of an extra text book so that your child could keep one text book at home and leave the other at school;
- receipt of homework assignments a week in advance. (In my own practice, I have one teacher who faxes homework assignment to the father of one her students.)

Designate "Focus" Time

Spend the last two weeks of summer encouraging a regular forty-five minute quiet focus time. This focus time should occur at the same time each day and consist of quiet reading, drawing, or writing. This sets up a regular routine for your child to follow so that returning to nightly homework sessions will not be a major adjustment once school begins.

Take Your Child on a Tour of School

Arrange for a tour of your child's school campus. This is particularly helpful for those students starting a new school, or entering middle school or high school. Before school starts, visit the campus with your child. If your child is starting middle school or high school, obtain a map from the school office and put it on your child's bulletin board. Later, when he gets his daily schedule, review the locations of his classrooms on the map.

Purchase Helpful School Supplies

Your next stop should be a business or stationery store for school supplies for your child. When choosing supplies, select color-coded and cued items, such as rainbow colored index cards, which can be used for study flash cards. These types of items help easily-distracted students tune in and stay focused. Encourage your child to select a sturdy clip board that can be used to carry information to-and-from class (the restless student needs a sturdy surface that moves when he needs it to). For older students, purchase mechanical pencils and pens with a rubber cushion around the grip (these are perfect for kids who hate to write), color highlighters, and one pen with several color ink cartridges for active note-taking. Post-its and a portable three ring paper punch are also valuable.

Another important item to purchase is a large piece of poster board on which your child can write (with colorful magic markers) a list of what she has to do nightly. Let your child select a large wall calendar for her room. Assignments, test dates, and due dates for papers can then be color-coded on this calendar. Also purchase a large notebook and a sturdy three ring binder with color-coded tabs for your child to use. Lastly, purchase a good daytime calendar for your child to write down daily reminders in.

Offer Your Child Interesting Organizing Systems

Encourage your child to use desk organizers, a file cabinet with brightly colored inserts, and boxes with information color-coded by subject. The use of colored file folders helps students organize written materials and separate class assignments into distinct groups. These types of systems add structure and order to your child's life while keeping the process of organizing interesting and fun.

Help Your Child to Stay Organized

As soon as your child brings home a schedule, locker combination, etc., immediately make ten copies of the information. Place a copy of this information in different places, such as in your child's notebook, on his bulletin board, and in his book bag so he will always have access to important information in case he forgets it. Throughout the year, encourage your child to make a list of what he needs to accomplish during a certain time period and remind him to keep this list with him at all times. If your child is having difficulty concentrating during class, especially those classes that involve lectures, suggest that he carry a portable tape recorder and record important information.

Encourage Goal-Setting

Take your child to a special place of her choice one day before school starts and ask her what she would like to do differently this school year and what goals she would like to accomplish. Discuss these goals and plan strategies together. Listen to what your child has to say and make certain she knows you value her input.

Do Your Homework

Make a note on your personal calendar to call your child's school about a month after school starts. This is your opportunity to talk with teachers to see how your child is doing in her classes. By doing this soon after the school year begins, you will know immediately if your child has weak areas that need your attention.

Be Positive

Speak in an understanding, positive manner to your child. For instance, instead of saying, "How could you forget your assignment book again?" try saying, "It's great that you have a phone buddy who you can call to get your assignment from." By speaking positively to your child, you will show him your support and let him know that it's all right to make mistakes.

Provide Your Child with Helpful Resources

If your child has had difficulty with spelling, make sure that her at-home school supplies include spell checkers, a good dictionary, and a thesaurus. There are excellent dictionaries now available on computer. Additionally, if your child's particular difficulties with attention have reduced her ability in comprehending reading material and she currently qualifies for learning disability services, you should consider purchasing or borrowing books on audiotape. The Recording For The Blind/Dyslexic Office offers books on tape for students whose reading comprehension is below grade level but have strong auditory skills. For information regarding Books on Tape, you may write to or call the Recording for the Blind/Dyslexia, 20 Rosell Road, Princeton, New Jersey, 08540. 1-800-221-4742.

In addition, if your child has excellent auditory recall skills and can often repeat information verbatim, she will benefit from hearing a book on tape first, then scanning the actual book. Should your child not meet the qualifications to receive special books recorded on tape through the school system, you can purchase books on tape at your local bookstores. Many cassette tapes of popular books and classics are available. Today many school textbook companies also offer their books on tape.

You *can* help make this year a successful school year for your child. But remember, *"Our goals can only be reached through a vehicle of a plan, in which we must fervently believe, and upon which we must vigorously act. There is no other route to success."* (Basil S. Walsh)

This article first appeared in the Summer 1996 ATTENTION!

Clare B. Jones, Ph.D. is a Diagnostic Specialist and Educational Consultant in Phoenix, Arizona. She is the author of two books on Attention Concerns: A Source Book on Attention Deficit Disorder for Early Childhood Professionals and Parents and Attention Deficit Disorder — Strategies for School Age Students.

Secondary School Transition: Planning for Success

by Rae Hemphill, CH.A.D.D. Chapter Coordinator

The transition into secondary school can be overwhelming and cause much anxiety in both the ADD adolescent and the parent. Many concerns arise regarding the new environment and how to manage it. Preparing for this journey can assist in adjusting to these changes and produce positive results.

Issues or concerns exist about the new school, changing classes, class scheduling, school communication, homework, and classroom interventions. Medication and teen advocacy are issues that are also of concern during the time a teen with ADD attends a secondary school program. Each of these issues can have a successful outcome, especially when a proactive approach is used. Anticipating issues and addressing them early as they relate to each individual teen can de-escalate concerns and prevent problems.

ORIENTING TO THE SECONDARY SCHOOL ENVIRONMENT

Attendance at a new school is like a new beginning and should be treated as such. You can prepare your teen with ADD for a smoother transition by scheduling a tour of the facility prior to the start of the new school year. You will want to locate the various service areas such as the library, cafeteria, administrative offices, and rest rooms. Using the teen's class schedule, walk from class to class noting any "walks" that could result in tardiness. Tardiness in secondary school generally is the result of socializing, searching for lost materials, or returning to the locker to retrieve forgotten items. For those long "walks", brainstorm with the teen how to reduce the amount of time it takes. If it seems impossible to reduce the time, discuss this item with the guidance counselor before it has a chance to become an issue with negative consequences.

The transition from one or two teachers to as many as seven can be quite disconcerting to the teen. All teachers will have their own style of presentation, body language, and expectations for the students. Each one will likely expect the teen to perform independently and not require monitoring. When a teacher is not willing to compromise with the teen on student expectations, s/he may have no other choice than to do "it" the teacher's way. As a parent, you will need to foster this environment as one which prepares the teen for the future. The teen needs to know that many situations occurring in adulthood — such as dealing with employers, which require rule-based actions and problem solving skills — are similar to having multiple teachers. Learning to deal with these expectations gives the teen experiences s/he can draw on in the future. Teens can be encouraged to express to the parent or guidance counselor reasonable requests for assistance.

CLASS SCHEDULING

The daily class schedule is an issue for many teens. The schedule, which is generally produced by a computer, may not perfectly "fit" the teen's needs or produce success. "Hand scheduling" of classes with the guidance counselor just prior to school opening could produce a more appropriate environment for learning. Consider using the following methods to create a schedule that betters meets your teen's needs:

- Schedule core academic classes, such as English, math, history, and foreign languages, early in the day if the teen is a "morning" person.

- Alternate core academic classes with electives if the teen needs a longer period of time to be mentally ready for the next academic class.

- Plan core academic classes when medication will be most effective.

- Request a teacher whose teaching style is a match to the teen's primary learning style.

- Request a teacher who has personal attributes which match the teen's and consider how the teen will relate to him/her.

Even though you may have used some or all of the above methods to facilitate your teen's schedule, selecting a class of study that may be "not working" can happen. If it does, take immediate action to change it to one that will likely produce better results. Take the following example into consideration: a teen has chosen a geometry class to fill a math requirement. If failing grades become quite evident approximately three to four weeks into the quarter and are caused by the inability to comprehend the subject matter, initiate immediate action with the guidance counselor to replace it with a different type of math where success can be more prevalent.

COMMUNICATING WITH THE SCHOOL

Parent communication with the school is a necessity for all concerned. Best results can be attained when a working partnership exists between the parents, teen's teachers, guidance counselor, school psychologist, school administration, and support staff. Employing a proactive approach will produce better results than one of reaction. Providing the school personnel with information of what has occurred in prior school years and what was successful in managing those issues will prepare them for what may occur during the teen's tenure in secondary school. Also, you will want to stress the need for feedback in the following areas:

- About class progress — assignments, tests, participation, comprehension of the subject matter, class participation, homework

- From teacher — find out how to contact each teacher and the best method for each of them to provide progress reports or notify you of other matters

- To monitor medication effectiveness — have teacher communicate changes in the teen's classroom behavior and ability to attend to assignments

- To monitor 504 progress — have teacher communicate how the classroom interventions are working and which ones are not working and should be replaced

Expressing your concerns and interest in your teen prior to the time problems or situations arise prepares school personnel for them. Awareness promotes the ability to monitor and take action before a situation has the chance to escalate. In some cases, methods employed by the teacher can eliminate a problem or greatly minimize it.

HOMEWORK HASSLES

Homework is the single school activity that can produce many issues and concerns in the areas of:

- Recording assignments and getting the materials home

- Planning time for homework to get done

- Doing the homework, consistently

- Turning in completed assignments on time

- Planning and completing long term projects

Each of these items requires organization and/or planning to reach a successful conclusion.

Homework assignment sheets or notebooks can be used by the teen to collect the assignments during the classroom period. A separate section or special place in the teen's notebook should house them. Have your teen collect names and phone number of students who would be willing to be called upon during a time of "crisis". These studymates can provide back up when an assignment is overlooked or a book is not brought home.

Homework will need to be completed along with other activities the teen is involved in. A routine time for doing homework should be established with the understanding that there will be exceptions. A "month-at-a-glance" type of calendar allows all activities — homework and non-homework activities — to be recorded. It provides a visual picture of what is happening on any given day. When a teen can see daily activities, such as a dentist appointment at 3 p.m. or soccer practice at 5 p.m., s/he can fit homework activities around them even though the routine homework time is different.

Homework should be done in an environment that is best for the teen. This may mean the teen will work best if music is being played. Some study better with the volume low while others need it louder. Still others may find that studying in a quiet room with the door shut is more productive. The teen should be allowed to choose the environment, and the parent should intervene only when progress is not being made. You will need to find creative ways to monitor your teen's progress without being a big intrusion.

Getting the completed assignments turned in is a common issue with teens with ADD. Homework can get "lost" between the time it is completed and the time it is to be turned in. One solution for this problem is for the student to have a pocket folder in his/her notebook where all completed work can be stored. If the student continues to lose work, one pocket folder per class may produce better results.

Probably the biggest homework issue is a long-term project, one that is assigned several weeks ahead of its due date — or in the case of a teen with ADD, one that you hear about the day before it is due. Some teachers will provide parents a list of long-term assignments and their approximate due dates for the entire year or each quarter. Once you know an assignment is due, assist your teen with planning the project. Help him/her to begin the planning by prompting him/her for what type of project will be done, what supplies will be required to complete the project, and what steps will be necessary to complete the project. More success occurs when dealing with small portions over a period of time.

NOTEBOOK ORGANIZATION

Organization of the teen's notebook can help produce success. The notebook can be to the student what a "planner" is to an adult. It can guide and facilitate the teen's actions and help keep items available for use. The following are suggestions for good notebook organization:

- A 1-1/2" to 2-1/2" D-slant notebook (it holds more than the traditional round ring notebook)
- Three-holed zippered pouch to hold pens, pencils, calculator, compass, protractor, and other items
- Three-holed ruler secured in the notebook
- Three-holed divider indexes — there should be one index for each class, one for assignments and calendars, and one for classmates' addresses and phone numbers (who can be called when an emergency exists)
- A good supply of three-holed notebook paper and one-quarter inch grid paper
- Three-holed pocket folder to transport worksheets and homework back and forth between home and school.

Daily, after all homework is complete, you should check the folder used to transport information to and from school to confirm that all assignments are complete and ready for transport to school the next day. Weekly notebook and backpack checks ensure all worksheet and notes have been three-holed punched and filed in the right section for future reference.

CLASSROOM INTERVENTIONS

Classroom interventions may be needed to assist the teen and allow him/her the ability to compete with peers. Interventions are plans that need to be individually selected to meet a specific need and can be changed or modified. The specific interventions should be matched to the teen's learning style. For optimal success, they should have the teen's agreement and participation when implemented. If there are many issues that need addressing, prioritize which ones should be dealt with first and be willing to negotiate on the strategies for improvement. Implement those that everyone agrees with and monitor them at predetermined intervals. Continue those that produce success and replace those that "just do not work".

MEDICATION EFFECTIVENESS

ADD teens who use medication as part of their treatment plan may have to make changes if its effectiveness diminishes. Some will require a dosage adjustment while others may require a different medication. Side effects that were non-existent when the teen was younger may become a problem during adolescence. If this should occur, you and your teen should discuss this issue with the prescribing physician. Another problem occurring in some teens is the refusal to take medication. Try to determine the reason for the refusal, since there may be a way for you, your teen, and the physician to successfully deal with it.

COMMUNICATING WITH YOUR TEEN

As teens progress through adolescence, they typically distance themselves from their parents. To maintain a good relationship with your teen, you may need to make changes in methods that have been successful in prior years. Peer or adult tutoring may have to replace parent tutoring. Communication with your teen should be brief and to the point as long discussions will cause the teen to "tune out". When that happens, you will be the only one who hears what is being said. Allow your teen the opportunity to participate in the decision making process. When making plans, offer them choices, solicit their opinions and ideas, and let them make the selections.

Emotional development and impulsive reaction in ADD teens contribute to moodiness above the normal changes in adolescence. You can affirm emotional outbursts by acknowledging, "I know you are frustrated about ... (the issue at hand)";. "I feel that way sometimes myself." Or you can get them thinking by asking "I wonder if ... (a method that might help)." Showing understanding for their emotions will help them better deal with the issue.

FROM ONE PARENT TO ANOTHER

The goal of all parents is to prepare their child for the realities of the real world. You need to provide the right environment for your teen to learn, but it is up to the teen to choose to learn. Become a consultant to your teen; do not do his/her work. If you have been instrumental in completing your teen's assignments, reduce your level of assistance gradually. Understand your teen's need for independence and self-sufficiency. Keep the communication lines open between you and your teen. All of these things are necessary for your teen to be able to assume the responsibility for his/her life after high school graduation.

Never underestimate your teen's abilities. Identify their strengths to use for coping and to feel good about themselves. Involve her/him in school meetings and encourage participation and input. Invite "ownership" by providing choices. Allow the teen to "stumble, fall, and pick herself/himself up" even though it may be difficult for you. You may be pleasantly surprised at how well s/he will adapt to the invited independence.

Now educated with the strategies that have been successful for others, you can be proactive by planning, using a "team" management approach, and involving your teen as much as possible to create success during the secondary school years. When it comes time for your teen to graduate, you will know it was worth each and every effort you put forth while assisting her/him in becoming a successful, independent, and self-sufficient young adult.

Rae Hemphill is the Chapter Coordinator of CH.A.D.D. of Northern Virginia. She has been active in her chapter for nearly ten years and initiated the creation of an adolescent committee to deal with the issues faced by parents of adolescents with ADD.

The Perplexed Perfectionist

by George W. Dorry, Ph.D.

After the celebration of an achievement, there is a sigh of relief from the perfectionist that, once more, the dream was enacted into reality. That happened yesterday when a child accomplished building the block structure which he had in mind, and it happened years ago when the Mayor of New York City cut the ribbon on the world's longest suspension bridge, the Verranzano Narrows Bridge. The positive side of perfectionism is the ability to conceive something of a higher order and create it (Silverman, 1993), to paraphrase T. S. Eliot (1958), the negative side of perfectionism is the gap between the conception and the creation. It falls on two groups of individuals as often as the sun shines: gifted children in general and gifted children with attention deficits.

Attention Deficit/Hyperactivity Disorder (AD/HD) is a neurochemically based deficiency in the areas of the brain that control selective attention and the "executive function" areas that direct planning, logistics, and a holistic overview of situations. The underlying condition of the attention deficit sometimes has a component of varying degrees of physical hyperactivity, hence the term Attention Deficit/ Hyperactivity Disorder (AD/HD). The fourth edition of the American Psychiatric Association's *Diagnostic and Statistical Manual* (DSM-IV, 1994) separates four types of AD/HD: Predominantly Inattentive Type; Predominantly Hyperactive-Impulsive Type; Combined Type; and Not Otherwise Specified (e.g., an adult with AD/HD who was hyperactive as a child, but not as an adult). Gifted individuals may have any of the four types of AD/HD.

Although only a limited number of gifted children have attentional difficulties of any type, children with AD/HD tend to be of higher intelligence than the average. While firm research findings are not yet available, it may be that highly gifted children have a higher incidence of AD/HD-like symptoms, if not diagnosable AD/HD.

Perfectionism is first on Tannenbaum and Baldwin's (1983) list of the shared characteristics of highly motivated, high IQ children vs. learning disabled children with high IQs. Among the many characteristics which individuals with AD/HD and the gifted have in common, perfectionism occurs with sufficient frequency to be worthy of consideration. Since the positive and negative sides of perfectionism apply to perfectionistic individuals whether they are children, adolescents, or adults, the ideas can be applied to gifted individuals of any age with or without AD/HD. We will, however, refer to children as the primary example.

PERFECTIONISM'S YIN AND YANG

For the sake of brevity, we will not debate whether perfectionism is good or bad. Let us instead accept a Taoist perspective which emphasizes the yin and yang, the acknowledgment of both positive and negative sides to perfectionism. If we start from that point of view, we can address the more productive issue of, "When is perfectionism useful for the individual's achievement and when is it a detriment?", so that we can minimize the negative and maximize the positive aspects of perfectionism.

May the force be with you: The struggle between good and evil in "Star Wars" can be an analogy to perfectionism's dual nature. The "force" is the positive drive to create something better and the satisfaction of achieving it, while the "dark side" can be anxiety and self-recriminating frustration when that achievement is not yet attained. As concerned observers, we want to see the motivating "force" as the individual strives for high achievements, but want him or her to avoid feeling anxiety, frustration, and lessening self-esteem.

Gifted children with AD/HD often have high personal and interpersonal expectations. However, they frequently experience underachievement because there is consistent variability in their performance. They are occasionally on target and as productive as expected. At other times they are susceptible to distractions from high levels of "internal" stimuli (thoughts) as well as from kinesthetic or external visual and auditory stimuli. Then they are not able to maintain the previous level of performance.

The gifted child with AD/HD is most often well intentioned, wanting to please and motivated towards achievement, but frustrated, because performance can vary without any apparent, identifiable motivational difference. The child may develop a learned strategy of perfectionism as over-compensation to increase the likelihood of achievement. For example, "If I demand that my homework is perfect, I have a better chance of getting it right."

Gifted children with attention deficits may have many of the same characteristics as gifted children with AD/HD, but performance is more within their control. Both groups are likely to be bombarded by high internal distractibility — "overexcitabilities" (Piechowski, 1979), and to have lower frustration tolerance for tasks without novelty or intrinsic motivational value. However, gifted children who do not have ADD can choose to persist if, for instance, the motivational value is changed by a highly rewarding outcome. The gifted child with AD/HD, for whom internal or external distracters prohibit maintaining attention to the task, may not be able to persist and perform. The level of impulse control is also a factor that can affect performance. However, as they reach the maturity of young adulthood, many individuals with AD/HD seem to develop greater impulse control; therefore, they are able to function more successfully.

THE PAYOFF FOR PERFECTIONISM

The perfectionism of gifted children with AD/HD has less chance to pay off than when the gifted child is without an attention deficit. The persistence of the child with AD/HD in the face of susceptibility to distraction is less likely to lead to achievement. The notion that bright individuals can always achieve the goal if they are persistent enough is a perfectionistic fallacy. Starting with high expectations, an attempt is made, but achievement is less than expected. The resulting frustration and anxiety over performance can lead to progressive performance decrements over time.

Anxiety over performance can take many forms: fear of failure, an "I can't do it" attitude, an obsessive set of thoughts about the task, or a compulsion to repeat the task in a perseverative manner. The possibility exists that gifted children with AD/HD are more susceptible to the forms of anxiety noted above than gifted children without AD/HD, but that hypothesis has not been empirically tested. The gifted child without AD/HD has a much higher likelihood of achievement than the gifted child with AD/HD if strong motivation, equal degrees of perfectionism, and a distracting environment in which to accomplish the task are the same. More frequent payoff to gifted children with AD/HD means that their persistent perfectionism will be reinforced. Their self-esteem and belief in their ability to accomplish the goal (the positive side of perfectionism) will be strengthened. The marked contrast between high expectations and the reality of consistently inconsistent performance can leave the child's self-esteem looking like a car after a demolition derby, and may, over time, discourage the child from attempting to try to do his or her best.

THE PERFECTIONISTIC PARADOX

One treatment technique in psychology is called prescribing the symptom. Rather than contend with an individual's perfectionism and potentially create resistance or entrench the individual in a defensive position, the strategy is to let this person continue to be perfectionistic, but modify the conscious thoughts about what it means to be the perfect perfectionist. This will increase the likelihood of behavioral change. The perfectionistic paradox is that to *be the best you can be, you must still accomplish this in the real world, which means acknowledging that there is a certain probability of error.* Some variables, like the weather, are simply outside of our control. Thus, we can only approximate the perfect solution to a problem.

By accepting the Perfectionistic Paradox, we can come closest to achieving a perfect solution if we *plan to minimize error.* The most straightforward way to accomplish that is to approach a goal through a gradual system of successive steps leading to the goal. The probability of error decreases as we achieve each progressive step successfully. Perhaps the following metaphoric fable can illustrate the situation.

POP'S RULE

At a beach house with a deck elevated above the sand, a large extended family gathered to baste themselves with oil of sacrifice to the sun god and seek respite from stress. Stress soon found them in its chameleon-like way (as it often does) and took the form of a multitude of merry munchkins constantly crying out to be carried up and down the stairs. The scene resembled the flow from an ant colony to and from the picnic. By mid-afternoon, the adults and the older children were approaching the limits of their frustration tolerance as sherpas to sand-covered toddlers.

The beloved grandfather of the clan (affectionately known as "Pop") ceased being observer and rose from the shaded comfort of his white wicker rocking chair to go to the tool shed. This aging Huckleberry Finn soon had a swarm of workers wielding hammers and saws to the task of building half-steps and a low handrail along one side of the staircase. Thus, the origin of **Pop's Rule: If they are not yet able to climb the whole staircase, help them to build half-steps so they can make it to the top on their own.**

Pop's Rule encourages the growth of independence, self-esteem, and pride in accomplishment. It conveys that **you can do it** without either an unrealistic expectation (too large a single step) or the impression that outside assistance is a prerequisite to accomplishment (being carried). Pop's Rule is a sequential thinker's problem-solving technique that can assist the non-sequential thinker through a cognitive cul-de-sac and generalize well to new situations.

To help a gifted child learn to operate on the basis of Pop's Rule requires starting with a child who wants to solve a problem. It is important to find a happy medium between dependence-inducing over-protection and unrealistic expectations of too much independence. Adults can assist a child without taking over ownership of the problem. Do not carry them up the stairs; help them to build half-steps so they can reach the top themselves.

In one case, Pop's Rule was taught in the course of therapy to a thirteen-year-old gifted boy with AD/HD who was motivated to learn new problem-solving techniques to avoid his parents' almost constant interventions. Further injury to his already wounded self-esteem was prevented by letting him define the need for his parents' assistance. When he felt he could not quite manage the next step, he would ask them to help design what had to be done; then he would politely ask them to leave so that he might build his science project himself. Many gifted individuals, particularly introverts, prefer to work in private. It enhances their sense of accomplishment to resolve the problem themselves and then show the finished product to the world. The boy was able to obtain limited consults from his parents, and yet retain his pride and the individual ownership of his creation.

The example above also demonstrates an important point. The application of Pop's Rule helped this child to create his science project with only limited consultation (as opposed to frequent intervention) from his parents. The process of learning to apply Pop's Rule was a series of help-steps down from the uncertain tight-rope of his dependence upon them to the solid ground of independent creation with minimum support. Pop's Rule can thus be used both to build steps of new learning and independence, and to step away from dependence in a gradual way.

Gifted children with AD/HD who are of the Predominantly Impulsive Type are much more likely to make an impulsive first choice at problem solution. If that choice fixates in a negative perfectionistic fashion, rather than allowing for review of alternative solutions, these children are less likely to achieve the best solution; this usually leads to negative consequences, such as frustration, and lowered self-esteem. Teaching them to use Pop's Rule will help to counteract their tendency to react impulsively. If they use a stepwise strategy, they are more likely to avoid an erroneous or non-optimal solution to the problem. Helping them to generalize Pop's Rule to new situations and to apply it independently will take time, but it is a worthwhile technique in a repertoire of problem-solving approaches.

Carefully structuring the environment, including our adult behavior, allows all gifted children and children with AD/HD to minimize anxiety and frustration by decreasing externally imposed demands that occur in goal achievement in a single step. Many AD/HD and gifted children already make those demands upon themselves. Helping them to learn Pop's Rule increases the possibility that they will experience the positive side of perfectionism more often.

To return to our example of the Taoist concept of yin and yang, of the balance between the positive and negative, the ideal would be for any individual, particularly the gifted individual with AD/HD, to accept the reality of errors as part of the balance between justifiable pride in accomplishment and occasional frustration when that accomplishment is not yet achieved. There will always be another step to take toward perfection. Absolute perfection may be impossible to attain. However, striving for excellence or doing one's best at the current step is a worthy, attainable goal.

Reprinted with permission of Understanding Our Gifted®, *a newsletter dedicated to helping gifted children reach their full potential, published by Open Space Communications, Inc., P.O. Box 18268, Boulder, CO 80308-8268.*

George W. Dorry, Ph.D., is a licensed psychologist and Director of the Attention and Behavior Center in Denver, Colorado, who specializes in the assessment and treatment of children, adolescents, and adults with ADD and AD/HD. He is one of the founding members of the Attention Deficit Disorder Advocacy Group (ADDAG) in Colorado and served as Chairman of the ADDAG Board of Directors from April, 1988 to January, 1995.

REFERENCES

Diagnostic and statistical manual of mental disorders (4th ed.) (1994 Draft). Washington, DC: American Psychiatric Association.

Eliot, T.S. (1958). The hollow men. In Leggett (Ed.), *Twelve Poets.* NY: Holt, Reinhart, & Winston.

Lind, S. (1993). Are we mislabeling overexcitable children? *Understanding Our Gifted* 5(5A), 1,8-10.

Piechowski, M.M.(1979). Developmental potential. In N.Colangelo & R.T. Zaffrann (Eds.), *New Voices in counseling the gifted* (pp. 25-57) Dubuque, IA: Kendall/Hunt.

Silverman, L.K. (1993). A developmental model for counseling the gifted. In L.K. Silverman (Ed.), *Counseling the gifted and talented* (pp. 51-78). Denver: Love.

Tannenbaum, A.J. & Baldwin, L.J. (1983). Giftedness and learning disability: A paradoxical combination. In L.H. Fox, L. Brody & D.Tobin (Eds.), *Learning disabled/gifted children: Identification and programming* (pp. 11-36). Baltimore, MD: University Park Press.

Webb, J.T. & Latimer, D (1993). *ADHD and children who are gifted* 522). Reston, VA: CEC

Summary of IDEA/Section 504

by Matthew D. Cohen, J.D.

With the issuance of its September, 1991 policy memorandum, the U.S. Department of Education confirmed what advocates and professionals serving children with ADD had been arguing for a long time: That children with ADD were potentially eligible for services under both the Individuals with Disabilities Education Act (IDEA) and Section 504 of the Rehabilitation Act of 1973. Parents and professionals who are seeking services from school districts for children suspected of or identified as having ADD must be aware of the significant differences between the IDEA and Section 504. There are also many considerations which may cause a parent to choose to pursue disputes over services through one statute, rather than the other.

The IDEA provides a highly detailed set of eligibility standards, procedures for evaluation, requirements with respect to services to be offered and details to be included in the individual education plan. It also provides a very specific set of procedural safeguards which relate to notice, right to hearing, type of hearing and confidentiality issues. By contrast, Section 504 is quite brief. It provides:

no otherwise qualified individual with disabilities in the United States shall, solely by reason of her or his disability, be excluded from the participation in, be denied the benefits of, or be subjected to discrimination under any program or activity receiving Federal financial assistance...(29 U.S.C. S 794)

Section 504 regulations define a person with a disability as any individual who has an impairment which substantially limits a major life activity. Learning and social development are included within the intended list of major life activities. As such, children with ADD who experience substantial impairment of learning or social development arguably should qualify as individuals with disabilities protected by Section 504.

The threshold with respect to the two statutes is whether the child is eligible for special education and related services — the IDEA requires that the child need both. The Section 504 regulations speak not of special education and related services, but rather of special education or related services. This distinction, seemingly subtle, is significant as a number of children with ADD may require various related services, without requiring any modification in their instructional program. Thus, while they may not qualify under the IDEA, they may qualify under Section 504. More importantly, the eligibility criteria under Section 504 are broader than the criteria for eligibility under the IDEA.

There are several advantages to being determined eligible under the IDEA. As earlier indicated, the IDEA has far more specific provisions with respect to the range of services to be provided, how the child's education plan is to be developed, and the procedural safeguards which are available if there are disputes with the public schools.

Under the IDEA, once the child has been identified as having a disability and an educational program has been developed for him or her, the school district cannot change or terminate services without giving notice to the parent. Further, if the parents object to the proposed change in placement by requesting a due process hearing, the current services must continue while any administrative or legal proceedings are pending. By contrast, services under Section 504 are far less clearly delineated. Procedural safeguards are also less specific and there is no comparable provision of services to be maintained while an administrative challenge is pending.

While Section 504 also allows for parents to challenge the failure of the school district to implement appropriate services, the school district has the option of appointing its own hearing officer, whereas under the IDEA the hearing officer is appointed through a process under the control of the state education agency. On the other hand, under Section 504, in addition to filing an administrative hearing request with the school district, a parent or professional may also file a complaint with the U.S. Department of Education, Office of Civil Rights, which has independent authority to investigate violations of Section 504 and to find school districts in noncompliance for such violations.

An additional advantage of Section 504 is that parents are able to recover damages if they end up filing civil actions under this law. The IDEA does not allow for the recovery of monetary damages, except in limited circumstances in the form of reimbursement of unilateral placements or compensatory education in response to inappropriate public school programming.

Parents and professionals seeking services for children with ADD should recognize that there is wide variability in how school districts will respond to these requests. The awareness of school districts will range form a complete understanding of their obligations to serve children with ADD under both the IDEA and Section 504, to only a limited understanding of how children with ADD fit into the overall eligibility scheme provided by the statutes.

Parents should also recognize that they do not have the right to choose whether their child will be determined eligible under one law or the other. Rather, they have the right to request that the child be evaluated to determine eligibility and that the child receive services under whichever law is determined to be appropriate to meet the child's needs. In order to be familiar with how the school district treats services to children who are identified with disabilities under Section 504, parents should request copies of their school district Section 504 plan. This is particularly true when a school district refuses services under the IDEA or when a parent is seeking to evaluate his of her options. If the school district indicates it does not have a 504 plan or is unwilling to respond to the parents' request, parents can contact a U.S. Department of Education Office of Civil Rights Regional Office for assistance in obtaining the necessary information. If the school district refuses services under the IDEA or Section 504 or both, the parent may choose to challenge this decision through a due process hearing.

This article first appeared in the November 1993 CH.A.D.D.er Box.

Matthew Cohen, J.D. is a partner at the law firm Monahan & Cohen in Chicago and an adjunct professor of law at Loyola University Law School. He is nationally recognized for his work in special education law and has considerable experience in health care and mental health law. He has been the principal litigator in a number of landmark special education cases. Mr. Cohen is the primary or collaborating author of several amendments to the mental health and special education laws of Illinois. He has lectured extensively on a wide variety of special education and law topics. Mr. Cohen serves on the editorial board of ATTENTION! and is chair of CH.A.D.D.'s Government Relations Committee.

UNITED STATES DEPARTMENT OF EDUCATION

OFFICE OF SPECIAL EDUCATION AND REHABILITATIVE SERVICES

THE ASSISTANT SECRETARY

<u>MEMORANDUM</u>   SEP I 6 1991

DATE   :

TO   :   Chief State School Officers

FROM   :   Robert R. Davila
                Assistant Secretary
                Office of Special Education
                    and Rehabilitative Services

                Michael L. Williams
                Assistant Secretary
                Office for Civil Rights

                John T. MacDonald
                Assistant Secretary
                Office of Elementary
                    and Secondary Education

SUBJECT :   Clarification of Policy to Address the Needs of
             Children with Attention Deficit Disorders within
             General and/or Special Education

I.   Introduction

There is a growing awareness in the education community that attention deficit disorder
(ADD) and attention deficit hyperactive disorder (ADHD) can result in significant learning
problems for children with those conditions. While estimates of the prevalence of ADD
vary widely, we believe that three to five percent of school-aged children may have
significant educational problems related to this disorder. Because ADD has broad
implications for education as a whole, the Department believes it should clarify State and
local responsibility under Federal law for addressing the needs of children with ADD in
the schools. Ensuring that these students are able to reach their fullest potential is an
inherent part of the National education goals and AMERICA 2000. The National goals,
and the strategy for achieving them, are based on the assumptions that: (1) all children
can learn and benefit from their education; and (2) the educational community must
work to improve the learning opportunities for all children.

---

[1]While we recognize that the disorders ADD and ADHD vary, the term ADD is
being used to encompass children with both disorders.

MARYLAND AVE. S.W. WASHINGTON D.C.

1

This memorandum clarifies the circumstances under which children with ADD are eligible for special education services under Part B of the Individuals with Disabilities Education Act (Part B), as well as the Part B requirements for evaluation of such children's unique educational needs. This memorandum will also clarify the responsibility of State and local educational agencies (SEAs and LEAs) to provide special education and related services to eligible children with ADD under Part B. Finally, this memorandum clarifies the responsibilities of LEAs to provide regular or special education and related aids and services to those children with ADD who are not eligible under Part B, but who fall within the definition of "handicapped person" under Section 504 of the Rehabilitation Act of 1973. Because of the overall educational responsibility to provide services for these children, it is important that general and special education coordinatetheir efforts.

II.   Eligibility for Special Education and Related Services under Part B

Last year during the reauthorization of the Education of the Handicapped Act (now the Individuals with Disabilities Education Act), Congress gave serious consideration to including ADD in the definition of "children with disabilities" in the statute. The Department took the position that ADD does not need to be added as a separate disability category in the statutory definition since children with ADD who require special education and related services can meet the eligibility criteria for services under Part B. This continues to be the Department's position.

No change with respect to ADD was made by Congress in the statutory definition of "children with disabilities:" however, language was included in Section 102(a) of the Education of the Handicapped Act Amendments of 1990 that required the Secretary to issue a Notice of Inquiry (NOI) soliciting public comment on special education for children with ADD under Part B. In response to the NOI (published November 29, 1990 in the Federal Register), the Department received over 2000 written comments, which have been transmitted to the Congress. Our review of these written comments indicates that there is confusion in the field regarding the extent to which children with ADD may be served in special education programs conducted under Part B.

A.   Description of Part B

Part B requires SEAs and LEAs to make a free appropriate public education (FAPE) available to all eligible children with disabilities and to ensure that the rights and protections of Part B are extended to those children and their parents 20 U.S.C. 1412(2); 34 CFR SS300.121 and 300.2. Under Part B, FAPE, among other elements, includes the provision of special education and related services, at no cost to parents, in conformity with an individualized education program (IEP). 34 CFR §300.4.

In order to be eligible under Part B, a child must be evaluated in accordance with 34 CFR §§300.530-300.534 as having one or more specified physical or mental impairments, and must be found to require special education and related services by reason of one or more of these impairments.[2] 20 U.S.C. 1401 (a) (1); 34 CFR §300.5. SEAs and LEAs must ensure that children with ADD who are determined eligible for services under Part B receive special education and related services designed to meet their unique needs, including special education and related services needs arising from the ADD. A full continuum of placement alternatives, including the regular classroom, must be available for providing special education and related services required in the IEP.

B.   Eligibility for Part B services under the "Other Health Impaired" Category

The list of chronic or acute health problems included within the definition of "other health impaired" in the Part B regulations is not exhaustive. The term "other health impaired" includes chronic or acute impairments that result in limited alertness, which adversely affects educational performanc. Thus, children with ADD should be classified as eligible for services under the "other health impaired" category in instances where the ADD is a chronic or acute health problem that results in limited alertness. which adversely affects educational performance. In other words, children with ADD, where the ADD is a chronic or acute health problem resulting in limited alertness, may be considered disabled under Part B solely on the basis of this disorder within the "other health impaired" category in situations where special education and related services are needed because of the ADD.

C.   Eligibility for Part B services under Other Disability Categories

Children with ADD are also eligible for services under Part B if the children satisfy the criteria applicable to other disability categories. For example, children with ADD are also eligible for services under the "specific learning disability" category of Part B if they meet the criteria stated in §§300.5(b) (9) and 300.541 or under the "seriously emotionally disturbed" category of Part B if they meet the criteria stated i §300.5(b) (8).

---

[2]The Part B regulations define 11 specified disabilities. 34 CFR §300.5(b) (1)-(11). The Education of the Handicapped Act Amendments of 1990 amended the Individuals with Disabilities Education Act (formerly the Education of the Handicapped Act) to specify that autism and traumatic brain injury are separate disability categories. See section 602(a) (1) of the Act, to be codified at 20 U.S.C. 1401(a) (1).

III.   Evaluations under Part B

A.   Requirements

SEAs and LEAs have an affirmative obligation to evaluate a child who is suspected of having a disability to determine the child's need for special education and related services. Under Part B, SEA's and LEAs are required to have procedures for locating, identifying and evaluating all children who have a disability or are suspected of having a disability and are in need of special education and related services. 34 CFR §§300.128 and 300.220. This responsibility, known as "child find," is applicable to all children from birth through 21, regardless of the severity of their disability.

Consistent with this responsibility and the obligation to make FAPE available to all eligible children with disabilities, SEAs and LEAs must ensure that evaluations of children who are suspected of needing special education and related services are conducted without undue delay. 20 U.S.C. 1412(2). Because of its responsibility resulting from the FAPE and child find requirements of Part B, an LEA may not refuse to evaluate the possible need for special education and related services of a child with a prior medical diagnosis of ADD solely by reason of that medical diagnosis. However, a medical diagnosis of ADD alone is not sufficient to render a child eligible for services under Part B.

Under Part B, before any action is taken with respect to the initial placement of a child with a disability in a program providing special education and related services, "a full and individual evaluation of the child's educational needs must be conducted in accordance with requirements of §300.532." 34 CFR §300.531. Section 300.532(a) requires that a child's evaluation must be conducted by a multidisciplinary team, including at least one teacher or other specialist with knowledge in the area of suspected disability.

B.   Disagreements over Evaluations

Any proposal or refusal of an agency to initiate or change the identification, evaluation, or educational placement of the child, or the provision of FAPE to the child is subject to the written prior notice requirements of 34 CFR §§300.504-300.505.[3] If a parent disagrees with the LEA's refusal to evaluate a child or the LEA's evaluation and determination that a child does not have a disability for which the child is eligible for services under Part B, the parent may request a due process hearing pursuant to 34 CFR §§300.506-300.513 of the Part B regulations.

IV.   Obligations Under Section 504 of SEAs and LEAs to Children with ADD Found Not
        To Require Special Education and Related Services under Part B

Even if a child with ADD is found not to be eligible for services under Part B, the
requirements of Section 504 of the Rehabilitation Act of 1973 (Section 504) and its
implementing regulation at 34 CFR Part 104 may be applicable. Section 504 prohibits
discrimination on the basis of handicap by recipients of Federal funds. Since Section 504
is a civil rights law, rather than a funding law, its requirements are framed in different
terms than those of Part B. While the Section 504 regulation was written with an eye to
consistency with Part B, it is more general, and there are some differences arising from
the differing natures of the two laws. For instance, the protections of Section 504 extend
to some children who do not fall within the disability categories specified in Part B.

A.   Definition

Section 504 requires every recipient that operates a public elementary or secondary
education program to address the needs of children who are considered "handicapped
persons" under Section 504 as adequately as the needs of nonhandicapped persons are
met. "Handicapped person" is defined in the Section 504 regulation as any person who
has a physical or mental impairment which substantially limits a major life activity (e.g.,
learning). 34 CFR §104.3(j). Thus, depending on the severity of their condition, children
with ADD may fit within that definition.

---

[3]Section 300.505 of the Part B regulations sets out the elements that must be
contained in the prior written notice to parents:

  (1) A full explanation of all of the procedural safeguards available to the parents
  under Subpart E;
  (2) A description of the action proposed or refused by the agency, an explanation
  of why the agency proposes or refuses to take the action, and a description of any
  options the agency considered and the reasons why those options were rejected;
  (3) A description of each evaluation procedure, test, record, or report the agency
  uses as a basis for the proposal or refusal; and
  (4) A description of any other factors which are relevant to the agency's proposal
  or refusal.

34 CFR §300.505(a) (1)-(4).

B.   Programs and Services Under Section 504

Under Section 504, an LEA must provide a free appropriate public education to each qualified handicapped child. A free appropriate public education, under Section 504, consists of regular or special education and related aids and services that are designed to meet the individual student's needs and based on adherence to the regulator requirements on educational setting, evaluation, placement, and procedural safeguards. 34 CFR §§104.33, 104.34, 104.35, and 104.36. A student may be handicapped within the meaning of Section 504, and therefore entitled to regular or special education and related aids and services under the Section 504 regulation, even though the student may not be eligible for special education and related services under Part B.

Under Section 504, if parents believe that their child is handicapped by ADD, the LEA must evaluate the child to determine whether he or she is handicapped as defined by Section 504. If an LEA determines that a child is not handicapped under Section 504, the parent has the right to contest that determination. If the child is determined to be handicapped under Section 504, the LEA must make an individualized determination of the child's educational needs for regular or special education or related aids and services. 34 CFR §104.35. For children determined to be handicapped under Section 504, implementation of an individualized education program developed in accordance with Part B, although not required, is one means of meeting the free appropriate public education requirements of Section 504.[4] The child's education must be provided in the regular education classroom unless it is demonstrated that education in the regular environment with the use of supplementary aids and services cannot be achieved satisfactorily. 34 CFR §104.34.

Should it be determined that the child with ADD is handicapped for purposes of Section 504 and needs only adjustments in the regular classroom, rather than special education, those adjustments are required by Section 504. A range of strategies is available to meet the educational needs of children with ADD. Regular classroom teachers are important in identifying the appropriate educational adaptions and interventions for many children with ADD.

---

[4] Many LEAs use the same process for determining the needs of students under Section 504 that they use for implementing Part B.

SEAs and LEAs should take the necessary steps to promote coordination between special and regular education programs. Steps also should be taken to train regular education teachers and other personnel to develop their awareness about ADD and its manifestations and the adaptations that can be implemented in regular education programs to address the instructional needs of these children. Examples of adaptations in regular education programs could include the following:

> providing a structured learning environment; repeating and simplifying instructions about in-class and homework assignments; supplementing verbal instructions with visual instructions; using behavioral management techniques; adjusting class schedules; modifying test delivery; using tape recorders, computer-aided instrction, and other audiovisual equipment; selecting modified textbooks or workbooks; and tailoring homework assignments.

Other provisions range from consultation to special resources and may include reducing class size; use of one-on-one tutorials; classroom aides and note takers; involvement of a "services coordinator" to oversee implementation of special programs and services, and possible modification of nonacademic times such as lunchroom, recess, and physical education.

Through the use of appropriate adaptations and interventions in regular classes, many of which may be required by Section 504, the Department believes that LEAs will be able to effectively address the instructional needs of many children with ADD.

C.   Procedural Safeguards Under Section 504

Procedural safeguards under the Section 504 regulation are stated more generally than in Part B. The Section 504 regulation requires the LEA to make available a system of procedural safeguards that permits parents to challenge actions regarding the identification, evaluation, or educational placement of their handicapped child whom they believe needs special education or related services. 34 CFR §104.36. The Section 504 regulation requires that the system of procedural safeguards include notice, an opportunity for the parents or guardian to examine relevant records, an impartial hearing with opportunity for participation by the parents or guardian and representation by counsel, and a review procedure. Compliance with procedural safeguards of Part B is one means of fulfilling the Section 504 requirements.[5] However, in an impartial due process hearing raising issues under the Section 504 regulation, the impartial hearing officer must make a determination based upon that regulation.

---

[5] Again, many LEAs and some SEAs are conserving time and resources by using the same due process procedures for resolving disputes under both laws.

V.   Conclusion

Congress and the Department have recognized the need to provide information and assistance to teachers, administrators, parents and other interested persons regarding the identification, evaluation, and instructional needs of children with ADD. The Department has formed a work group to explore strategies across principal offices to address this issue. The work group also plans to identify some ways that the Department can work with the education associations to cooperatively consider the programs and services needed by children with ADD across special and regular education.

In fiscal year 1991, the Congress appropriated funds for the Department to synthesize and disseminate current knowledge related to ADD. Four centers will be established in Fall, 1991 to analyze and synthesize the current research literature on ADD relating to identification, assessment, and interventions. Research syntheses will be prepared in formats suitable for educators, parents and researchers. Existing clearinghouses and networks, as well as Federal, State and local organizations will be utilized to disseminate these research syntheses to parents, educators and administrators, and other interested persons.

In addition, the Federal Resource Center will work with SEAs and the six regional resource centers authorized under the Individuals with Disabilities Education Act to identfy effective identification and assesment procedures, as well as intervention strategies being implemented across the country for children with ADD. A document describing current practice will be developed and disseminated to parents, educators and administrators, and other interested persons through the regional resource centers, network, as well as by parent training centers, other parent and consumer organizations, and professional organizations. Also, the Office for Civil Rights' ten regional offices stand ready to provide technical assistance to parents and educators.

It is our hope that the above information will be of assistance to your State as you plan for the needs of children with ADD who require special education and related services under Part B, as well as for the needs of the broader group of children with ADD who do not qualify for special education and related services under Part B, but for whom special education or adaptations in regular education programs are needed. If you have any questions, please contact Jean Peelen, Office for Civil Rights; (Phone: 202/732-1635), Judy Schrag, Office of Special Education Programs (Phone: 202/732-1007); or Dan Bonner, Office of Elementary and Secondary Education (Phone: 202/401-0984).

CHAPTER 3

ADOLESCENCE AND THE SOCIAL CONTEXT

An Introduction by Robert Brooks, Ph.D.

McLean Hospital, Belmont, MA

Director, Department of Psychology

Faculty, Harvard Medical School

I have worked with many adolescents with ADD and their families in my role as a psychologist. Every interaction I have had with these adolescents has provided me with information about their lives and has challenged me to articulate the concepts that guide my interventions with them. The articles included in this section about the "social context" address several of these concepts, including the importance of (a) being empathic, (b) involving adolescents in their own treatment, especially through education, (c) helping these youth to develop self-control skills, and (d) placing the spotlight on strengths and resilience rather than on pathology.

In the beginning of my career I had no idea what I was doing as a therapist, a feeling that most likely is experienced by all novice clinicians. It is difficult for me to believe that during those early days I actually asked hyperactive patients to "have a seat" or to "try harder to pay attention." In many ways I blamed the very adolescents I was supposed to be helping by referring to them as "resistant" and "oppositional." I began to feel frustrated by my inability to reach my patients, and upset by the "blame game" in which I was engaged.

It was at this point that I realized something that seems so obvious now. How could I be of help if I did not understand what my patients with ADD were experiencing? How could therapists be effective unless they truly practiced empathy and attempted to understand the world through the eyes of their patients? In my quest to become more empathic I began to ask those in my care to describe and write about their lives; as I read their stories I came to appreciate the struggles and pain that these youngsters experience. Many of these adolescents who I had so glibly called "resistant" because of my lack of understanding were dealing with feelings of low self-esteem, a sense of incompetence, and often a loss of hope. What they needed was less blame and more support.

First person accounts such as that written by Alan Brown provide rich and poignant information about the lives of adolescents with ADD, accounts that can enhance our ability to be empathic. Would teachers so easily write, "Needs to concentrate more on answers; Needs to turn in all work; Needs to follow directions," if they appreciated how accusatory these comments could sound? We must give more than lip service to being empathic. We must practice it at all times even when we are frustrated with an adolescent.

A characteristic of high self-esteem is the belief that you have some control over what is occurring in your life. Thus, an important feature of my interventions with adolescents is to reinforce a sense of ownership by educating them about their disorder, by enlisting them as active participants in developing and implementing their treatment plan, and by providing them with opportunities to nurture their problem solving and decision making skills. Articles offering advice to parents on how to talk with and educate their adolescents about such issues as medication are of great importance. The more comfortable parents are in discussing these issues, the more effectively they can communicate the information to their adolescents and the more successfully adolescents can apply what they are taught. Much the same, strategies for developing self-control skills as discussed by John Taylor are essential in assisting adolescents to gain increasing control over their behavior and strengthen their self-esteem.

In my workshops for educators and mental health professionals, I often ask who has taken a course on abnormal psychology or the psychopathology of childhood. Most acknowledge that they have. However, when I next ask who has taken a course on resilience, almost no hands are raised. It is interesting how often we subtly — or not-so-subtly — place the spotlight on deficits and disorders rather than on strengths and how often we fail to ask questions about what factors help children at risk to overcome adversity and become resilient. I believe we must increase our knowledge of these factors that promote resilience and use this knowledge to guide our interventions. We must identify and reinforce what I call the "islands of competence," or areas of strength in each child, instead of spending most of our energy diagnosing deficits.

We need more researchers and clinicians like Mark Katz who help us to understand the power of the human mind and spirit to confront adversity, who provide us with information about what we can do as caregivers to improve the prognosis of all adolescents with ADD, and who paint a picture of hope rather than despair. I would love to see the day when courses on resiliency are offered as frequently as courses on pathology, when thoughtful articles and books about resiliency are readily available, and when parents and other caregivers appreciate the role they can play in fostering hope and in saving our youth. Articles such as those written by Mark Katz remind us that no adolescent should ever be written off.

The articles in this chapter, taken together, capture the importance of fostering empathy, self-esteem, empowerment, resilience, and hope. It is difficult to think of more significant themes for those of us who are raising, educating, or working with adolescents with ADD.

Building Conscience and Self-control Skills in Children and Adolescents with AD/HD

by John F. Taylor, Ph.D.

The methods discussed in this article, like most of those portrayed in Helping Your Hyperactive Attention Deficit Child *and the audiotape* Answers to ADD: Social Skills Training, *can be used by any parent or teacher. Teaching these techniques to children and teens can best be accomplished by using skits, group discussion, or role playing to supplement didactic instruction.*

METHODS TO ENHANCE PROBLEM SOLVING

To most people, trying harder means working faster on a task. For the adolescent with AD/HD, however, the best way to improve performance is to slow down and think about each step. Tell the child: "When you want to try hard at something, that means slow down so you are sure to do it correctly." One of the most useful self-reminding statements is: "Stop and think: what do I need to do next?"

To aid decision making and problem solving, teach the adolescent to break down tasks into these simple steps: (1) Know the Problem: What are your needs, deadlines, resources? Break tasks down into parts; (2) Identify the Choices: generate possible approaches, using similar experiences with other problems as a starting point; (3) Try the Best One: Filter the possible approaches and weigh pros and cons to decide which would be the best to try; (4) Evaluate: Choose key indicators of progress and use a timetable of expected results. Modify the approach until the situation is resolved or the goal is accomplished. Notice that these four steps can be represented by the acronym **KITE**.

METHODS FOR CONTROLLING ANGER

Anger control training is one of the most consistently needed forms of intervention to assist children and teens who have AD/HD. Wholesale problems with anger control are generally much more pronounced when there is comorbidity with a conduct disorder. Don't expect to have a calm discussion about anger control when the adolescent is out-of-sorts; talk after he/she has calmed down. Decide together what can be done next time to prevent a similar outcome and train the adolescent to become aware of the early signs of anger. What happens first? Do you clench your fist? Do you tell yourself something is unfair? Do you tell yourself you are not going to let someone get away with something? Another method is a regular check-in on frustrations, which is especially helpful for adolescents who are extremely volatile and short-tempered. The adolescent writes down descriptions of frustrating moments during the day in a special notebook and discusses the concerns with a caring adult on a regular basis at home or at school.

Invite the adolescent to tell an adult. An instant-service version of the daily check-in, this technique allows the child to come to you whenever anger starts to develop. "Just come to me and say, 'I'm starting to feel angry'. I will stop doing whatever I'm doing, listen to your concerns, and give you advice about what you can do."

Teach this universal assertion technique: the "three-part way to get others to stop bugging you." The adolescent states how she feels, asks for what she needs in order to feel better, and makes a deal with the other person of the win-win variety. The entire statement would be something like: "When you do that, I feel frustrated and confused. Please don't do that; do this instead. If you do it that way, I'll do what you ask." If the adolescent has trouble with the entire three-part message, substitute a basic assertion statement such as "That bothers me; please stop it" . . . "Please don't do that to me" . . . or "Please stop doing that." Introduce the statement as a special "trick" or "magic phrase" to use whenever the child senses a build-up of frustration toward others.

Teach the adolescent to use the self-reminders "stay calm" and "stay in control," which are more helpful than "don't get angry." This method transforms anger into determination to remain self-controlled and trains him/her to own responsibility for one-half of the confrontation.

METHODS TO HANDLE UNDESIRABLE FRIENDSHIPS AND INFLUENCES

If you have concerns about peer influence, involve the child in other activities that don't include the less desirable peers. Strengthening the adolescent's refusal skills will also be helpful. Encourage more wholesome relationships by offering new prospective friends in competition. At school, for example, plan activities that pair the adolescent with likely prospects for wholesome friendships. Once you have established more wholesome peers as possible new friends, contrast the desirability of the two groups of peers. Discuss the qualities of a good friend and compare both groups of peers against those standards. Don't force the issue, but plant the seeds for the adolescent to consider standards for whom to befriend.

TEMPTATION RESISTANCE TRAINING

Here are several key steps to help an impulsive, needy-for-friends adolescent learn to refuse invitations to mischief:

Lower the attractiveness of temptations. This is the best way to help the adolescent become unimpressed with temptation thoughts given by peers. Sit down with the child and say something like: "Let's play a special game of listing all of the ways those children have of trying to convince you to get into mischief. I know a couple of them to start our list. Then you help me add some more. 'Everybody does it . . . you are a chicken if you don't . . . we won't get caught . . . just this once would be o.k. . . . I did it so you have to do it too . . . if you were really my friend you'd do it . . . it will be fun . . . I won't do what you want me to do unless you do this for me . . . I dare you.'" Continue with the adolescent's assistance, then explain that each one of those approaches is a lie rather than a truth. Each is a distortion intended to manipulate and to rob him/her of power and self-control.

Provide self-reminder statements having to do with self-determination issues, such as: "I will control me and not let others control me . . . They are trying to control me — I won't let them . . . Stop and think, what should I do now? . . . If I do that, what will happen? (undesirable consequences) . . . If I refuse, what will happen? (desirable consequences)."

Practice refusal statements. Have the adolescent practice saying "no" and stating refusals such as: "no thanks . . . not me . . . absolutely not . . . You can get into trouble if you want to, but not me . . . I don't want to . . . that's dumb . . . that's wrong and I won't do it . . . forget it . . . no way." Teach the child to say "no" and suggest a better idea. The adolescent quickly changes the subject rather than debating the issue with the peer. Teach him/her to give two "no's", then leave. The adolescent needs to settle the matter by giving two refusal statements, then leaving the scene. Leaving comes after the refusal, not before it. Staying and arguing with the peer leads to becoming persuaded or bullied into following along.

These are only a few of the methods parents can use to help their adolescents with ADD build both their self conscience and self-control skills. As new challenges arise, parents must develop their own strategies to help their adolescents with ADD develop appropriate social skills, but the suggestions mentioned in this article may be able to serve as a helpful resource.

John F. Taylor, Ph.D. is an authority on AD/HD, writing the first book providing in-depth discussion of family relationship issues in ADD families, including sibling rivalry, self-esteem, parent's emotional stress, and marital dysnfunctions. He is President of ADD Plus, a consulting, training, and publishing organization.

From Challenged Childhood to Achieving Adulthood: Studies in Resilience

by Mark Katz, Ph.D.

In a moment, you'll read a letter written to the CH.A.D.D. newsletter by a very concerned mom, who's worried about what lies in store for her sixteen-year-old son Kurt. Kurt's a hard worker, who tries his best at school, despite having to contend with long-standing attention and learning difficulties. It's likely that few people who know Kurt really appreciate what he's had to endure. Fewer likely appreciate his strength and courage. This is changing, however, thanks to a new field of study that's highlighting sources of resilience and protective influences that help young people successfully overcome many childhood adversities.

In responding to the letter that Kurt's mom wrote, I tried to provide an overview of this field of study, which we feel offers great hope and opportunity to kids like Kurt, and to the mothers and fathers who try so hard to buffer them. Here then, is the letter from Kurt's mom, followed by my reply.

> My sixteen-year-old was diagnosed with ADD when he was a little boy. He also has learning disabilities in reading and math, and school has been a constant struggle. Even so, I have received very few comments about behavior problems from his teachers over the years. While Kurt is miserable in the classroom (he says that the school day is "about 20 hours long") he shines in music and theater, and has many good friends. People who hear him play trumpet in the pep band or see him act in plays (he is very clever) assume he will be a big hit in life. However, his grades are mostly C's, and he says he wants no more of school after graduation. The high school counselor says only two words: vocational school, but I can't imagine him doing anything dull or routine. As his friends make plans for college, he's noticeably down, already anticipating feeling like a "failure" after high school. Do you have any advice for helping a teenager like this plan for his future?

We've been trying to learn as much as possible about the lives of successful adults who struggled in school as children and teenagers. We always anticipated that these people were out there in great numbers. We underestimated ourselves. The numbers appear to be larger than we ever thought. The problem is, their stories have not received much attention. I anticipate that Kurt will someday join the ranks of these individuals, who, by the way, we see as extremely resilient and courageous people. We feel that we have much to learn from these individuals, and that the lessons that they can teach us will someday prove extremely valuable in helping other children having to contend with similar adversities.

Many successful adults who struggled in school were, like Kurt, talented in a variety of areas. Looking back over their school histories, however, their strengths may not have extended to reading, mathematics, or subjects requiring organizational skills. It probably shouldn't surprise us that for many of these individuals, their identities formed around the few things that they struggled most with, as these areas comprised the vast majority of activities they were required to do during their years in school. Their wide-ranging gifts seemed to do little to alter their views of themselves. Make no mistake — these individuals were very talented. Some were gifted in their ability to solve problems in unique and inventive ways. Some were gifted artistically and creatively. And some were extremely talented in the way that they related to people. What they were not gifted in were such things as reading, spelling, multiplying, dividing, remembering where they put things, or doing things that required a lot of repetition. As children, some of these individuals also found school to be very boring. During their school years, they were stimulation seekers, always looking for exciting things to do.

So herein lie a couple of questions that I'm sure greatly concern you, and which, for some time now, have also greatly concerned us. First, how can we help these children and teenagers start to see themselves more accurately, that is, as individuals with multiple talents who aren't strong within specific academic and/or attention areas? And secondly, how can we help steer multi-talented young people, who may not be strong within specific academic-related areas, into career paths that will provide them the opportunity to showcase and nourish their talents? The world needs people with different talents and gifts. But as I heard Rick Lavoie once say, the world can be kinder to children with learning disabilities than schools are.

Our search for answers to these questions has led us to the growing field of research on human resilience. For some time now, researchers and clinicians have been studying the lives of individuals who overcame various childhood adversities. these researchers and clinicians include (but are not limited to) Emmy Werner, Ph.D.; Norman Garmezy, Ph.D.; Michael Rutter, M.D.; and Robert Brooks; Ph.D.

Let me briefly share with you some of the findings we've come up with that are helping us guide many young people, and which may also be of some help to you.

Successful individuals who overcame earlier childhood adversities, at some point, began to define themselves more around their multiple talents than around their few areas of vulnerability. The fact that they had areas of talent and areas of vulnerability didn't distinguish them from most of us.

Many of these individuals had the good fortune of being provided with opportunities to express their talents in meaningful ways, and to have their talents recognized and valued by others, particularly others who they saw as important people in their lives. So talents and abilities need outlets for expression. Ever notice how happy Kurt is after a good acting performance? There's a favorite cartoon we have, which hangs on some of our office walls. The cartoon is of a man looking inquisitively into the face of a small bird, who sits perched on a branch of a tree. The man asks the bird, "Do you sing because you're happy?" To which the bird replies, "No. I'm happy because I sing."

Being able to showcase our talents, and to have them valued by important people in our lives, helps us define our identities around that which we do best. This is how people develop a sense of mastery. The reverse is true as well. If you spend a disproportionate amount of your life doing the few things you do poorly, and do these things around important people who see you only in this light, you're apt to define yourself in harsh and devaluing ways.

Every time I refer to this issue of providing opportunities for children to showcase their special gifts and talents, I'm reminded of Eugene Lang, and the I Have A Dream Foundation. As the story was told to me, and as I remember reading about it in newspaper articles, Eugene Lang, a very successful businessman, was asked to give a speech to a 6th grade assembly at an elementary school in East Harlem. It was a school that he himself attended many years earlier as a child. During his speech, which he delivered in the early 1980s, he told the children that if they stayed in school, he would pay for their college education after high school graduation. If you asked these children's teachers before Mr. Lang's speech whether or not their students would someday attend college, what do you think their replies would be? Reportedly, not many students attending this elementary school ever made it to college. Many years have passed since the speech. The children are now college age. And recent reports indicate of the fifty-one students that Mr. Lang agreed to support, forty-seven earned their high school diplomas or GED, and approximately 90 percent are expected to complete at least two years of college.

Many successful adults who didn't do well in school also often speak of a very important person in their lives who might have served as a mentor, or who might have been very skilled at something they were skilled at, and who made them aware of new career paths. Someday, there will be professionals who are trained in identifying and opening up career paths for multi-talented individuals who aren't gifted within specific academic-related areas. Many counselors today think of vocational schools as the only career path for children who didn't do well in school. Now don't misunderstand me. Vocational school serves as an extremely valuable role in training individuals to do valued, needed jobs. The point here is that in the future, as we become more knowledgeable about the many different paths that successful adults took to get where they are, vocational school will serve as one viable option. If your dream can be realized through vocational school, then that may prove to be your path. It also may provide you with an opportunity to learn a skill to support yourself while you pursue another dream that may carry with it greater risks, but which compels you to at least give it your very best try.

Researchers who study the ways in which individuals overcome earlier adversities in their lives often speak of turning point experiences. For some individuals, turning point experiences can unfold over an extended period of time. For others, they can occur by virtue of brief, chance encounters. Sometimes, one experience, or one encounter, begins a process in which an individual starts seeing him or herself in a completely different way.

Another thing that we're learning about successful adults who struggled in school is that somewhere during their life span they found different words, a different language, that helped then legitimize the pain and demoralization they experienced in their earlier school years. They stopped defining themselves in negative ways. They came to understand that they tried their best, that there were things that they could and couldn't control, and that they may have actually done pretty well under the circumstances.

Many of these successful adults also cite the presence of a special person in their lives, who served as a buffer or protective influence. Often, but not always, this was a parent. This special individual, time and again, was there to dry the child's tears and encourage him or her to go on and try their best. The child's frustration and pain, and the special person's frustration and pain, often persisted for years and years. In the long run, however, being there time and again counted, more than words could convey; a caring concerned individual who stood by them unconditionally, and who always thought of them as special.

To the concerned parent who wrote this letter, I encourage you to consider purchasing Dr. Howard Gardner's book, *Multiple Intelligences: The Theory In Practice.* Howard Gardner has been instrumental in helping us appreciate that people have multiple intellectual capacities, each of which carries special value and importance to society. His body of work has also helped dispel the myth that intelligence can be measured with one single score. Some schools around the country are developing their curriculum around multiple intelligences theory. In these schools, the range of intellectual capacities are nourished and valued.

And finally, a brief message to Kurt. While you may not realize it, you represent a group of individuals who possess a type of resilience that has become the focus of many professional people around the country. These people (of which I am one) feel that individuals like yourself have many lessons to teach. Bear in mind that your friends have no real idea what school has felt like for you. You've been tested in ways that your friends haven't. You've stood strong, despite what likely have been some very stressful times. Individuals like yourself often become stronger as a result of this. It's like you develop "psychological antibodies." Future stresses down the road somehow don't seem so big. This isn't always the case for children who sailed through school smoothly. Some of these children have escaped having to contend with significant obstacles in their path. These obstacles will likely appear someday, in one form or another. They too will be tested, like you were. I hope they can stand up as well.

You and your school counselor share something in common. Neither of you know much about the potentially wonderful things that lie in store for you in the future. I hope that you can spend some time getting to know, or perhaps even working around, special people who love doing the same things that you love doing. Some of these endeavors sound as though they involve theater and music. Volunteer your time working around these people at your local colleges and universities that teach music and drama, and see if they have any ideas. It's important that you speak with people who feel passionately about the areas of talent that you possess, and who have carved out successful careers for themselves. These people may have ideas that you haven't thought about.

In closing, let me just say, Kurt, that I'm typing this article a few hours after returning from the movies, where I just saw *Schindler's List.* It was directed by Steven Spielberg. The story told to me about Steven Spielberg was that he didn't do so great in school. In fact, I heard that he did pretty poorly. The family lived in Arizona. Steven kept asking his mother to take him out to the desert so that he could make a movie. One day when he was still in elementary school, Steven Spielberg's mother wrote him a note excusing him from school, took him out to the desert, and let him start making his movie — talent meeting opportunity. Keep in mind that talents like his are ones that usually aren't highlighted and nourished in most schools. He is, nonetheless, extraordinarily talented. In the future, Kurt, when our society becomes more aware of the diversity of human talents, and the need to nourish all of them, there will be more options for students like yourself. For now, you're going to have to a bit of a trailblazer. But you're in some great company.

*This article first appeared in the
May 1994 CH.A.D.D.er Box.*

Dr. Katz is Director of Learning Development Services, an educational, psychological, and neuropsychological center in San Diego, CA. He is also Supervising Psychologist at San Diego Center for Children.

From the Newsroom to Your Living Room — Talking to Teens About Methylphenidate Abuse

by Jeff Rosenberg

From ABC's 20/20 to Newsweek to local news outlets, reports of abuse of stimulant medications such as methylphenidate are receiving a great deal of attention. The news reports may range from the responsible to the sensational, but undoubtedly and understandably, every report about the abuse of prescription medications greatly concerns parents of children with ADD.

"We have formed a scientific study group to examine the issue of methylphenidate abuse," says CH.A.D.D. National President Mary Richard. "The study group, which includes many of the leading researchers in the field, will review the latest research, data, and information on reported abuse of methylphenidate. Their work will help us determine whether the anecdotal reports presented by the media are indicative of a growing trend."

"The latest data that we have seen, and consultations with experts around the country, suggest that abuse is not widespread. We are, however, extremely concerned about the reports and taking them very seriously. Our children are growing up, many becoming teenagers who are now facing challenges and issues they did not have to worry about when they were younger. We believe that parents need to talk to their children about the issue of methylphenidate abuse."

"I generally try to reassure parents," reports Thomas Giroux, Ph.D., a clinical psychologist at the Kellar Center in Fairfax, Virginia. "We don't see that many adolescents who are abusing their medication. But certainly in the drug-abusing community, there are people who would abuse anything."

TALK TO YOUR CHILD ABOUT METHYLPHENIDATE ABUSE

Parents and clinicians, alike, agree: parents should talk to their pre-adolescent and adolescent children about substance abuse and the role of peer pressure. "Based on my discussions with teenagers, some kids are asking other kids if they know somebody taking methylphenidate, and some teenagers I know have been approached by other kids asking to buy their methylphenidate," reports Howard Schubiner, M.D., an Associate Professor at Wayne State University who practices at Children's Hospital of Michigan.

"Children need to be prepared. They need to be able to resist such an approach. They need to understand the danger of someone taking their medication without medical supervision, and that it could have serious consequences for them, as well," Schubiner warns.

JoAnne Evans, a parent of two teenage boys with ADD and CH.A.D.D.'s Immediate Past President, says, "In light of the media attention about possible abuse of methylphenidate, it makes talking to your child even more important. Without a doubt, every parent should be talking to their child frankly about the issue."

"Parents do need to have a frank discussion about this issue with their children," agrees Giroux. "The fact that abuse has been brought up as a concern by shows such as 20/20, makes it imperative that parents talk to their children about how to handle the situation if someone approaches them and says, 'Hey, let me have some of your medication.'"

WHEN AND HOW TO TALK

Many experts feel that by the time children reach age twelve or middle school, parents should discuss substance abuse issues with them. But it is one of the tougher issues for parents and children to talk about, especially when your child is a teenager. "Parents need to get rid of some of their own anxieties about medication and abuse," says Bruce Pfeffer, M.D., a developmental pediatrician in Fairfax, Virginia. "I'm much more concerned about parents who refuse treatment for their child. What I see in my practice — and many of my colleagues report the same thing — is that the child with ADD who receives treatment is less likely to get into problems with substance abuse than the child who is not treated."

Giroux agrees, saying, "I don't think teenagers with ADD who are taking medication are at greater risk for substance abuse. In some ways, they might be less prone to abusing it because by the time they reach adolescence, they understand the proper role and handling of medication."

It is important to keep your own anxieties in check and put them in perspective. But even the most "laid-back" parent will feel stressed and anxious when discussing a difficult and sensitive topic with an adolescent child. "A good parent should listen to his or her adolescent, and that's hard for all of us," says Pfeffer. "I think it's fair to ask a teenager, 'Are you worried about this?'" Avoid lecturing, he cautions. Pfeffer points out that it can help to have another important adult in the child's life bring up the issue, such as a pediatrician or school counselor. "I can say things to my fourteen-year-old patients that I can't possibly say to my own teenager," Pfeffer notes.

A good way to broach the subject is to put it in context. "Bring the topic up in conjunction with a television show or an article about the issue of methylphenidate abuse," says Schubiner. "'Hey, I read something in a magazine that seems important. Why don't you read it and then let's talk about it,' is a good way to begin. The first step is to bring things up in a nonjudgemental way, to ask what your child knows or thinks about it. Because what he or she thinks is very important."

WHAT TO SAY

CH.A.D.D. strongly believes that every child needs to understand ADD and its treatment. "Make sure your child understands why he is taking medication, what the medication does, and how it fits into his overall treatment plan," says Richard. Children need to know that methylphenidate, when taken properly and under the direction of a physician, is safe and effective. But they also need to understand that, like many other medications, if taken without medical supervision, methylphenidate can be dangerous.

"Parents should give their children strategies for handling questions about the medication they take and, most certainly, strategies in case they are approached by other kids asking for their medication," says Evans. "What I've told my own children is, if anyone asks for some of your medication, you say 'No. This medicine is prescribed only for me by my doctor,' and then walk away. If it becomes a problem, children should be encouraged to go to an adult at school or to their parents."

"Parents also need to be aware of the rules and procedures at their child's school for handling and dispensing prescription medications," adds Richard. "Don't assume that personnel at your child's school are knowledgeable about ADD and the medications used in its treatment, and don't assume that they are as sensitive to the issues, such as confidentiality, as they should be. Ask questions."

The best advice? Open up a dialogue with your teenager about this and other important issues. Don't preach or lecture, but discuss. Listen to your teenager — he or she knows much more about what's really happening out there than you do. If the normal parent-teen struggles are getting in the way of a dialogue, enlist the help of someone outside of the family, such as your child's doctor, teacher, or coach, or a member of your church or synagogue. And be sure to learn about school rules for medications and how those rules are put into action.

*This article first appeared in the
Winter 1996 ATTENTION!*

Jeff Rosenberg is President of Rosenberg Communications, a communications firm located in the Washington, D.C. area that specializes in media relations and publications. He is the Executive Editor of ATTENTION! magazine and Managing Editor of CH.A.D.D.er Box newsletter.

THINGS TO TALK ABOUT WITH YOUR CHILD

- A complete understanding about ADD
- Why your child is taking medication
- How medication fits into the treatment plan
- Strategies for handling questions about ADD and medication
- Strategies for dealing with peer pressure and requests to share/sell medication

THINGS TO CONSIDER

- How and where medication is stored in your home
- School rules and procedures for handling and dispensing medication
- How much medication to have in the home at any one time

Attention Deficit Disorder Through the Eyes of a Young Teen

by Alan Brown

I often wondered why I wasn't in group time in kindergarten. The teacher sent me in the corner to play with a toy by myself. Because of being singled out, I didn't know why or what it was. Toward the middle half of first grade, the teacher called my mom in for a conference. She was telling my mom, "I'm always having to call on Alan: 'Alan, be still, please. Yes, you can sharpen your pencil for the third time. You have to go to the bathroom, again?'" That evening, my teacher educated my mom. She told my mom about Attention Deficit Disorder. My teacher suggested taking me to the doctor and letting him run some tests. Mom and I went to see the doctor. After some testing, the doctor put me on methylphenidate. Within about two weeks the teacher said I was completing my homework, making good grades, and feeling good about myself. Although we (my Mom and I) thought our battle was won, we had no idea what adventures were waiting for us.

Second grade went by. I was doing all right in school. My teacher would usually write on my report card, "Alan worked hard this six weeks. Encourage him to read at home." I hated to read; it was so hard to understand what I had read. I loved to play outside, run in the field near my house, and ride on my bicycle — a free spirit.

By the time I got to third grade, things were getting off track. I felt like nothing I did was right. I would try to do good work. My teacher would write on my papers: "Needs to concentrate more on answers; Needs to turn in all work; Needs to follow directions."

I really didn't think my teacher liked me. She was very stern, never seemed to smile, and was always watching me....Fourth grade was the year everything fell apart!

Before school started my mom took me to see the doctor, like we did every year. The doctor prescribed the same dose of methylphenidate I had taken the year before. He didn't want to raise my dosage unless he really had to.

The first six weeks passed and I didn't do very well, but the doctor said it might be the new school year or getting settled in and used to a new teacher. My mom told the teacher the doctor was considering raising my methylphenidate dosage. The teacher said something had to be done because my grades were low. I wasn't always prepared for class, was slow getting my books out, and always needed to go to my locker because I had forgotten something. My doctor did raise my medication to one pill in morning and one pill at lunch. Everyone in the room would say, "Dummy has to go take his pill."

My teacher wanted to make me concentrate better, so one day she put my desk in the far corner, separated from the rest of the class. A few days passed. I still wasn't finishing my work on time, but I was trying to do the work correctly. The teacher didn't care; it wasn't finished. She then put a refrigerator box around my desk so I couldn't see anyone in class. I could hear as other kids in class would make fun of me. It really hurt; I was ashamed of myself and mad at my teacher. I couldn't tell my mom, because I might get in trouble.

I hated school, didn't like my teacher and started not liking myself. Imagine a nine-year-old going through this day after day. It was hard to face the next day. A week passed, and I poked holes in the cardboard, so I could see who was making fun of me. I started peeping through the holes, making the other kids laugh. The teacher would get so annoyed. So I became the class clown. I was expelled for two days. When my mom found out what was going on, boy, did she get angry.

She was mad that the teacher would do this and mad that the principal allowed it, and no one could see what this was doing to me.

Mom called my doctor, explained what was going on, and asked him to recommend a specialist. We needed some help! I remember my mom cried over the phone. It scared me. I thought I was really in trouble, but instead, she put me in her lap, kissed my cheek, gave me a hug and said, "You're special to me, and I love you. Together we are going to get through this." It made me feel good because Moms can always fix everything.....

The next day Mom explained that we were going to meet someone special, someone I could talk to. I was kind of nervous. This person was a licensed clinical social worker. She was nice. I played games while we talked. After a while I felt like she was a friend. It was time to meet with the principal to return to school. Mom and I went to the office. The principal wanted to give my place to a more deserving student, a higher academic achiever. It would make the school look better. At that point Mom asked about my rights as a handicapped student. She didn't like the thought that no one seemed to care what they had done to me, and she said so. At that point the principal made a phone call to one of his friends, also a principal. It had something to do with Mom not going to the school board meeting to discuss this matter. I was going to a new school, a school close to where my mom worked, thanks to that phone call.

On the way home that day, Mom explained to me that what they had done to me wasn't right, and they should be ashamed. She said that there were a lot of smart, successful people in this world who were not happy with themselves. She said, "It's more important in life to be happy and know within yourself that no matter what comes your way, you can survive." Academics are important but self worth is, too.

The new school was a more positive atmosphere; my grades came up. The doctor changed my medication to a slow release pill so I didn't have to leave class to take it anymore.

Fifth grade came along. It was great! I had the best teacher; she smiled a lot and was flexible, yet had a structured day planned. One day I remember she asked me to go to the closet and get the book, *Charlotte's Web*. I went to the closet and found the most wonderful book, *King of The Wind*. A story about a horse. I hid the book, *Charlotte's Web*, and told the teacher I couldn't find it but that this horse book was there and I really liked horses. All along the teacher knew those books were in that closet. She thought if *King of The Wind* looked that interesting to me, maybe it would be worth doing instead of *Charlotte's Web*. After reading the book, I wrote a report about the story. The teacher was so impressed. She posted the book report in front of the class and made a comment on my report card. I was so proud — proud of myself. I was on track again; life was great. My parents were going to be so proud. Sixth grade came, and I did fairly well. I had to change classes. It was hard to adjust to better organization skills. I color-coded folders for classes and kept a schedule of where and when classes were.

Seventh grade was a little rocky, but I made it. There were more students. I kind of got lost in the shuffle. By eighth grade it was a struggle every day. More peer pressure to fit in, and I was going through a lot of changes — puberty.

I would find myself daydreaming a lot, wanting to be with my grandfather. In the summer I got to spend a lot of time with him. Grandfather owned his own business, and taught me a lot. Learning was fun that way. It was hands-on learning. Anyway, that year my report card read, "Needs to finish work. Didn't turn in all papers. Needs to show more effort." I dreaded every day. Sometimes I even cried when I was by myself. How could I get these people to understand me? I went into automatic shut-off; everything seemed negative with school.

Summer came. I needed a break, I worked with my Grandfather. That summer my family spent a lot of time preparing me for high school.

High School! What a big step! I was growing up. More things were going to be expected of me. I wanted to fit in and not be a jerk or dork. My parents warned me about wrong crowds and told me high school grades were really important to my future. What pressure! My mom talked to the guidance counselor about my having ADD. The counselor assured her I would do just fine.

I was really nervous the first day, but guess what — all freshmen are. The first six weeks went by. Not all of my teachers had taken the time to read my school records. They didn't realize I had ADD. Boy, did things get out of hand.

Later that year, when mom went in for a conference one of my teachers said, "I would never have guessed Alan had ADD." Mom looked surprised. The teacher said, "He dresses so nice, has a clean hair-cut and shows respect for teachers. He doesn't get into trouble." Mom rolled her eyes but didn't say anything until we got into the car. "Alan, that teacher doesn't understand about ADD. Anyone can get it. It's not a shame to have ADD. At least we know what we are dealing with. Remember, build on your strengths rather than magnify your weaknesses. Ignore that teacher's comment. She needs to be better educated in this field. School isn't just for ABC's anymore!"

I wanted to belong. I acted tough, even started to tell lies. I told stories that made me look big in people's eyes, but everyone knew they were lies. I just made things worse. In high school you are with a lot of people everyday. You meet lots of teachers. Some teachers are there just to earn a paycheck, and there are a few who really care about the students they have. I had such a teacher. She took time for me, time to try to understand me better. When I needed someone to stand up for me, this teacher did. Once, a teacher asked everyone to write a story as if they were in a make-believe world. She asked me about my ideas. I replied, "I deal in the real world." This really puzzled the teacher. I am fifteen now and I have to deal in the real world. Dreaming is nice. Being a student with ADD takes all my energy to meet the goals I have set for myself.

Through my years in school so far, I've been through a lot. My mom says I have a good heart; I care about those in need. I am not dumb. You can't always measure smartness by tests. I feel I'm doing better in school. The school psychologist has become an important tool for me. I can talk to him when I get a teacher who doesn't understand, if I disagree with something, or if I'm just having problems. It helps to talk to someone who understands. What I am trying to say is NO MATTER WHAT COMES MY WAY I CAN SURVIVE. I have those who really care, and from that, I draw my strength.

This article first appeared in the Winter 1995 ATTENTION!

CHAPTER 4

THE FAMILY

An Introduction by Samuel Goldstein, Ph.D.
Clinical Instructor, Department of Psychiatry,
University of Utah School of Medicine
Staff Member, Primary Children's Hospital and the
University Neuropsychiatric Institute

As we stand on the threshold of the 21st century, the future of our children appears bright. Yet this brightness reflects a mixed blessing. Certainly the technological, academic, and vocational opportunities for our teens appear limitless. Yet it may be the best of times *and* the worst of times. Statistical trends demonstrate that crimes by and against children and adolescents continue to increase. A significant percentage of our children grow up in poverty. The psychological health, fabric, and function of an increasing number of families continues to deteriorate. In the face of such trends — suggesting that, in their daily lives, our children face increased stress and pressure — it is not surprising that children with ADD are more vulnerable than ever before and facing greater struggles.

It would seem that as our treatments to relieve the symptoms of ADD become more refined and efficient, the present and future lives of children with ADD would become brighter. Yet this does not appear to be the case. In almost every instance, relief of symptoms may bring improved functioning; but symptom relief for ADD has not been demonstrated to be synonymous with improved long-term outcome.

That is not to suggest that treatments for ADD — medicine, parent training, educational interventions, and psychosocial treatments — are not beneficial. It is that they alone do not appear to change the life course for children with ADD. As has been repeatedly demonstrated from longitudinal studies — studies following children from birth into their adult years — in almost every instance, biological risk such as that leading to

ADD is mediated by environmental experience. Thus, the forces that impact the child with ADD day in and day out appear to be the best and most powerful predictors of their future outcome. It is this environmental foundation upon which we place our ADD treatments.

This environmental foundation contains factors that increase risk for problem outcome (e.g., poverty) and those that protect or insulate children. Among the latter, the most powerful predictors of children's life outcome are related to family issues. Parents' availability, competence, and their ability to develop a warm, nurturing, supportive relationship with their child, and, most importantly, to build a sense of self-esteem and emotional security in their children are critical. These appear to be the best predictors of what happens to all children, including those with ADD. If the environmental foundation, of which the most important component is the child's family, is unsound, even the best treatments for ADD will be unsuccessful.

This chapter contains articles to help parents of adolescents with ADD build in these important protective factors. Adolescent authority, Arthur Robin, provides parents of adolescents who have ADD with a set of practical, realistic guidelines. Dr. Robin also provides tips to help parents communicate effectively with their teens. I provide a discussion that will help parents to understand sibling relationships and deal with the often intense sibling rivalries that children and adolescents with ADD often experience. Finally, Rick Lavoie applies his ever-popular touch to questions related to designing effective home environments.

Golden Rules of Survival
For Parents

by Arthur L. Robin, Ph.D.

I. **Golden Rules of Survival For Parents**

    A. Learn as much as you can about ADHD

    B. Understand the implications of adolescent development

    C. Develop coping attitudes and reasonable expectations

    D. Establish clear-cut house and street rules

    E. Problem solve issues with your adolescent

    F. Communicate assertively but respectfully

    G. Use professional help wisely

    H. Take vacations regularly

    I. Practice forgiveness and maintain a sense of humor

II. **Personal Education about ADHD**

    A. Learn as much as you can about ADHD from books, videos, CH.A.D.D. meetings, workshops, therapists, others.

    B. Make these resources available to your teenager, but don't push them on him/her.

III. **Implications of Adolescent Development**

    A. Adolescents are becoming independent of parents

    B. For ADHD teens, their minds are usually far behind their bodies in maturity

    C. Some conflict is normal. Pick your issues wisely.

    D. Teens reject parental ideas/values in favor of peer ideas/values

    E. Teens have a great need to have nothing wrong with them. They reject disabilities and their treatments.

    F. Teens are more likely to do what you want if they think it was their idea.

    G. Adolescents needs reasons for rules.

    H. ADHD adolescents already have fragile self-esteem. ADHD adds insult to injury. Increased defensiveness and sensitivity to criticism.

    I. Forgetfulness often looks like defiance. Impossible to separate them out.

    J. Impulsiveness fuels increased conflict.

    K. Hyperactivity translates into badgering parents.

IV. **Coping Attitudes and Reasonable Expectations**

    A. Unreasonable expectations

        1. Flawless academic performance perfectionism

        2. Perfect driving records perfectionism

        3. Compliance with a smile obedience

        4. More freedom will always end up in disaster; ruination

        5. They do bad things to get parents angry; malicious intent

        6. Adolescent will appreciate all your efforts; need for approval

        7. Adolescent will love to take their medication

    B. Reasonable Expectations

        1. Satisfactory grades

        2. Genuine effort at school and at homework

        3. Adhere to basic societal norms for living in family.

        4. Will occasionally mess up when given more freedom, but it usually won't result in disaster

        5. Misbehavior is only occasionally intended to anger parents

        6. Teen tolerates medication with hesitation

    C. How to change your unreasonable expectations?

        1. Recognize you control your thoughts and feelings

        2. Increase your awareness of distorted thinking

3. Actively challenge it
4. What is the evidence for a belief?
5. What is the worst thing that can happen?
6. What do other parents say about this?
7. Rehearse positive self-statements

V. **Discipline: The Skills of Parenting**

A. Parents run out of power by the time their children reach adolescence

B. Simply dictating to teenagers doesn't always work

C. Involving teens in decision making, e.g. democratic approaches to discipline work best

D. But how do you negotiate with a hostile, out-of-control adolescent? You don't

E. Divide the world of issues into two categories:
   1. Non-negotiables issues — short list of bottom-line rules for living in a civilized family
   2. Negotiable issues — everything else

F. Non-Negotiable issues — reflect your values
   1. House Rules
      a. No drugs, smoking, alcohol
      b. No violence, destruction of property
      c. Treat people with respect
      d. Respect others' privacy
      e. Parent home when friends come over

   2. Street Rules
      a. No drugs, alcohol
      b. Violence only for self-defense
      c. Attend school
      d. Tell parents where you are going, and call if your plans change
      e. Parents must meet friends before you go driving with them

G. Monitoring and enforcing rules
   1. Very difficult. No simple approaches
   2. In 2 parent families, work as a team
   3. In 1 parent families, enlist others as supports
   4. Be consistent and highly structured
   5. Post rules and review them often
   6. Be awake at curfew time
   7. Strive for balance between detachment and overinvolvement
   8. Establish consequences for compliance: telephone, car, allowance, groundings, work details, video games, etc.
   9. Project your authority
   10. Enlist outside help if you can't enforce rules

VI. **The Negotiable Issues: Problem Solve Mutually**

A. Rationale for problem solving — give and take. Each person gives his/her ideas, and together, you try to work at a compromise that everyone can live with.

B. Steps of Problem-Solving — you hold a family meeting to practice these steps. You may be able to do this on your own, but in many cases, you will need a professional therapist to help get the process started.

   1. Problem Definition
      a. Each family member makes a clear, short, nonaccusatory statement of what is bothering him/her and why.
      b. Family members take turns defining the problem. They, then paraphrase back each other's problem definitions to check understanding.

   2. Solution-Listing (brainstorming)
      a. List as many ideas as possible
      b. Take turns listing ideas
      c. Anything goes — be creative
      d. Just because you say it, you don't have to do it
      e. Don't evaluate the ideas
      f. Think up outlandish ideas to lighten the atmosphere and creativity
      g. Family member writes down ideas
      h. Continue until there are several "workable" ideas, usually there are 6-8 ideas

   3. Evaluation/Decision Making
      a. Family member take turns evaluating each idea
      b. Will the idea solve my problems?
      c. Will the idea solve the others' problems?
      d. Is the idea practical?
      e. Considering b-d, do I vote "+" or "–"?
      f. Record your ratings in columns on paper next to your ideas
      g. Evaluate all of the ideas on the list
      h. Then, were there any rated "+" by every one?
      i. If yes, go ahead to implementation planning using these ideas
      j. If no, follow suggestions below:

   4. Resolving an Impasse by Splitting Down the Middle
      a. Pick idea on which family came closet to consensus
      b. Brainstorm alternatives which "bridge" the differences on this solution
      c. Evaluate the compromises and try to reach a consensus

5. Implementation Planning
   a. Work out the implementation details
   b. Will do what, when, where, etc.
   c. What will be the consequences for compliance vs. noncompliance?
   d. Who will monitor compliance?
   e. Write out a behavioral contract if needed
   f. Consequences may involve reinforcement/ punishment
   g. Performance prompts (reminders) may be necessary with ADHD teenagers
6. Put the solution into action and see how it goes
7. Re-negotiation (if needed): If solution failed, renegotiate after analyzing reasons for failure.

VII. **Communicate Assertively but Respectfully**

A. Review the following list of communication habits in a family meeting.
   1. Which bad habits does the family exhibit?
   2. What is the impact upon family relations?
   3. Which good habits do they exhibit?

B. Pinpoint communication change goals

C. Rehearse positive alternative behaviors

D. Monitor several communication habits at a time, and give each other feedback throughout the week.

E. Repeat these steps as often as necessary to change patterns communication.

VIII. **Use Professional Help Wisely**

A. Find a professional you can work with. Arrange to check in with this professional several times per year. This is the "dental checkup" model of follow-up.

B. Periodically, you will need some more intensive help.

IX. **Practice Forgiveness and Maintain a Sense of Humor**

A. Forgive your adolescents for the things they will do which they cannot help

B. Forgive yourself for your inevitable mistakes

C. Keep a sense of humor. Remember, above all else, while ADHD is lifelong, adolescence is a temporary condition.

NEGATIVES	POSITIVES
1. Call each other names	Express anger without hurt
2. Put each other down	"I am angry that you did ___ ."
3. Interrupt each other	Take turns; keep it short
4. Criticize too much	Point out the good and bad
5. Get defensive	Listen, them calmly disagree
6. Lecture	Tell it straight and short
7. Look away from speaker	Make eye contact
8. Slouch	Sit up, look attentive
9. Talk in sarcastic tone	Talk in normal tone
10. Get off the topic	Finish one topic, then go on
11. Think the worse	Don't jump to conclusions
12. Dredge up the past	Stick to the present
13. Read others' mind	Ask other's opinions
14. Command, Order	Request nicely
15. Give the silent treatment	Say what's bothering you
16. Make light of something	Take it seriously
17. Deny you did it	Admit you did it, or nicely explain you didn't
18. Nag about small mistakes	Admit no one is perfect; overlook small things

Arthur Robin, Ph.D. is the Chief of Psychology at Children's Hospital of Michigan and Professor of Pediatrics at Wayne State University School of Medicine. Dr. Robin is the author of many chapters and articles;, a professional text, Negotiating Parent-Adolescent Conflict; *and a videotape,* ADHD in Adulthood: A Clinical Perspective and ADHD in Adolescence: The Next Step.

REFERENCES

Barkley, R. (1990). *Attention Deficit Hyperactivity Disorder: A Handbook For Diagnosis and Treatment.* New York: Guilford Publications.

Gordon, M. (1993). *I Would If I Could: A Teenager's Guide to ADHD.* Syracuse, New York: GSI Press.

Parker, R.N. (1992). *Making the Grade: An Adolescent's Struggle with ADD.* Plantation, Florida: Impact Publications.

Quinn, P.O. *ADD and the College Student.* New York: Magination Press, 1994.

Robin, A.L. (1993) *ADHD in Adolescence: The Next Step.* A Videotape produced by Practice Development Workshops, 101 Pleasant Street, Suite 101, Worcester, MA 01609.

Robin, A.L., & Foster, S. L. (1989) *Negotiating Parent-Adolescent Conflict: A Behavioral Family Systems Approach.* New York: Guilford Publications.

Also, watch for my chapter in Dr. Russell Barkley's forthcoming book on parenting ADHD children and adolescents.

Talking With Your Teen:
Communication Tips From an Expert

by Arthur L. Robin, Ph.D.

Consider the following conversation between Mrs. Jones and her fourteen-year-old son, Andrew, who has ADD.

Mrs. J: "How was school today?"

Andrew: "Fine" (averts his glance; ten seconds of silence).

Mrs. J: "Do you have any homework today?"

Andrew: "Nope" (kicking the table, leaving the room).

Mrs. J: "Are you sure? Where do you think you're going?"

Andrew: (halfway to the front door) "See you later."

Mrs. J: "Don't you leave this house! (angry). Last week you lied. You had five overdue math assignments, according to your teacher. Get back in here now!" (screaming)

Andrew: "Get off my case. You never trust me. You're always snooping around with my teachers."

Mrs. J: "Trust you?" (sarcastic laugh). "How can I trust someone who lies to my face over and over. You lied about the chores; you lied about where you were last night. Homework is very important. We are talking about your future."

Andrew: "(bored stiff and very restless, hanging off the front door) "This is getting old. You treat me like a baby. I'm sick of this . . ."

Mrs. J: "Watch your tongue!" (very angry).

Andrew: (sarcastic) "Watch your tongue! What are you going to do? Tell Dad again? He doesn't do diddly . . ."

Does this conversation sound familiar? Let's stop and ask ourselves what is going wrong. We must resist the temptation to blame either mother or son. Given the interactions between biology and family/environmental conditions in ADD, blame has no place in our vocabularies. Instead, we could better say that mother and son are stuck in an unfortunate, negative communication logjam. Before you know it, a seemingly innocent question elicits a negative response. The other person carries it one step further, and an escalating crescendo of unpleasant communication builds, heading for an explosive finale. Such showdowns have been found to be more common in families with adolescents who have ADD than in other families.

Mrs. Jones' first question, "How was school today?" seems innocent, as does Andrew's first response. However, most teenagers with ADD are defensive about discussing school, even when asked in a non-critical manner, since inside they often feel badly about their poor academic performance. It takes very little to set off a negative response, especially at the end of the school day, when they are fatigued and on edge. In addition, teens with ADD fail to realize that their parents may be genuinely interested in school, not just on a witch hunt to uncover their latest mistake.

When your teenager returns home after school, try to sense his/her mood before you ask about school. Give him or her a cooling off period, a brief time to unwind. If you sense that your teenager is in a bad mood or had a tough day at school, try to be empathetic. Mrs. Jones could say, in a tentative, empathetic manner, something like, "Andrew, it looks like you had a rough day in school. Do you want to talk about it?" If Andrew refuses to talk about it or starts to "bite off" his mother's head, Mrs. Jones might say, "I'm not criticizing, just asking. We will leave it for later."

It is useful to develop a routine and schedule around homework that can be carried out even on a bad day. This prevents unnecessary negative communication at a time when Mrs. Jones can expect Andrew will be touchy.

How can you change such bad communication habits? As a family therapist, I teach parents and adolescents to: (1) become aware of the most common sources of negative communication; (2) monitor their own and their families' communication style as they talk; (3) assertively give each other feedback about negative communication; (4) practice positive behaviors, replaying the scene, and (5) praise each other for good communication.

Review the following list of common negative communication habits and positive alternatives with your family. See if you can follow these steps to better communication. Don't expect perfection, and try to deal with one negative communication habit at a time.

Check if your family does this:	Try to do this instead:
☐ Call each other names	Express anger without hurt
☐ Put each other down	"I am angry you did _____."
☐ Interrupt each other	Take turns; keep it short
☐ Criticize too much	Point out the good and bad
☐ Get defensive	Listen, then calmly disagree
☐ Lecture	Tell it straight and short
☐ Look away from speaker	Make eye contact
☐ Slouch	Sit up, look attentive
☐ Talk in sarcastic tone	Talk in normal tone
☐ Get off the topic	Finish one topic, then go on
☐ Think the worst	Don't jump to conclusions
☐ Dredge up the past	Stick to the present
☐ Read others' minds	Ask others' opinions
☐ Command, order	Request nicely
☐ Give the silent treatment	Say what's bothering you
☐ Make light of something	Take it seriously
☐ Deny you did it	Admit you did it, or nicely explain you didn't
☐ Nag about small mistakes	Admit no one is perfect; overlook small things

This article first appeared in the January 1994 CH.A.D.D.er Box.

Arthur Robin, Ph.D. is the Chief of Psychology at Children's Hospital of Michigan and Professor of Pediatrics at Wayne State University School of Medicine.

Dr. Robin is the author of many chapters and articles, a professional text, Negotiating Parent-Adolescent Conflict; *and a videotape,* ADHD in Adulthood: A Clinical Perspective *and* ADHD in Adolescence: The Next Step.

Sibling Rivalry: When Brothers and Sisters Don't Get Along

by Sam Goldstein, Ph.D.

Many parents, and even some professionals, assume that hostility and jealousy between brothers and sisters is part and parcel of multi-children families. Yet it is likely that there are just as many families in which siblings develop close relationships as those in which siblings develop deeper antagonisms or indifference to each other. With two or more children in a family, it is quite likely that there will be some degree of bickering or arguing. Quarreling among siblings is one of the most often cited complaints by parents. Some parents feel that quarreling may reflect the lack of a happy, harmonious relationship in the home. Others accept this pattern as consistent with their own childhood experiences.

It is unknown how the term "sibling rivalry" was coined to refer to conflicts between siblings. Parents and professionals use this term to describe negative experiences. One never thinks of sibling rivalry as being a good thing. It is important, however, for parents to understand that some degree of squabbling, teasing, and competition among siblings is normal. In most families, brothers and sisters develop a liking and loyalty to each other that outlasts these minor irritations. Rivalry can be considered normal if brothers and sisters share mutual satisfactions as well as frustrations. However, when siblings become overwhelmed by violent impulses, harbor grudges, and overreact, families are in trouble.

It is not surprising that families raising children with emotional, behavioral, or developmental problems report greater degrees of sibling rivalry. Often, symptoms of attention deficit hyperactivity disorder (AD/HD) are as disruptive to siblings of the child with AD/HD as they are to the child's parents. However, it has not been demonstrated that quality of sibling rivalry in families raising a child with AD/HD is different. Rather, the quantity of rivalry may often be greater and more intense. This is especially true in regards to sibling conflicts when an elder sibling suffers from AD/HD. Given this state of affairs, parents of children with AD/HD can benefit from general knowledge and suggestions offered to all families.

Researchers suggest that siblings become more competitive and rivalries intensify with increased age. Rivalry is often prevalent in older siblings when they are fairly close in age. Some researchers suggest that the older child may feel replaced by the younger. Rivalry also tends to be greater with two children of the same sex. Many families experience a period of sibling jealousy when a new baby enters the family. In most cases, parents can defuse the situation by actively involving siblings in the baby's care.

Among the more obvious reasons for siblings to develop more serious relationship problems include the fact that their dependency and need for parental love and attention can cause them to resist sharing parental time. Parental favoritism can also spark resentment in other children. At times, hostile feelings a child may have toward a parent can be taken out on a younger sibling. Additionally, older siblings may act out a parent's favoritism towards other siblings. Finally, when one sibling has to live in the shadow of the achievements of another talented sibling, this sibling's frustration and anger may be taken out on the child garnering more positive attention.

When sibling rivalry begins to permeate the family, it is time for parents to intervene. Parents need not tolerate frequent, destructive teasing where the goal is to destroy the sibling's self-esteem. Physical aggression should also not be tolerated. Once a pattern of aggression, teasing, and squabbling is established between siblings, almost any little event, including a wrong look, can trigger a fight.

Here are some tips for dealing with sibling rivalry:

- Avoid comparing one child with another. Treat everyone in the family fairly. Watch out for favoritism. Subtle signs of favoritism might include babying one child, belittling another child's interests or performance, calling one child by more affectionate terms, spending more time with one child, or spending more money on one child. Family therapists suggest that parents should not rely on their judgment in terms of favoritism but regularly ask their children how they feel.

- Try to spend some quality time each day or a few times per week with each of your children. Let the child be the center of your attention. This is a time for listening, caring, and mutual enjoyment.

- Encourage separate experiences for your children. Avoid asking older children to let younger siblings tag along. Arrange for your children to spend time each day apart. Encourage different friends and activities.

- If one child in the family suffers from a medical, educational, or behavioral disability, recognize that the additional time you spend with this child must be compensated for with your other children. Be up front about this issue and make time for everyone in the family.

- Act quickly if you see a pattern of conflict developing between two siblings. At times, in such situations, professional guidance and assistance is beneficial.

- Try to ignore bickering, squabbles, or disagreements. Let your children learn to work these problems out by themselves. However, when you do intervene, there are a number of cardinal rules to follow. These have been well summarized by psychologist, Dr. Thomas Phelan.

  (1) When you intervene, it is best to discipline both children rather than just one. Although one child may be the instigator, in most situations, each child has a way of provoking the other in ways you may not recognize.

  (2) When your children are fighting, never ask "who started it?" or "what happened?" When you do, the response will usually be "he did" — "no, she did," etc. This discussion usually leads to fruitless arguing and does not solve the problem. Often, things get worse. Hold both children responsible unless the situation is unusual.

  (3) Never expect an older child to act in a more mature fashion than a younger child during a conflict. Do not goad the older child by suggesting he or she should be able to put up with teasing from a younger child. This will only further fuel the younger child's pattern of behavior and increase the older child's anger and frustration.

  (4) When you intervene, the best option is to separate the siblings for a forced time out.

- In many situations, it is helpful to offer a reward that must be earned by both children. If either child complains about the other, neither earns the reward. This forces each child to act more carefully with the other and avoids unnecessary conflicts.

- In some situations, it may be helpful for you to act as a referee, helping each child present his or her point of view and assisting in working out an even compromise. This teaches siblings effective problem-solving skills.

When siblings develop a repeated pattern of hostility, aggression, teasing, and anger towards each other, parents should take the issue seriously. Children must be protected from all forms of physical and psychological abuse by one another. While disagreements are common for most individuals living within the same household, parents should not accept frequent, angry squabbles among siblings as normal family behavior. Often, with some time and effort, the reasons for sibling rivalry can be understood, and in many situations, dealt with successfully. Parents must also recognize that in extenuating circumstances, when their efforts at intervention are not successful, the help of a trained mental health professional can be invaluable for gaining a better understanding of family dynamics and an improvement in family relationships.

This article first appeared in the January/February 1996 CH.A.D.D.er Box.

Sam Goldstein, Ph.D. is a clinical instructor in the Department of Psychiatry at the University of Utah School of Medicine and is a staff member of the Primary Children's Hospital and the University Neuropsychiatric Institute. Dr. Goldstein has authored a number of guides for parents and teachers concerning attention and language problems in children, award-winning videos, and journal articles.

Life on the Waterbed:
Mainstreaming on the Homefront

by Richard D. Lavoie, M.A., M.Ed.

As a school director and consultant, I spend a good deal of time working with the families of special needs children. Whenever I work with a family of five — including my own — I always try to keep the following analogy in mind:

"A family of five is like five people lying on a waterbed...whenever one person moves, *everyone* feels the ripple."

If any member of the family is experiencing turmoil, all family members are directly or indirectly effected. This analogy is particularly significant for the family wherein attention deficit disorders (ADD) or learning disabilities (LD) are present. The mother, the father, the siblings, and the extended family develop unique problems and needs as a result of their involvement with the child's difficulties. Mindful of this, our school often conducts community workshops that are designed to meet these unique needs. "Dads Only," "Siblings Only," and "Grandparents Only" workshops provide family members with the opportunity to discuss their feelings openly among others that are experiencing similar challenges.

This article is designed to focus upon the unique needs of the parents of a child with ADD/LD. These devoted parents often focus so much energy upon the needs of their child that they may fail to recognize or acknowledge the myriad emotions that they are experiencing themselves. As a result, they may be confused or concerned by their feelings. By learning to understand their emotions, parents are not only better able to cope with their own feelings, but also are able to be more effective, empathetic, and productive parents.

Our field has only recently come to realize that the child with special needs often exacts a tremendous emotional toll on parents. Many practitioners now feel that the parental reaction to the diagnosis of ADD or LD is more pronounced than any other type of exceptionality.

Consider the following: If a child is severely retarded or physically handicapped, the parent becomes aware of the problem in the first few weeks of the child's life. However, the preschool development of the child with ADD or LD is often uneventful and, therefore, the parent does not suspect that a problem exists. When they are informed of the problem by elementary school personnel, a typical first reaction is to deny the existence of the disability.

I have dealt with hundreds of parents of special needs children throughout my career. There are two phenomena that have always confused me about parents who are faced with this challenge. The first is what I refer to as the "discrepancy of professional perception" phenomenon. It has been my experience that like-thinking professionals often differ strongly in their perceptions about the same set of parents over a period of time. For example, a middle school counselor may report that he found Mr. and Mrs. Johnson to be very contrary, combative, and resistant towards school personnel, while, some years later, the high school administrator reports the Johnsons are cooperative, collegial, and respectful towards school personnel. What causes this phenomenon?

Secondly, I have often been puzzled by sets of parents who are able to agree on nearly all decisions that they make in their lives. They can reach a consensus on the selection of wines, movies, table lamps, and wallpaper, but they are completely unable to agree on issues regarding their child who has ADD. The care and education of the child becomes a major source of conflict and tension between the couple. How is a couple able to reach agreement on so many topics, yet unable to reach a "common ground" on issues related to their child?

Both of these mysteries were clarified for me when I discovered the pioneer work of Eleanor Westhead and Sally Smith. These practitioners have developed a theory that fully explains these two puzzling phenomena. They propose that the parents of the child with ADD or LD actually go through a "mourning process" following their being informed of their child's disorder. This process consists of a totally unpredictable series of emotional states or stages. There is no predictive factor regarding the order in which the parent experiences these stages. Neither is there any predictability to the number of stages that a parent goes through or the length of time that the parent spends in each stage. This "roller coaster of emotions" can have a profound impact upon the parent and his/her interactions with the child, other family members, and school personnel.

These "Stages of Acceptance" (and their related reactions) are as follows:

Denial:
"There is really nothing wrong!"
"That's the way I was as a child — not to worry!"
"He'll grow out of it!"

Blame:
"You baby him!"
"You expect too much of him!"
"It's not from my side of the family!"

Fear:
"Maybe they're not telling me the real problem!"
"Is it worse than they say?"
"Will he ever marry? go to college? graduate?"

Envy:
"Why can't he be like his sister or his cousins?"

Mourning:
"He could have been such a success, if not for the ADD!"

Bargaining:
"Wait 'til next year!"
"Maybe the problem will improve if we move! (or if he goes to camp, etc.)"

Anger:
"The teachers don't know anything."
"I hate this neighborhood, this school, this teacher, etc."

Guilt:
"My mother was right; I should have used cloth diapers when he was a baby."
"I shouldn't have worked during his first year."
"I am being punished for something and my child is suffering as a result."

Isolation:
"Nobody else knows or cares about my child."
"It's you and me against the world . . . no one else understands."

Flight:
"Let's try this new therapy . . . Donahue says it works!"
"We are going to go from clinic to clinic until somebody tells me what I want to hear!"

These stages and emotions will seem very familiar to most parents of special needs children. I have discussed this theory with hundreds of parents and the great majority of them report that they have experienced these stages as they have taken the "school journey" with their special needs child. There is great validity to the Smith and Westhead theory.

This "Stages of Acceptance" theory provides a viable explanation for the two phenomena outlined earlier; the reason that the two professionals disagreed so strongly about the Johnsons is that the couple had reached the Acceptance Stage by the time the child reached high school. The middle school counselor was working with the parents during the chaotic period of ever-changing stages and emotional states.

More importantly, however, this theory provides valuable insight into the impact that parenting of a special needs child can have on a married couple. Parents must realize that they will certainly *not* go through these stages in synchrony. That is, Mom and Dad may find that they are in stages that are different from the stage that their spouse is experiencing. These stages are often in direct conflict with one another (e.g., blame vs. guilt, isolation vs. flight, etc.) because each parent is viewing the situation from entirely different perspectives. Therefore, communication is very difficult and conflict is quite likely. Each partner must recognize the other's right to travel through these stages and respect the feelings and attitudes inherent in each stage.

The goal of this process is, of course, to reach acceptance. Only at this stage is the parent able to make child-oriented decisions that are unclouded by undue emotionality or adult agendas. The Acceptance Stage is best illustrated by *Welcome to Holland* by author and advocate, Emily Pearl Kingsley:

"I am often asked to describe the experience of raising a child with a disability to try to help people who have not shared that unique experience to understand it, to imagine how it would feel. It's like this:

When you are going to have a baby, it's like planning a fabulous vacation trip — to Italy. You buy a bunch of guidebooks and make your wonderful vacation plans. The Coliseum, Michaelangelo's David, the gondolas in Venice. You may learn some handy phrases in Italian. It's all very exciting.

After months of eager anticipation, the day finally arrives. You pack your bags and off you go. Several hours later, the plane lands. The stewardess comes in and says, 'Welcome to Holland.'

'Holland?!?' you say. 'What do you mean, Holland? I signed up for Italy! I'm supposed to be in Italy. All my life I've dreamed of going to Italy.'

But there's been a change in the flight plan. They've landed in Holland and there you must stay.

The important thing is that they haven't taken you to a horrible, disgusting, filthy place, full of pestilence, famine, and disease. It's just a different place.

So you must go out and buy new guidebooks. And you must learn a whole new language. And you will meet a whole new group of people you would never have met.

It's just a different place. It's slower-paced than Italy, less flashy than Italy. But after you've been there for awhile and you catch your breath, you look around, and you begin to notice that Holland has windmills, Holland has tulips, Holland even has Rembrandts.

But everyone you know is busy coming and going from Italy, and they're all bragging about what a wonderful time they had there. And for the rest of your life, you will say, 'Yes, that's where I was supposed to go. That's what I had planned.'

The pain of that will never, ever go away, because the loss of that dream is a very significant loss. But if you spend your life mourning the fact that you didn't get to Italy, you may never be free to enjoy the very special, the very lovely things about Holland."

Below are some further thoughts on this theory and its ramifications for parents and professionals.

- Experience tells us that parents with less day-to-day involvement with their child tend to remain longer in the Denial Stage.

- Teachers, counselors, administrators, physicians, and other professionals should be aware of these stages. They should recognize that these stages are normal, natural, and necessary and should make no attempt to derail or "speed up" the mourning process.

- Parents should be aware that the child may be going through a similar series of stages. Again, this accounts for the communication difficulties that many families experience. Imagine a scenario wherein a child and his parents sit at the kitchen table to discuss the recent report card. Dad is in the denial stage, Mom is in the flight stage, and the child is in the anger stage. Little wonder that no effective and productive communication can take place. This is a recipe for tension and conflict.

- Parents should keep in mind that reaching the acceptance stage does not mean that you have achieved permanent, infallible wisdom and peace. Whenever there is a major change in the child's situation (e.g., changing schools, going away to camp, etc.), the parent often re-enters the maelstrom of guilt, envy, anger, etc.

The parenting of a child with ADD or LD presents a formidable challenge. It is important to understand the emotional impact this situation can create. Just remain mindful that children with ADD or LD have the same three basic needs that all children have: understanding, structure, and unconditional love.

This article first appeared in the Summer 1995 ATTENTION!

Richard D. Lavoie, M.A., M.Ed. is Executive Director of Riverview School, Cape Cod, MA, a member of the Professional Advisory Board of the Learning Disabilities Association, and the Executive Producer of FAT City: How Difficult Can This Be? *and* Last One Picked, First One Picked On: The Social Implications of Learning Disabilities. *(Videos distributed by PBS Video.)*

CHAPTER 5

ADVOCACY

An Introduction by Matthew D. Cohen, J.D.
Member, CH.A.D.D. National Board of Directors

AD/HD and adolescence is something akin to fuel being added to a fire. With adolescence comes adversity; the frustrations of academic, behavioral, and social challenge; and increased disruption to the child, the family, and school. As a function of the magnification of AD/HD symptomatology, and the consequences of that symptomatology in the form of intolerant and often punitive responses from home, school, and community, advocacy for teenagers with AD/HD becomes especially important. The articles which follow explore the role of advocacy for adolescents in a number of contexts, using a number of different approaches.

Outside of the family, the school milieu is unquestionably the most important setting in which children with AD/HD function. The success or failure of children in the school setting is very much dependent upon the willingness, skill, and flexibility of the school at working with the student and family to assist them in managing this difficult time. As children grow older, the behavioral manifestations of AD/HD at school, including inattentiveness, impulsivity, off-task behavior, and disorganization, often present themselves in adolescence as defiance, academic non-compliance, and more serious behavioral difficulties, sometimes including aggression against others. As the teenager becomes more frustrated with the reaction of adults, he or she also reacts negatively and a cycle of confrontation develops. In this context, the regular education disciplinary procedure becomes especially problematic; many children with AD/HD will be disciplined and, in the worst cases, suspended or expelled from school for behavior directly related to their AD/HD, and indirectly related to the failure of the school system to appropriately respond to it.

Beyond discipline, it is important for parents of children with or suspected of having AD/HD to be well-versed in the overall rights of children with AD/HD within the school context. Not only do special rules apply with respect to discipline if the child is appropriately identified and found to be eligible for special education services, but the child can qualify under either special education (IDEA) or Section 504 for a wide variety of accommodations, supports, and special services.

Regrettably, the struggle to meet the needs of an adolescent with AD/HD does not end in secondary school. Instead, the issues that create difficulty in secondary school persist into college and beyond. The two articles in this chapter relating to the right to accommodations in colleges and universities, and the rights of individuals with AD/HD in society at large as articulated in the Americans with Disabilities Act (ADA) are especially important. Just as children with AD/HD do not automatically receive the support that they need in the public schools, there are also very specific procedures that must be followed in order to secure appropriate accommodations from private or public colleges in the admission process, in college testing and, in receiving accommodations once enrolled.

Similarly, the ADA offers protections covering qualifying exams, job applications, the interview process, and on-the-job accommodations for persons with AD/HD in the workplace.

Finally, and consistent with the need for self-advocacy in adulthood, this chapter includes an article on self-advocacy at the high school level. Educational systems in general are not yet fully responsive to the needs of children with AD/HD. To the extent that adolescents are able to act on their own behalf in securing the support and the modifications that they need, this will not only serve them well in high school but will be an important skill for them as they enter adulthood. This chapter also provides invaluable guidance for helping teenagers become their own, best advocates.

If AD/HD and adolescence is like adding fuel to the fire, advocacy — including self-advocacy — must be seen as a way of preventing the fires from spreading and bringing the fires that are already raging under control. Hopefully, this chapter will assist adolescents and their parents in developing effective advocacy techniques.

The Americans with Disabilities Act and Its Impact on People with ADD

by Lei Ann Marshall-Cohen, J.D.

The Americans with Disabilities Act of 1990 (ADA) is a federal civil rights law that extends broad protections against discrimination to people with disabilities. The Act is divided into substantive sections called titles. Title I covers private employers with fifteen more workers. Title II applies to all units of state and local government and prohibits discrimination in both employment and the provision of programs and services. Title III applies to privately owned businesses that are open to the public and governs both access to goods and services and physical access to facilities. This article will explore these three titles of the ADA and discuss the ways in which adults with an attention deficit disorder (ADD), parents of children with ADD, and professionals that work with patients or clients with ADD may benefit from the law.

The threshold question in determining whether a person is entitled to the protections of the ADA is whether the individual meets the definition of a person with a disability. The ADA defines a person with a disability as an individual who:

(1)   Has a physical or mental impairment that substantially limits a major life activity;

(2)   Has a history or record of such impairment;

(3)   Is perceived as having such an impairment.

The ADA does not link disability to a particular category or diagnosis. Rather, the definition is deliberately subjective, and turns on whether the person's impairment substantially limits the performance of one or more major life activities such as learning, caring for oneself, seeing, hearing, walking, or working. For example, two individuals may each have a diagnosis of ADD. One may have a very mild case that does not impact on the performance of any major life activities. This person would not be considered a person with a disability for purposes of the ADA. The second individual, however, may have substantial limitations with respect to learning, working, or other activities. This individual would be protected by the Act.

The employment title (Title I) of the ADA provides that an employer cannot discriminate against an employee on the basis of a disability in any aspect of the employment relationship. Such covered activities include the application process, testing, interviewing, hiring, assignments, evaluations, discipline, medical examinations, compensation, promotion, on-the-job training, layoff/recall, termination, leave, and benefits. An individual seeking protection under this title must demonstrate that he or she is a person with a disability and a qualified individual with a disability. For purposes of Title I, a qualified individual with a disability is a person who has the skill, experience, and education for the job and can perform the essential functions of the job with or without reasonable accommodation.

Generally, the ADA requires employers to make reasonable accommodations to the known disabilities of their employees and after a specific request for such an accommodation has been made. This is an area with potentially significant benefits for people with ADD. Reasonable accommodation has been defined as: "Modifications or adjustments to a job application process, work environment, or the way in which a job is customarily performed or benefits provided that enable a qualified individual with a disability to be considered for the position, perform the essential functions of the job or enjoy the benefits of employment in the same manner as other employees." Examples of reasonable accommodation include part-time or modified job schedules, job restructuring, provision of auxiliary aids and services, modifications to a job site or work site and job reassignment. There may be circumstances where an adult with ADD is qualified to perform the job functions but requires some modification at the work site. For example, an individual with ADD who is receiving multiple oral instructions from a supervisor may benefit from having the supervisor dictate such instructions onto a tape or put them in written form so as to provide greater structure and organization.

Prior to making a job offer, an employer can not ask questions concerning the existence or nature of a disability. For example, a question on an employment application that asks, "Are you currently taking any prescription medication and if so, for what?" would be impermissible as it would identify the existence of a disability. Reasonable accommodation is also available before a job offer is even made. For example, an applicant with ADD may require some modifications in the administration of an employment test if the test is administered in a heavily trafficked reception area. The applicant may request a small, quiet room in which to perform the job test.

The law creates a counter-balance in the area of accommodation: employers are not required to provide an accommodation that is found to cause an "undue burden." Although undue burden has historically been determined on the basis of cost, the ADA makes clear that other factors will be considered in making such determinations; these include size of the employer, number of sites operated by the company, and the impact of the accommodation on the business. The types of accommodation that are likely to be requested by an individual with ADD, such as environmental modifications at the work site or supports in terms of how the job instructions are provided would generally be considered reasonable.

Title I also contains strict requirements with respect to confidentiality of disability-related information. Employers are required to maintain two personnel files on an individual: one related to job status, promotions, and evaluations, and a separate file containing any medical or medically-related information such as health insurance applications forms, health insurance claim forms, or other disability-related materials.

Although medical testing prior to a job offer is prohibited by the ADA because it may reveal a disability, drug testing is not so limited. It is critical that an applicant or employee who is asked to undergo a drug test be given the opportunity to identify, in a confidential manner, prescription medications which he or she may be taking. This is especially important with respect to people with ADD who are taking prescription medications which are often controlled substances that will show as a positive on a drug screen. The confidentiality requirements discussed above also extend to disclosures required of an employee in this situation.

Finally, the ADA requires that employees be provided with equal access to benefits. One recent area of concern is that some people with ADD are being denied health insurance on the basis of a pre-existing psychiatric condition. Although initially such an individual should seek a clarifying letter from his or her treating doctor to indicate that ADD is neurobiological disorder, the employer, if benefits are made available, is obligated to provide insurance to all employees and not just to those without disabilities. This may require the employer to seek alternative insurance if a particular

employee is rejected for coverage. This is a developing area of the law and how much courts will require of individual employers is not yet clear.

The U.S. Equal Employment Opportunity Commission (EEOC) is responsible for the enforcement of Title I. An individual charging an employer with discrimination under the Act must first file a charge with the EEOC and allow the EEOC time to evaluate the charge before such an individual can go into federal court. Complaints must be filed within 180 days of the alleged discriminatory act. Remedies include back pay, front pay, hiring, provision of an accommodation, job reinstatement, and restoration of benefits. In situations where an individual can show intentional discrimination, compensatory and punitive damages may be available.

Title II of the ADA applies to all units of state and local government, and prohibits discrimination against people with disabilities with respect to the programs, services, or activities of those entities. Title II prohibits discrimination in employment by public employers. Finally, Title II contains extensive regulations concerning accessibility to publicly owned public transportation systems.

The general non-discrimination requirements of Title II include (1) assuring equal opportunity to participate in programs, delivery of programs, and services in the most integrated setting appropriate: (2) prohibiting use of methods of administration or practices that are discriminatory; and (3) reasonable modification of policies, practices, and procedures when necessary to avoid discrimination against people with disabilities, unless to do so would fundamentally alter the nature of the program or service offered or create an undue burden. Also, public entities cannot use eligibility criteria that screen out or tend to screen out people with disabilities unless necessary for the provision of the service or activity. Finally, all state and local government entities must ensure program accessibility to all programs and services operated by the entity.

One category of Title II coverage of significance to people with ADD is public education. It is not yet clear what the program accessibility requirement of the ADA adds to the rights and responsibilities delineated in the federal special education law, the Individuals with Disabilities Education Act (IDEA). What is clear, however, is that education programs not reached by IDEA, such as community college or other adult education programs are covered. As such, requesting such modifications as provision of a quiet room for testing or permission to tape record a class to be replayed later for purposes of note taking would be considered appropriate requests under the ADA.

Another example illustrating the applicability of the program access requirement would be in the area of recreation. A community may offer a summer day camp program with a one-to-fifteen staff-to-camper ratio. If the program is appropriate for a child with ADD in all other respects, but that child requires closer supervision than the existing staff ratio can provide, parents may request provision of an extra counselor at that camp or session as a possible modification of a program, service, or activity. Individuals with disabilities cannot be charged to offset costs associated with providing such program access. However, if provision of a request would impose undue financial and/or administrative burdens on an entity in light of all available resources, it may be permissible for the public entity to only pay a portion of the cost. Such determinations must be made on a case-by-case basis.

Title II is enforced by both the EEOC, for employment charges and the U.S. Department of Justice (DOJ) for other charges. Under some circumstances, an individual can also file directly in federal court for injunctive relief and, in certain cases, damages.

Title III of the ADA covers privately owned businesses that serve the public. Although some private clubs and all religiously controlled entities are exempted, the scope of Title III is very broad and reaches over 50 million businesses in the United States. Basically, Title III provides that no individual with a disability may be denied the full and equal enjoyment of the goods and services of a place of public accommodation. This broad mandate is further refined through a series of specific requirements insuring provision of services in a manner that is equal and in a setting that is integrated. In addition, businesses are required to make reasonable modifications in their policies, practices or procedures, provide auxiliary aids and services where appropriate, and are prohibited from using eligibility criteria that screen or tend to screen on the basis of disability. Finally, there are extensive regulations providing structural access in new construction and alterations. Again, the counter-balance built into the law is that such modifications are required unless it fundamentally alters the nature of the service or causes an undue burden. A typical example where Title III would affect an individual with ADD is with respect to private schools including nursery schools, private universities, or other privately operated entities such as SAT exam preparation course offerings. If an individual with ADD requires a reasonable modification such as longer

time for the taking of tests or creating a quieter, less distracting setting for test taking, these would be examples of modifications contemplated under this Title.

Title III can be enforced directly in the courts. Injunctive remedies are available such as court orders providing particular modifications. Damages are not available through a private lawsuit under Title III. However, an individual can also file an administrative complaint with the U.S. Department of Justice which has responsibility for administrative enforcement of Title III. The Department of Justice can seek compensatory damages on behalf of an individual and also has the authority to assess penalties against entities that have violated the Act. There is no provision for punitive damages under Title III.

It is important for individuals with ADD, parents of children with ADD, and professionals who work with patients or clients with ADD to understand the full scope of the ADA and the ways in which the ADA may benefit such individuals. The ADA is but one weapon in an advocate's arsenal. It should be viewed as a tool to be used together with other laws that prohibit discrimination on the basis of disability. Moreover, it should be used, since the law is only effective if individuals who experience discrimination utilize its protections and take a stand against wrongful and discriminatory conduct. To do so is especially challenging with a hidden disability such as ADD — but no less important.

This article first appeared in the
Winter 1995 ATTENTION!

Lei-Ann Marhsall-Cohen, J.D. provides expertise on legal issues relating to the Americans with Disabilities Act (ADA) and disability rights law. Ms. Marshall-Cohen has served as a consultant to major corporations, hospitals, state, and local agencies and not-for-profit organizations on ADA compliance, as well as providing training on the ADA, disability awareness, and other disability rights issues. She successfully litigated two of the first ADA cases filed in Illinois, has written extensively on ADA, and was awarded the Council on Disability Rights' Gnawing Gargoyle Award for public policy in 1992.

Legal Rights and Accommodations for College Students with ADD

by Lei-Ann Marshall-Cohen, J.D.

College students today have more clearly defined legal rights and access to more reasonable modifications of the policies and practices of the school they attend than they did in the past. The Americans with Disabilities Act of 1990 (ADA), a landmark federal law prohibiting discrimination on the basis of disability nationwide, includes specific protections for college students. The ADA applies to both public and private colleges and universities. If a college or university is a recipient of federal funds, it is also prohibited from discrimination on the basis of disability under the Rehabilitation Act of 1973. Finally, state law or city or county ordinances may be available that prohibit discrimination on the basis of disability. Each of these avenues of protection will be discussed below.

The ADA is divided into substantive sections called titles, that establish the rights of people with disabilities and the responsibilities of public and private entities to provide services in a non-discriminatory manner. It is these provisions of the ADA that are of great significance for students with ADD. The threshold question in determining whether the law is applicable is whether the student meets the definition of a person with a disability. The ADA defines a person with a disability as an individual who:

(1)   has a physical or mental impairment that substantially limits a major life activity;

(2)   has a history or record of such impairment; or

(3)   is perceived as having such an impairment.

The ADA does not link disability to a particular category or diagnosis. Rather, the definition is deliberately subjective and turns on whether the person's impairment substantially limits the performance of one or more major life activities. Major life activities are defined to include seeing, hearing, walking, learning, or working. Recently, the federal regulations were modified to include thinking, concentrating, and interacting with others as examples of major life activities that bring an individual within the definition of a person with a dis-

ability. This modification clarifies that an individual with ADD is protected by the ADA if these major life activities are substantially limited.

An individual with a disability must also meet the criteria of being a "qualified individual with a disability." This means that the individual must meet the general requirements for participation in the program or activity offered by the private or public entity. For example, a student seeking admission to a college or university must meet certain objective criteria, such as the completion of high school with a certain grade point average. These objective requirements are equally applicable to students with and without disabilities.

Title II of the ADA applies to all units of state and local government. The Title contains a broad mandate that prohibits discrimination against people with disabilities in all programs, services, or activities of such public entities. The general non-discrimination requirements of Title II include:

(1)   Assuring equal opportunity to participate in the programs and services in the most integrated setting appropriate;

(2)   Prohibiting the use of methods of administration or practices that are discriminatory; and

(3)   Requiring reasonable modification of policies, practices, and procedures when necessary to avoid discrimination against people with disabilities.

These requirements must be met unless doing so would fundamentally alter the nature of the program or service offered, or create an undue burden on the public entity. Also, public entities cannot use eligibility criteria that screen out or tend to screen out people with disabilities unless necessary for the provision of the service or activity. Finally, all state and local government entities must ensure program accessibility to all activities offered by the entity.

Education programs such as community college, adult education programs, and public universities are covered by the provisions of Title II. Requesting such modifications as provision of a quiet room for testing or permission to tape record a class to be replayed later for purposes of note-taking are the kinds of reasonable modifications contemplated under the ADA. Since many students with ADD have difficulty concentrating or paying attention in a noisy environment, reasonable modifications for these students may include a quiet place for testing, assignment of a carrel for studying in a quiet part of the library, or even a housing assignment to a dormitory designated as a "quiet dorm." Other reasonable accommodations may include use of an FM listening system to diminish external sounds and use of a laptop computer to facilitate note-taking.

Some students may have ADD together with other recognized disabilities such as learning disabilities. These students may require other modifications, such as an extension of the time in which to take an exam or permission to create a work product on a computer to compensate for handwriting difficulties. These are also examples of reasonable modifications covered by the ADA.

Determinations as to the reasonableness of a requested modification are made on a case-by-case basis under the Act. Individuals with disabilities cannot be charged to offset any costs associated with providing program access. However, if provision of a modification would impose undue financial or administrative burdens on a school in light of all available resources, it may be permissible for the school to pay only a portion of the cost. Again, these determinations are based on the individual circumstances.

The provisions of Title II that apply to college students are enforced by the U.S. Department of Justice (DOJ). Individuals may file administrative charges directly with DOJ, which are typically routed to the Office of Civil Rights of the U.S. Department of Education, for investigation and possible compensation. Under some circumstances, an individual can also file directly in federal court for injunctive relief and, in certain cases, damages.

Title III of the ADA covers places of public accommodation, meaning privately owned entities that serve the public. Title III provides that no individual with a disability may be denied the full and equal enjoyment of the goods and services of a place of public accommodation. In delineating this mandate, the law states that private entities are required to make reasonable modifications in their policies, practices, or procedures, to provide auxiliary aids and services where appropriate, and are prohibited from using eligibility criteria that screen or tend to screen on the basis of disability.

Most private universities are included within the reach of Title III of the ADA. However, religiously controlled entities are expressly exempt from this part of the federal law. For example, a Catholic university that is controlled by a board with a majority of representatives of the Catholic church would be considered a religiously controlled entity under the ADA. Thus, a private college or university that is controlled by a religious entity would not be covered by the ADA. However, if the private religious school receives federal financial assistance, it will be covered by the Rehabilitation Act of 1973 (Section 504).

As was true in the public university setting, the provisions of Title III can be used as the basis for reasonable modifications that assist the student with ADD in functioning effectively in the classroom. Examples of such modifications may include a quiet place for testing, extension of test time, permission to use a tape recorder or computer for note-taking, and other modifications.

There are also particular requirements in Titles II and III of the ADA that relate to preparatory courses and administration of entrance exams for college, medical, law, or graduate school, and other professional or licensing exams. Title III of the ADA specifically requires that organizations that offer courses such as the preparation courses for the college SAT or ACT entrance exams and preparation courses for such exams as the LSAT or MCAT examinations provide materials in appropriate formats, insure accessible settings, and make other reasonable modifications for students with disabilities. In addition, under the requirements of Title II, the actual administration of such exams, if controlled by a public entity, such as the Board of Bar Examiners for future attorneys, must be provided in an accessible location and an accessible manner. Thus a college student who has been receiving the modification of testing in a quiet location has a basis to request such modification for the law school entrance exam, in law school, and in the eventual taking of the bar exam for licensing.

Title III can be enforced directly in the courts. Injunctive remedies, such as court orders providing for particular modifications, are available. Damages are not available to a private litigant under Title III. However, if an individual has filed an administrative complaint with the U.S. Department of Justice, DOJ can seek compensatory damages on behalf of an individual and also has the authority to assess penalties against entities that have violated the Act. There is no provision for punitive damages under Title III.

Students with disabilities are also protected from discrimination by the Rehabilitation Act of 1973, typically referred to as Section 504. The Rehabilitation Act prohibits discrimination on the basis of disability by any entity that receives federal financial assistance. Many colleges and universities, both public and private, are covered by the Rehabilitation Act because such schools typically receive federal funding in such areas as student financial aid or research grants. The language of the Rehabilitation Act is very broad and it does not contain the specific examples concerning higher education that are present in the ADA's legislative and regulatory history. However, there is an extensive body of administrative decisions and case law under Section 504 that makes clear the non-discrimination obligations of such institutions. Moreover, this wealth of administrative and judicial decisions is available to assist in the interpretation of the requirements of the ADA. Finally, Section 504 may provide a basis to reach a private religiously controlled school that is exempt under Title III, but receives federal financial assistance.

Many states also have broad civil rights laws that expressly include people with disabilities as a protected class. In order to determine whether such laws are applicable, one must look at both the definition of disability and the identification of activities or entities regulated by the state law. Some state's civil rights acts have specific provisions that relate to higher education. Also, particularly in major metropolitan areas, cities or counties may have enacted ordinances that prohibit discrimination on the basis of disability. Under some circumstances, the procedures for handling complaints under these laws may be more efficient or may provide alternative remedies to those that are available under federal law.

The legal rights that are available to students with disabilities can be used as effective leverage in advocating for change in student programs at the local level. Obviously, they also provide a judicial or administrative remedy where necessary. Most colleges and universities have student services departments that are familiar with the protections of the law. Students and their families are encouraged to educate themselves in order to advocate for their rights more effectively.

*This article first appeared in the
Fall 1996 ATTENTION!*

Lei-Ann Marhsall-Cohen, J.D. provides expertise on legal issues relating to the Americans with Disabilities Act (ADA) and disability rights law. Ms. Marshall-Cohen has served as a consultant to major corporations, hospitals, state, and local agencies and not-for-profit organizations on ADA compliance, as well as providing training on the ADA, disability awareness, and other disability rights issues. She successfully litigated two of the first ADA cases filed in Illinois, has written extensively on ADA, and was awarded the Council on Disability Rights' Gnawing Gargoyle Award for public policy in 1992.

The Limits of Discipline Under IDEA and Section 504

by Matthew D. Cohen, J.D.

Neither the Individuals with Disabilities Education Act (IDEA) nor Section 504 directly address the question of what rights and obligations schools have with respect to the discipline of children with disabilities, particularly for behavior related to their disabilities. Despite the absence of explicit reference to disciplinary safeguards, these laws, nonetheless, have been found by the courts to provide important safeguards for children with disabilities from improper discipline. A recent federal policy letter on disciplining students with disabilities (4/26/95), as well as a recent circuit court decision, shed light on the rights of students with disabilities in discipline situations.

Perhaps the most important safeguard under the (IDEA) is that it provides an absolute right for children with disabilities to receive an education, without any limitation or restraint. This means that even if children with disabilities are subject to discipline and may be excluded from the program in which they are enrolled due to misbehavior, they are still eligible to receive some form of continuing services from the public schools. By contrast, under Section 504, children with disabilities are entitled to protection from discrimination by the public schools, even if disciplinary procedures are being implemented. However, services may be discontinued if it is determined that the child's behavior is not related to his disability and he is excluded from school for more than ten days, if this is true for regular education students.

A second critical safeguard in IDEA relates to the notice and due process provisions of that law. IDEA requires that parents receive notice from the school district prior to any proposed change in the special education placement of a child with an identified disability. That notice must include notice of the parents' right to request an impartial due process hearing to challenge the school district's proposed change in placement. If a parent files a request for a due process hearing, the school district may not change the child's placement during the time that the adolinistrative and legal proceedings initiated by the parents are pending. Again, on its face, this

may not appear to have any direct significance with respect to the issue of discipline.

The United States Supreme Court made the connection between these procedural safeguards and discipline in the landmark decision, *Honig v. Doe.* In this case, the Supreme Court held that the disciplinary exclusion of a child from school, either by suspension in excess of ten school days, or expulsion, constituted a change in educational placement. If the child has an identified special education disability, the school district must determine whether the child's behavior is related to his/her disability prior to exclusion from school for more than ten days. If a child's behavior is determined to be related to his/her disability, the school should not exclude the child for an excess of ten days, but instead should utilize the IEP process to develop additional interventions that will address the disability-related behavior. Alternatively, if the child's behavior is not related to the disability, the school district has the option of proceeding with normal regular education disciplinary procedures.

However, in either instance, according to the United States Supreme Court, if the parent initiates a request for an impartial due process hearing, the school cannot go forward with the exclusion from school or with the change in placement until all administrative and legal challenges are resolved. Thus, whether or not the behavior is related to the disability, under most circumstances, the parent can file a request for a due process hearing and effectively delay, circumvent, and in some instances, overturn the school district's efforts to discipline the child through exclusion from school.

The only exception to this procedure identified by the Supreme Court in *Honig,* was a situation in which the child presented an immediate danger to him/herself or to others. Under these circumstances, the Court prescribed that school districts should seek an emergency court order permitting them to change the placement of the child despite the fact that a due process hearing had been requested by the parents. Another exception was recently created by Congress. This exception states that if a student brings a firearm to school, he/she may be suspended for up to forty-five days. While the school must continue to provide some service during the period of exclusion, if the parents file for due process during this period, the interim placement will be maintained while due process is pending.

Not only has the *Honig* decision been interpreted to limit the ability of schools to suspend or expel students who have already been identified as having a disability by the school system; it has also been interpreted to limit the ability of the schools to suspend or expel those students who are within regular education, who should have been evaluated for the existence of a disability and/or determined eligible for special education. Thus, if a parent concludes that the child's behavior warranted a special education evaluation or that the child should have been in special education, the parent may request a due process hearing while the regular discipline procedures are pending, and the regular disciplinary procedures may not go forward until the special education issues are resolved. If it is determined that the child either should be evaluated for special education or is eligible for special education, then all of the procedures described above with respect to special education safeguards will apply.

In a significant expansion of the protection offered by *Honig,* the United States Court of Appeals for the Eighth Circuit further limited the ability of the school district to unilaterally exclude a child from school, even in an emergency situation. In *Light v. Parkway C-2 School District,* the Eighth Circuit held that the school district must not only demonstrate that the child poses an immediate danger to self or others, but also must show that an attempt has been made to provide behavioral intervention to control the behavior within the existing school placement to minimize the likelihood of injury to self or others, before seeking emergency permission from the Court to change the child's placement by excluding the child from school or putting the child in a different program. The significance of the *Light* decision is that it conveys that school districts have an affirmative duty to identify and respond to the need of the child whose behavior is at issue, even if there is some concern relative to the potential impact of that behavior on other students. While this may seem in many respects as a gross imposition on the discretion of schools to act to preserve safety and security, it is consistent with the overall mandate of IDEA that children with disabilities be served in the least restrictive environment and be provided with services that are tailored to their individual needs.

Whether due to these procedural requirements or for unrelated reasons, some school districts resort to referral to the police and/or juvenile court as a response to student misconduct within the schools. While this may be appropriate with student behavior involving acts of severe physical aggression, it is often occurring for relatively minor misbehavior, which could be regarded as illegal, such as disorderly conduct, minor property damage, threatening behavior, and a variety of other behaviors which are inappropriate, but do not constitute an immediate physical threat to self or others. Several courts have recently held that it is inappropriate for a school district to utilize referral to police or the juvenile courts under these circumstances and that the same special education procedural safeguards described above apply with respect to such referrals. This issue is now pending before the Sixth Circuit Court of Appeals in *Morgan v. Chris L.*

The analysis above relates to safeguards under IDEA. The Office for Civil Rights, which enforces Section 504, has adopted the general position of *Honig* as applying under Section 504 as well. OCR has stated that under §504, a suspension in excess of ten school days or an expulsion, where the behavior is related to the child's identified disability, is a change of placement subject to procedural safeguards. However, in dramatic contrast to the safeguards under IDEA, there is no "stay put" or "frozen placement" provision in Section 504 or its regulations. Thus, even though a parent may challenge a suspension or expulsion under Section 504, the school is not precluded from implementing the discipline while the Section 504 challenge is pending. This gives the child substantially less protection than is afforded under IDEA.

Under both IDEA and Section 504, there is an obvious question as to how the ten-day limit on suspension is calculated. Under IDEA, the U.S. Office of Special Education Programs has recently opined that the ten-day limitation is reset if the child's placement is changed mid-year. Thus, for example, if a child is in a regular education-based program, is suspended for ten days, and is subsequently transferred to a self-contained program mid-year, the school could suspend the child for an additional ten days without triggering the change in placement provisions. This provision has not been adopted by the courts (nor has it been rejected). I personally disagree with this interpretation, but it is being widely utilized by school districts.

A related and frequent question revolves around the use of brief suspensions of less than ten days, which when aggregated, add up to ten or more days. Here, OCR has opined with respect to §504 and OSEP has opined with respect to IDEA, that several suspensions for related behaviors in a relatively close proximity of time, which in total exceed ten days, will be regarded as triggering the ten-day limitation. It remains unclear as to how much time can elapse between suspensions or how much of a pattern in behavior needs to be present for this interpretation to apply.

It is the author's personal belief that any suspensions, regardless of passage of time or relatedness, in the course of a year, which in the aggregate exceed ten days, trigger procedural safeguards. Further, it is the author's belief that part-day and in-school suspensions, which lead to an interruption in the provision of services and programs provided for in the IEP, also should be included in the ten-day calculation.

It should be noted that the determination that a child's behavior is related or unrelated to his/her disability is not dependent on the child's disability label. While there will be a stronger presumption that inappropriate behavior is related to the disability of a child identified as severely emotionally disturbed, it will often be connected to the disability for a child identified with a disability due to AD/HD. In fact, a child who is mentally retarded may demonstrate misbehavior due to difficulty understanding rules, expectations, or social conventions. A child with LD may have behavioral difficulties as an outgrowth of emotional responses to the learning disability. Many schools use an improper test of relatedness based on whether the child knows right from wrong and has the capacity to control his or her behavior. These tests are inappropriate and unsupported in the regulations and case law. In fact, it is often the case that children with AD/HD know right from wrong and can control their behavior some of the time. If this test were legitimated, these children would be completely denied the procedural protections to which they are entitled in disciplinary situations.

The IEP, and particularly the presence or absence of behavioral goals and objectives and a behavior management plan may have significant impact on how a child's behavior is managed and how procedural options are assessed. If a child is demonstrating problematic behavior, it is important that behavioral goals and a behavior management plan be developed.

Often behavior management plans place the onus on the child. For example, Johnny will take his medicine on time, write down all assignments in an assignment notebook, and seek out help if he is angry. If Johnny can do these things reliably and independently, fine. But in all likelihood, the reason Johnny is in trouble is that he does not do these things reliably or independently. Under these circumstances, the plan must outline the assistance the adults will provide, as well.

Parents are generally cautioned against agreeing to provisions in behavior management plans that appear to waive the child's rights, such as allowing for suspension "as needed."

A final note: Even if a child is not in special education nor does the parent feel it appropriate to file for due process because of the failure to evaluate a child or place the child in special education, some minimal due process protections are constitutionally mandated for all students, and many states have statutory requirements for suspension and expulsion that go beyond the minimal constitutional requirements. Thus, consultation with a knowledgeable attorney may be advisable if suspension or expulsion is pending.

This article first appeared in the October/November 1995 CH.A.D.D.er Box.

Matthew Cohen, J.D. is a partner at the law firm Monahan & Cohen in Chicago and an adjunct professor of law at Loyola University Law School. He is nationally recognized for his work in special education law and has considerable experience in health care and mental health law. He has been the principal litigator in a number of landmark special education cases. Mr. Cohen is the primary or collaborating author of several amendments to the mental health and special education laws of Illinois. He has lectured extensively on a wide variety of special education and law topics. Mr. Cohen serves on the editorial board of ATTENTION! *and is chair of CH.A.D.D.'s Government Relations Committee.*

Advocacy for Adolescents: Training Teens to Take on their Own Troubles

by Janice Bleakney and Karen Wiles

He sits in the center of the classroom, ears tuned to the teacher's lecture, eyes following the teacher's every movement. It all makes sense. It all seems so clear. Now it comes . . . the assignment, the independent work . . . the opportunity to prove to the teacher that he does remember, that he does understand. The mathematical concept is right there — in the book. The formula is right there — on the board. But the steps to the solution, that arithmetical journey that seemed so straightforward minutes before with the teacher as tour guide, now looms like a tortuous train with unknown dips and switchbacks, devoid of signposts, or even helpful hints. Who does he ask for help? His classmates, who are all busily navigating journeys of their own — getting someplace — understanding? Pull it out of the textbook? That didn't work the last several times he tried. There's no other choice left but to ask the teacher. The one who has already explained it three times — to everyone — including him.

"Mr. Jamison?"

"Yes, Brett?"

"I don't get this."

"Well, Brett, what is it that you don't understand?"

"Everything!"

(*Translation:* "Mr. Jamison, if I knew what I didn't understand, I wouldn't be standing up here in front of everybody else who already understands it because they're smarter than I am, taking this risk that you'll think I'm stupid because I'm always the one who comes up to your desk telling you I don't get this — Mr. Jamison, I DON'T KNOW WHAT I DON'T KNOW!!!)

Brett is lost. Lost in the process of math. Gone is the memory of those clearly delineated, numbers, "don't-you-dare-do-them-out-of-sequence" steps. Those steps that could take him from listening, through understanding, safely to the destination of: "I can accurately demonstrate what I know." This journey is often quite a brief one. It takes only a minute to move from a long division problem with no solution, through to the answer. But the road map of predetermined, spatially oriented, precisely ordered steps is a confusing path to a youngster with ADD who cannot hold the procedural sequence within his active working memory while he calculates to an accurate answer.

The search for an answer can be frustrating for the child with ADD who does not have the sustained attention to stay with a prolonged operation — who may be distracted — then cannot re-engage in the steps to solution. A child who is not in tune to visual detail — who drops a sign, or misreads a "+" as an "x." A child who may or may not also have a learning disability in visual/perceptual processing. These roadblocks may occur in any journey: through reading, written language, history. These are real barriers. These are not excuses — they are explanations. They are explanations that a teacher might understand and respect. They are valid foundations upon which a request for accommodations in testing or instruction might be based. They are the underpinnings for advocacy.

Advocacy often appears to be a parent's job. It seems to fall under the category of protection — protecting one's young from harm, from failure. Indeed, for the primary school youngster, the parent is his or her most important and passionate advocate. But once a child reaches junior high or high school, most parents are automatically disqualified from advocacy. The fact that they are parents (and are inherently "uncool" and, quite possibly, incapable in their teenager's eyes) is the element that dismisses them from this role. Who then becomes a youngster's champion? The youngster her or himself. The very ones who, in the end, must understand and accept his disability, and who must proactively seek solutions that make a difference. That is why as parents, and as caring professionals, one of our most important goals should be to help the child with ADD and/or Learning Disabilities develop into an informed and effective self-advocate.

Student self-advocacy can begin successfully in the later elementary grades (4th, 5th). Indeed, many youngsters with ADD and/or LD possess incredible verbal fluency and social sophistication that are invaluable assets to negotiation. Those words "overly social" and "gregarious," which heretofore have appeared in report cards as negatives now can be recognized as strengths and brought to bear for the student's own benefit.

The steps in training youngsters as self-advocates are identical to those used in training their parents:

- Identify the student's individual strengths as a learner.
- Identify what his other abilities are and how those affect classroom performance.
- Identify and request reasonable accommodations in testing and instruction.

Students who engage in advocacy training can be mature and secure enough to accept their differences, as well as believe in and maximize their strengths. The development of a student "Self-Advocacy Worksheet" must be done utilizing the student's own words, words which he or she will comfortable using — ultimately by him or herself — in negotiation. Advocacy Worksheets differ in length and sophistication depending on the age of the child. The single most important element in successful student self-advocacy is that the student can self-examine, self-accept, and (through support and practice) become self-sufficient in this process.

A student who is developing advocacy skills must learn the concrete preparatory steps to negotiation:

- Don't go up and try to advocate before or after class.
- Make an appointment with the teacher.
- Write the date and time on your worksheet.
- Have copies of your worksheet for everyone who will be there.
- Review your worksheet before your meeting.
- Arrive on time.
- Attitude Check — negotiation. NOT confrontation.

The training of a student as self-advocate must include role playing and rehearsal. At Educational Tutoring and Consulting, we develop the worksheet as an exercise in self-realization, self-acceptance, and self-empowerment. We utilize the worksheet as a guide — a game plan — for the student to follow in advocacy meetings with his or her teacher(s). We recommend that the worksheet be put in the teacher's box prior to the first meeting. The coordinator working with the student role plays advocacy sessions prior to meeting with the teacher and accompanies the youngster to the first in-school advocacy session. She acts as an initiator, the one who models that first step (that critical step that so eludes our youngsters): "Mr. Jamison, Brett has developed a thoughtful plan for participating successfully in your classroom. He would like to present it to you and work with you in developing some solutions for him as a student, . . . Brett?"

("HEY, MR. JAMISON, NOW I DO KNOW WHAT I DON'T KNOW!")

Sample Advocacy Worksheet: 6th Grade Student

STRENGTHS:
I am good at expressing myself verbally.
I am very artistic (with watercolors).
I have good computer skills.

LEARNING DIFFERENCES:
Attention Deficit Disorder.
Language: Phonetic Memory (spelling).
Written expression (on demand).

WHAT HAPPENS TO ME IN THE CLASSROOM:
I have a hard time with the organizational and pacing of long-term assignments.
I cannot screen out environmental stimuli like outside movement or a ticking clock.
I sometimes have a short fuse, and I often react impulsively.
I have a difficult time taking notes.

WHAT WOULD HELP ME IN THE CLASSROOM:
Chunk long-term assignments. Ask for these "chunks" on a daily/weekly basis.
Balance lectures with visual delivery: charts, timeliness, mind maps, etc.
Give me an outline of the lecture in advance.
Give me a reading guide before I start.
Let me demonstrate my knowledge.
Modify my testing procedures (more time/oral tests).
Allow someone to take notes for me (using carbonless paper).

This article first appeared in the January 1994 CH.A.D.D.er Box.

Janice Bleakney is a co-founder of Educational Tutoring and Counseling in Mercer Island, WA. She has been a teacher and counselor for grades 7-12 and was instrumental in the establishment of one of the first alternative high school programs in Washington State.

Karen Wiles, M.A. is a former school and special education teacher. She is a director at Educational Tutoring and Counseling. She has been a faculty member and guest lecturer at the University of Maryland and is an adjunct faculty member at Seattle Pacific University.

CHAPTER 6

BEYOND HIGH SCHOOL

An Introduction by Kathleen Nadeau, Ph.D.
Director, Chesapeake Psychological Services, Bethesda, Maryland

This chapter, which focuses on choices and challenges beyond the high school years, is perhaps one of the most crucial and most hopeful chapters offered in this collection.

Adolescents nearing the end of high school have already survived some of the hardest challenges for a young person with ADD. Even without ADD, adolescence is often stressful. This is a time of personal insecurity as adolescents seek to understand themselves, to establish greater freedom and independence, and to find acceptance among their peers. Teens are exposed to many new challenging, exciting, and, at times, frightening experiences within a very short period of time. To add insult to injury, high schools tend to be organized in a very "ADD-unfriendly" fashion. High school is full of multiple, competing demands — demands for prolonged concentration on topics which may hold little interest, repeated forced shifting of focus of attention with no regard for individual rhythm and interest, and multiple visual and auditory distractions. All of these stressors: the "internal" stressors which accompany sexual development and the search for identity, peer acceptance and independence, and the external stressors of high school years, combine to greatly intensify the challenges of ADD.

After the intense challenges of the high school years, many teens with ADD, as well as their parents, may look ahead with worry and anxiety, feeling ill-prepared for the increased independence and responsibility that awaits them. It is important for teens with ADD and their families to realize that some of the most difficult challenges are already behind them. During post-high school years, for the first time, teens who have ADD have a much broader range of choices available to them, allowing them to become much more pro-active in creating or selecting an environment that takes advantage of their strengths and de-emphasizes areas of difficulty.

The two key words for adolescents with ADD as they enter the years beyond high school are choices and challenges. The huge increase in the range of opportunities available to them means that they have the chance to make more "ADD-friendly" choices, whether at school or at work. At the same time, teens leaving high school face many new challenges as they enter a period in their lives when greater independence is expected of them. One of the greatest challenges will be to take over responsibility for managing their ADD — seeking appropriate services and treatment, making decisions, and developing habits that allow them to function in an increasingly adult fashion. Both teens with ADD and their parents, however, should realize that learning to take on the responsibilities of adulthood is a gradual, joint process, as parents relinquish responsibility and control, while their adolescents learn to take the reins.

Whether adolescents with ADD select college or the workplace, they (as well as their parents) should keep in mind that neither choice is set in stone. These are years to gain experience and to learn life management skills. A choice to enter the workplace may later translate into a decision to return to school, as the adolescent with ADD may pinpoint an area of career focus and be able to return to school with increased motivation and purpose. Similarly, if a teen with ADD first goes to college, but decides that this is not a good decision for him or her, there are many ADD-friendly workplace opportunities that do not require a college degree.

The articles included in this chapter have been chosen to help post-high school teens with ADD make good choices — choices that are good for ADD and good for their unique talents and interests. These articles focus on college selection and college survival techniques for those teens who make the choice to go on to higher education. Other articles focus on alternatives to college and strategies for succeeding in the workplace. Armed with the information contained in this excellent selection of articles on the years beyond high school, post-high school teens will be much better prepared to take charge of their ADD and to approach the challenges of young adulthood with confidence and optimism.

The Key Steps to Selecting a College For Students with ADD

by Marybeth Kravets

The college search process for students with ADD requires many of the same strategies, techniques, and assessments that it does for students who do not have ADD. However, students who have special needs have special reasons why they need to be selective with their college choices. Any college receiving federal funds must comply with the law and provide reasonable accommodations. However, finding the right fit goes beyond reasonable accommodations. There is no crystal ball that can look into the future, but there are several key steps that should help students with ADD search and select colleges that are well suited for their individual needs. These key steps are:

accepting
assessing
prioritizing
disclosing
testing
identifying criteria
exploring
touring
interviewing
applying
selecting
accommodating
succeeding

ACCEPTING

The most important ingredient in selecting a college is accepting the diagnosis of ADD. This process could be affected significantly by the length of time that has elapsed since the diagnosis was made. A recently-made diagnosis may have a greater emotional effect than a diagnosis made at an earlier age. Students diagnosed in elementary school have had time to learn about their disorder and make adjustments to enhance their behavior and learning. Students diagnosed later, such as in high school, however, have not had time to understand the disorder and master all of the compensatory skills and techniques.

However difficult it may be, acceptance is essential for success in life. Acceptance means that the student with ADD and his/her parents understand the diagnosis and the accommodations that will be necessary in college. Acceptance and understanding are fundamental to the student's ability to self advocate. It is important that college-bound students with ADD be comfortable with their disability. The student should be able to:

- **Articulate** the disability and the impact on his/her learning
- **Identify** his/her strengths and weaknesses
- **Accept** accommodations
- **Describe** accommodations used in high school
- **Identify** services needed in college

ASSESSING

Students may be socially, chronologically, and emotionally ready, but not academically ready for college-level work. It is important to do an assessment on all levels to determine overall readiness.

To assess emotional/social readiness, students should evaluate their:

__ Ability to make and keep friends
__ Ability to deal with setbacks
__ Appropriateness in conversations
__ Ability to read body language
__ Level of interaction with peers and teachers
__ Ability to describe feelings
__ Level of independence
__ Ability to follow rules
__ Coping skills
__ Self-esteem & positive self-image

To assess academic readiness, students should:

__ Review the high school curriculum
__ Evaluate the degree of difficulty of courses
__ Look for signs of upward grade trend
__ Look for mainstream courses
__ Look for willingness to take risks
__ Look for willingness to accept accommodations

Not every student will begin high school taking college preparatory courses, and many colleges admit students who were enrolled in modified, remedial, or special education courses. However, most four-year colleges will ultimately look for evidence of upward challenge and mainstream college preparatory courses by the student's junior year.

Students and parents must remember that:

- college professors are not trained to teach to different levels of academic ability
- students are responsible for what they needed to learn in high school
- students need to be prepared to tackle difficult college level courses
- reviewing college entrance and exit course requirements is imperative
- very few colleges offer remedial or individualized courses
- students need to experience mainstream, college prep courses during high school.

PRIORITIZING

College brochures and promotional materials typically show pictures of students smiling and having fun on campus and feature the institution's outstanding facilities; videos highlight academic offerings, activities, residential life, and comments from happy students and faculty. All of this information is important in establishing selection criteria. However, students with ADD must begin their search by identifying and prioritizing the most important criteria in their ultimate selection. To do this, students should rank their priorities. What is most important?

__ Extended testing time
__ Distraction free environment for testing
__ Small classes
__ Priority registration
__ Advising system
__ Counseling available
__ Course substitution
__ Advocacy available
__ Tutoring
__ Readers
    __ Scribes
    __ Notetakers
    __ Audio tapes of lectures & texts
    __ Use of calculator on exams
    __ Use of word processor with spell check/thesaurus on exams
    __ Time extension for assignments
    __ Skills Courses
    __ Support groups
    __ Distance from home
    __ Psychologist available

__ Particular major
__ Fraternities/sororities
__ Warm /cold climate
__ Sports
__ Other

DISCLOSING

Colleges cannot ask any questions on a college application regarding disabilities. They can, however, suggest that students provide additional information that may be useful in the admission process or they can provide information about the resource people on campus who can discuss disability services with the student. Thus, the decision to disclose or not remains with the student. Although a student's willingness to disclose his/her ADD on a college application indicates acceptance of the disorder, many students and parents fear that this information could be detrimental in the admission process. The truth of the matter is that colleges cannot deny admission solely based on information about a disability, and in fact, at many colleges, self-disclosure is used in a positive way to be more flexible in an admission decision. Following are a few common questions students with ADD and their parents typically ask:

- Will colleges look negatively at this disclosure?
  NO. Colleges are far more interested in academic success and ability to compensate.
- Will the admission staff understand the disability?
  YES/NO. If they don't, they should seek advice from a knowledgeable source.
- Do colleges deny admission because a student has ADD?
  NO. Not only is this illegal, it is impractical. Students with ADD can be as successful in college as students without ADD.
- Should students disclose the disability?
  YES. Disclose the disability and provide supportive documentation describing when it was diagnosed, as well as strategies used to compensate.
- Should students submit a personal statement about the ADD?
  YES. Students should show their acceptance of ADD and a perspective of their learning history, strengths, weaknesses, and goals.

TESTING

Many students — whether or not they have ADD — are concerned about the importance of standardized testing (ACT or SAT). Following is a list of tips that may serve as an aid in taking standardized tests:

- Familiarity could result in better performance, so student should be prepared

- Untimed tests don't benefit all students; students are encouraged to seek guidance
- ACT/SAT grant permission to take tests non-standardized
- Official documentation of the disability must be submitted to ACT/SAT
- All colleges accept non-standardized administration of the ACT/SAT
- Most colleges require ACT/SAT
- Not all colleges use the results in the same way
- Rarely will an admission decision be based solely on an ACT/SAT

Students who were diagnosed with ADD late in their high school years and very close to the time for taking ACT/SAT, and students who do not take other high school tests/exams in an untimed setting, should be aware that these circumstances often raise a "red flag" from the college's perspective. Colleges might question why ADD suddenly "appeared" in the student's junior year or why the student didn't take other high school tests untimed. This caution is just a reminder that it is very important for all students to provide documentation and explanation to colleges that identify their reasons for the submission of non-standardized test scores.

RECOMMENDING

Students should ask for recommendations from teachers and counselors who know them well and can describe them in positive terms. The purpose of a recommendation is not necessarily to "recommend" admission for a candidate, but rather to provide a 3-D picture of the student. The recommendation can come from a teacher in a course that was difficult, but one in which the student showed perseverance, motivation, and a willingness to keep working in spite of problems. The important aspect of recommendations is to identify where the student was and is now — not to predict where the student will be tomorrow, next week, or next year.

Recommendations should:

- Provide a "user friendly" explanation of ADD
- Highlight the student's strengths and weaknesses
- Describe strategies used to cope and compensate
- Demonstrate motivation and determination
- Show evidence of creativity
- Assess maturity
- Use specific examples
- Discuss challenges of curriculum and academic success

INTERVIEWING

College interviews can be an important part of admission decisions. If interviews are optional and a student interviews well, then he/she should, by all means,

request one. If, on the other hand, face to face interviews cause the student great anxiety and are not required, then he/she should opt for a group orientation or a tour of the campus. By law, colleges cannot require an interview for students with ADD unless they require interviews of all candidates. However, if the college has a special admission process for students with ADD or the interview may be used to help the student who does not meet admission criteria, then an interview can be requested. Interviews provide students an opportunity to research a particular college and determine if it would be a good match, and they allow the interviewer to learn about the student, answer the student's questions, and gather information to help in the admission decision.

The interviewer may ask:

(1) When was the ADD diagnosed?
(2) Can the student describe the disability?
(3) How does ADD affect the student's learning?
(4) What services or accommodations will be needed in college?

The interviewer will be documenting whether:

(1) Questions are answered by the student or parent
(2) The student exhibits motivation
(3) The student has realistic goals
(4) The student shows signs of being independent and a self-advocate

Students and parents may ask:

(1) What is the philosophy of the college regarding students with ADD?
(2) What are the admission requirements?
(3) Can entrance course requirements be waived or substituted?
(4) Is there an alternative admission plan?
(5) What documentation is required?
(6) Who is responsible for admission decisions?
(7) Are there fees for services?
(8) Is there a limit on tutoring?
(9) How are professors notified of the student's disability?
(10) What services and accommodations are available?
(11) How many students on campus are identified as having ADD?
(12) What is the success rate of students with ADD?
(13) How is the faculty provided in-service training on working with students with ADD?

TOURING

Most people would not buy a house sight unseen. This is also true in selecting a college. Students need to identify what they want and need in a college environment before making a decision to attend. Videos and view books are useful, but pictures might convince a student that it never snows in Minnesota or that all college classes are taught in small groups outside on a beautiful spring day. Therefore, students are encouraged to visit colleges they are interested in to get a true perspective about its environment. While touring campuses, students should:

- meet with service providers
- verify that necessary services will be available
- walk the campus
- observe the surrounding area
- talk with students
- taste the food
- visit residence halls
- read about "hot topics" in the school newspaper
- take a formal tour
- attend classes
- talk with professors in the major of interest
- take notes
- take pictures
- attend a social activity (while parents do something else)
- keep a chart to rank colleges

SELECTING

If students with ADD follow the key steps outlined in this college search process, they should ultimately be prepared to select a reasonable number of colleges that would be the right match. In making a selection, students should make sure they have:

- talked with their counselor, teachers, and family
- verified their comfort level in articulating their disability
- understood their needs
- prioritized the criteria for success in college
- assessed academic and emotional readiness
- read college materials
- taken ACT/SAT standardized or non-standardized tests
- written a personal statement disclosing their ADD
- identified appropriate colleges
- requested recommendations from teachers/counselors
- visited campuses for interview/tour
- submitted applications
- submitted official ACT/SAT scores
- given permission to release ADD documentation to colleges

Sample Criteria Chart

CRITERIA	COLLEGE A	COLLEGE B	COLLEGE C
General Information			
1. # of students			
2. Location			
3. Competitiveness			
4. Cost			
5. Fee for services			
6. Majors offered			
7. Admission criteria			
8. Documentation required & how recent			
Accommodations			
1.			
2.			
3.			
4.			
5.			
6.			
Student's Thoughts			
1. Pros-Positive			
2. Negatives			
3. Parents' Thoughts			

Once the student's role in the application process is complete, colleges begin their selection process to determine the student's admissibility.

ADMITTING

Colleges make admission decisions based on different factors and in different ways:

- computer-generated test scores, class rank, grades, and courses
- committee evaluations assessing each applicant individually
- flexible admissions for students who self-disclose a disability
- special admission for students deficient in admission requirements
- student interview with the director of support services
- decision by director of admission
- decision by admissions and support services
- faculty admission committee
- "Open Door admissions"

Even a denial does not necessarily mean the student cannot attend that college. If a student with ADD is denied admission to a college, he/she should inquire about an "appeal process" that allows admission in different ways, such as through summer admit, conditional/probational admit, limited course load admit, or concurrent enrollment in a community college and four-year college with a limited number of credits at each institution.

Yes, Students with ADD Should Consider College

Colleges pledge that they are dedicated to assuring each student an opportunity to experience equity in education. The law guarantees access to "reasonable accommodations" as long as these accommodations do not compromise the academic integrity of the program.

Examples of "Reasonable Accommodations" include:

- additional time to complete tests, coursework, or graduation
- substitution/modification of specific courses for degree requirements not essential to program of study
- adaptation of course instruction
- notetakers
- calculators
- auxiliary aids, taped texts, readers, computers, scribes, recorders

SUCCEEDING

Students should keep in mind that the first college they are admitted into does not have to be the only one they attend. They do not have to give a four year commit-ment to the first college they attend. On the contrary, the "college road" can be taken in several steps. For instance, a student may begin at a college that provides the appropriate environment and support and complete a successful first year or two, and then transfer to another college. There are many colleges that offer "open door admission," admitting any student with a high school diploma. Sometimes these colleges provide the most appropriate services and/or accommodations for students with ADD. It is important that students stay focused on attaining a college diploma — not on what college they'll be receiving their degree from or which college decal will be displayed on their car bumper.

In summary, to be successful in college, students should:

- be self-advocates
- be independent
- be able to articulate their disability
- have an understanding of themselves
- develop compensatory strategies
- learn better organization skills
- learn how to manage their time
- make a schedule for study time and stick to it
- plan ahead for lengthy or difficult assignments
- know their strengths and weaknesses
- be realistic
- be able to take notes or know how to get notes
- develop writing skills
- develop reading skills
- be computer literate
- tape lectures and clearly mark each tape
- review class notes as soon as possible and review often
- be comfortable with their disability
- have good judgment
- attend all classes
- sit in the front of the classroom
- be willing to work longer and harder
- plan three hours of study time for each hour in class
- be willing to ask for assistance
- check their understanding of assignments
- seek advice from their advisor
- develop a four year plan for their college courses
- visit a career counseling center early in their college careers

Parents need to:

- stay involved
- know their child's rights
- promote self-esteem
- be proud of their child's accomplishments
- encourage motivation, taking some academic risks, and independent learning

There are thousands of students diagnosed with ADD. The good news is that the future for these individuals is bright. College-bound individualss with ADD are typically talented, intelligent, capable students who have developed strategies for compensating for their disorder. However, to ensure success, students need to be open-minded to educational interventions, including classroom accommodations, compensatory instruction, or in some cases, placement in special classes or resource programs. If students with ADD can establish realistic goals and learn to channel their energy appropriately, they can pursue their dreams and achieve success in college.

This article first appeared in the Fall 1996 ATTENTION!

Marybeth Kravets is the College Consultant at Deerfield High School, Deerfield, Illinois. Ms. Kravets is the President-Elect of the Illinois Association For College Admission Counseling and the Chair of the Membership Committee for the National Association for College Admission Counseling. She is also the co-author of The K&W Guide To Colleges For The Learning Disabled.

Using Strategies and Services for Success in College

by Lois J. Burke

More and more college campuses across the nation are enrolling students with ADD. College is challenging for many students, but it can be particularly challenging for students with ADD, especially if strategies for successful management of the disorder are not employed. Students with ADD need to be aware of, and apply when necessary, some key strategies that can help foster success in the college environment.

ADVOCACY

On most college campuses, students with disabilities are responsible for informing necessary personnel about their need for assistance and/or accommodations. The key to advocacy is knowledge about what ADD is. Oftentimes, college students with ADD find that they may be in a position of educating faculty members and other personnel about the disorder. It is very important that students with ADD know their legal rights in order that they may obtain the most appropriate education possible. A disability services office can be very helpful in this area as office personnel can provide students with guidance on addressing faculty and staff regarding accommodations and services that are needed.

SELF AWARENESS

It is also very important that individuals with ADD educate themselves and understand how the disorder impacts them. Some of the ways to become more aware include reading books and other resources, talking to professionals who are experienced in the field of adult ADD, and talking with other adults who have been diagnosed with ADD. These types of opportunities can be provided through participation in adult ADD support groups or through local and national organizations like CH.A.D.D.

Students with ADD also need to have a good understanding of how they respond to certain situations. Some important questions that can lead to this level of awareness are: "How do I react to failure?"; "How do I react to stress?"; "What do I do when I become overwhelmed?"; "How do I relate to others when I'm taking medication?"; "How do I relate to others when I'm not taking medication?".

Some other helpful keys students should use to develop a strong sense of self awareness are:

Making time for transitions. It is important that college students with ADD leave time between their classes and/or activities in order to take a break from the structured environment of the classroom, gather thoughts, get a snack, or do something to relax before another class begins. This procedure can aid in reducing the stress that commonly accompanies college.

Becoming aware of physical surroundings. Students should figure out what environments promote the best learning situations for them. For instance, do they concentrate better in an environment with no noise, some noise, or white noise? It is important that they consider both visual and auditory distractions as well as any temptations that are present in their study environments. A student may find it difficult to study in her apartment, for example, because of the many temptations that exist there, such as household chores or favorite television programs. Students should try to choose environments that can provide them the most optimal learning environment and the fewest temptations and distractions.

Learning strengths, weaknesses, and learning style. Students with ADD often excel in areas like reading and written expression, but have difficulties in subjects such as math. By recognizing their strengths and weaknesses, students can more appropriately plan for academic courses and balance course loads. Also, by understanding the type of learning style they have, students can better learn how to study and prepare for classes. For instance, some students require breaks between academic classes for optimal learning. Therefore, taking a few courses that provide recreational activities, such as aerobics or a sport, or classes that are not necessarily of an academic nature but are interesting and fun, may help students to relax and serve as a necessary break from academic stress.

Utilize counseling. Students are encouraged to seek counseling if they are in need of help getting on task or keeping their focus — especially if the initial diagnosis of ADD was not made until adulthood. Counseling can help address any personal issues that have resulted from past experiences. If comorbid conditions such as depression are present, a personal counselor can provide additional support and help students develop strategies and techniques for effectively managing their ADD and related problems. Additionally, academic needs, such as time management and organizational skills can be addressed by disability services providers at many colleges and universities throughout the country.

USE OF AVAILABLE ACCOMMODATIONS AND SERVICES

Typical services and accommodations in the college environment for students with ADD include a distraction-free space for testing and extended time on exams (usually time and one-half). For some students, the extra time provides an opportunity to take needed breaks. For other students, simply having a quiet space is a major benefit. Some students are easily distracted during the typical classroom setting, especially when other students finish exams before they do and are moving around and making noise.

Priority scheduling of classes is also beneficial for students with ADD as it allows them to schedule more appropriately for academic success. For example, some students are most alert in the morning; others are more alert in the afternoon. Priority scheduling allows students to schedule classes at times during the day when they are typically at their best.

Other services that are commonly available on college campuses include tutoring, access to personal counseling assistance, medication management, and stress reduction workshops. Students should investigate whether a peer support group exists if they feel that meeting other college students with ADD would be helpful. Some students may also benefit from assistance with note taking or on a rare occasion, a reader for exams.

USE OF EFFECTIVE TIME MANAGEMENT AND ORGANIZATIONAL STRATEGIES

The key word in developing skills in these areas is "effective." In many cases, developing or establishing structure can be a very effective tool in managing ADD. Some effective time management strategies can include using check lists and/or a daily planner, periodically writing notes about important information, and using a watch with a chime. Many students find it helpful to plan daily; others like making weekly plans. Whichever planning method is chosen, it is important that students with ADD set realistic deadlines and break large tasks into smaller,

more manageable parts. If a student with ADD requires assistance in this area, a disabilities counselor who is familiar with organizational and time management strategies can be helpful. Some colleges have classes or workshops that provide assistance in effectively managing time and developing organizational strategies.

SETTING PRIORITIES

Students with ADD must try to set realistic goals for themselves. To do this, it may be helpful for the student to establish goals for each week, quarter, or semester. While students should plan for success when they establish their priorities and set their goals, it is also important that they not set themselves up for failure by attempting to accomplish too many tasks in too short a time period. They should also keep in mind that, even with the best attempts, some failures are inevitable. However, instead of seeing failures as stumbling blocks, students should try to learn from their failures and make appropriate adjustments to ensure more positive results in the future.

USE AVAILABLE CAMPUS RESOURCES

In addition to using the disability services office, it is important that students learn what other resources are available on campus, such as quiet study rooms, tutoring facilities, libraries, and computer equipment. Getting to know personnel in the disability services office can be very useful, as they often have contacts in key departments and offices on campus, and knowing the right person to contact often saves time and frustration when it comes to addressing a number of issues and concerns.

These are but a few key strategies that may assist the college student with ADD in being successful in the college environment. Students typically develop strategies of their own during their college years, but the suggestions outlined above can serve as a preliminary guide. By avoiding negative, self-defeating behaviors and habits, such as not taking prescribed medication properly, and employing appropriate strategies like the ones highlighted in this article, students with ADD can achieve success in college.

This article first appeared in the Fall 1996 ATTENTION!

Lois J. Burke is a Counselor at the Office for Disability Services at The Ohio State University. She works with students who have been diagnosed as having learning disabilities and ADD. Ms. Burke has been in the field of service provision for students with disabilities for over ten years and regularly makes presentations regarding accommodations and services for college students with learning disabilities. Her most recent presentations have focused on working with the college student with ADD.

Planning for the Future: Alternatives to College

by Robin Hawks

"*I probably should be going to college — all my friends are and that's what my parents want me to do. But I never liked school, and I don't know how I'll be able to deal with it for another four years!*" *Statements like these are common of high school seniors with ADD. For many, school has been difficult and unenjoyable and the thought of going through more schooling after graduating from high school is often unbearable. The prevalence rates of AD/HD in childhood is estimated to be approximately 3 to 5 percent (APA). Research has suggested that a substantial number (30 to 70%) of children who have ADD will continue to experience symptoms in adulthood (Barkley). One of these symptoms, according to research, manifests itself in a substantial comorbidity between ADD and learning disorders (Hooper & Olley, 1996). In fact, one study found that 63% of a learning disabled sample population also had ADD (Cantwell 1991). While individuals with ADD can certainly achieve success in college, it is not always the best — nor the only — option. There are a number of alternatives to the college environment that may be more suitable for those with ADD. Several of these alternatives are highlighted below.*

TRADE AND TECHNICAL SCHOOLS

One alternative for individuals with ADD who do not choose to attend college is to attend a trade or technical school. In keeping with comorbidity rates between AD/HD and learning disorders, nearly 30 percent of adults with a learning disability receive a degree from a trade or technical school, according to *LDA Newsbriefs*. The National Association of Trade and Technical Schools reports that there are over 10,000 such schools in the United States. These schools offer training in 100 different careers, such as cosmetology, automotive repair, and computer training. There are a number of benefits for individuals who choose to attend a trade or technical school. Not only do they receive hands-on experience and guided practice in and learn the special skills that are required for the occupations of their choice, but they are also receiving training that is the most up-to-date; most trade and technical schools have connections with the labor force so their curriculums are updated based on the requirements of local employers. *The Handbook of Trade and Technical Careers and Training*, which is published by the National Association of Trade and Technical Schools, may be a helpful resource for those interested in pursuing this route.

MILITARY SERVICE

Individuals with ADD who receive passing scores of the Armed Services Vocational Aptitude Battery (ASVAB) may want to consider the military as a alternative to college. Military service is an option for individuals with ADD who perform well in structured and routine environments. Those individuals who have significant difficulty following rules and are oppositional to authority figures will not want to pursue this option, as a willingness to adhere to strict regulations and disciplinary standards is an essential ingredient for military success. It is important to note that adults with ADD who require medication to manage their disorder may not be eligible for military service. Failure to disclose any pre-existing condition may result in discharge from the military.

APPRENTICESHIPS

Another alternative for individuals with ADD who do not wish to attend college is to enroll in an apprenticeship program. Apprenticeship programs provide an opportunity for participants to learn a trade while in the work environment. Administered by the Department of Labor, apprenticeship programs are available in over 425 occupational areas, such as heating and air conditioning (Levinson, 1993). The specifics of the arrangement are worked out between the apprentice and the employer; however, general guidelines regarding the hours of training, wage, evaluation methods, and related academic instruction are provided. For more information, contact your local labor department.

EMPLOYMENT

For some individuals with ADD, seeking employment opportunities may be the best option to pursue following graduation from high school. Employment can be obtained through a number of channels, including state employment commissions, newspaper advertisements, job lines, and the individual's network of family and friends. Many states have automated labor exchange systems that assist in the job search process. Those choosing this alternative should recognize, however, that employment brings its own unique set of demands. Common weaknesses for the individual with ADD in the employment arena include:

Failure to report to work on time;

Failure to listen and follow instructions properly;

Taking on responsibilities not assigned as job tasks;

Being sensitive to criticism;

Taking too long to complete job tasks.

The Americans with Disabilities Act (ADA, P.L.101-336) "guarantees all citizens with disabilities equal access to employment, public accommodations, state and local governmental services, transportation, and communication" (Krieg, Brown & Ballard, 1995). This act requires that employers make reasonable accommodations for the disabled employee of which ADD may qualify. To learn more about accommodations and strategies for success in the workplace, consult *Succeeding in the Workplace,* by Patricia Horan Latham, J.D. and Peter S. Latham, J.D. In addition, the Job Accommodations Network, which can be accessed by calling 1-800-AOA-WORK, is also a valuable source of information regarding employment issues.

VOCATIONAL REHABILITATION SERVICES

Rehabilitation services are available for individuals with ADD provided that the condition constitutes a substantial barrier to employment. Section 504 of the Rehabilitation Act of 1973 (P.L. 93-112) affords individuals with disabilities, including ADD, consideration for services. Individuals qualifying for these services, which include vocational counseling, evaluation, training, and job placement assistance, often benefit greatly. There is no upper age limit for application to vocational rehabilitation. There are three important points that individuals seeking vocational rehabilitation services should be aware of, however: (1) there is no legal obligation on the part of the rehabilitation agency to pay all of an individual's training costs; (2) vocational rehabilitation is an eligibility program — not an entitlement program; and (3) the application process can be intimidating, as there is a set of involved procedures to follow. For additional information regarding vocational rehabilitation services, readers are encouraged to contact their local or state vocational rehabilitation program. HEATH Resources Center also publishes *Vocational Rehabilitation Services — A Student Consumer's Guide.*

SELF AND OCCUPATIONAL AWARENESS

Before choosing a post-secondary pursuit, it is critical for young adults with ADD to take into account their personal characteristics as well as the characteristics of the environment in which they are considering. ADD is as much apart of an individual as his likes and dislikes, and must be considered when choosing alternatives after high school. It is the author's experience that individuals who "own," "embrace" and "attend to" their ADD are the most successful in any environment when compared to their peers who deny the impact of the disorder in settings other than academic ones.

Sources such as the *Dictionary of Occupational Titles* (U.S. Employment Service, 1981) and the *Occupational Outlook Handbook* (U.S. Department of Labor, 1982) can be used to promote occupational awareness (Levinson, 1993). Career interest inventories can also provide individuals who have ADD with a time efficient method of matching interests to various job titles. For example, *Holland Self Directed Search* (Holland, 1985) takes approximately fifteen minutes to complete and results in an occupational code that pinpoints the individual's most dominant career interests (i.e., realistic, social, investigative, enterprising, artistic, and conventional). The individual then matches the code to the appropriate job titles that correspond with the code. While this system does not address aptitude, it does provide a direction for self and job exploration. Other sources, such as computerized career information systems, (e.g., SIGI) may be beneficial for individuals to explore. These systems generally guide the individual through a series of career-based interest questions resulting in a code that is matched to various career types. Information pertaining to the job duties, qualifications, occupational outlooks, and salaries of a particular career are also often provided.

Additional information about careers that cannot be accessed through written means can be obtained via informational interviews or job shadowing. Individuals with ADD are encouraged to contact persons who have careers they may be interested in pursuing and ask if they can arrange for an informational interview or a job shadowing experience. Job shadowing allows the individual with ADD the opportunity to follow a professional of the individual's choice for a day to gain first-hand experience about a particular job. For persons with ADD, this arrangement can be an extremely valuable experience as their often limited attention span makes gaining career information through books or other written resources troublesome. Informational interviews or job shadowing experiences are informal, arranged easily, and expose the individual to the subtle nuances of a job.

For individuals with ADD, planning for the future beyond high school can be a stressful time, as many graduates dread the thought of enduring more schooling. It is important for these individuals to realize that success is not only achieved through a college degree — there are a number of options that high school graduates with ADD can pursue other than attending college. The items highlighted in this article serve as an example of the many alternatives to college individuals with ADD have available to them.

This article first appeared in the Fall 1996 ATTENTION!

Robin Hawks is in private practice as Director of the Center for Learning Potential and a part-time instructor of special education at James Madison University.

RESOURCES

HEATH Resource Center
One Dupont Circle, Suite 800
Washington, DC 20036
800 544-3284

Job Accommodations Network
West Virginia University
809 Allen Hall
Morgantown, WV 26506
800 ADA-WORK

National Association of Trade and
Technical Schools
2021 K Street N.W.
Washington, DC 20006
202 296-8892

REFERENCES

Adelman, P. B. & Vogel, S. A. (1993). Issues in the employment of adults with learning disabilities. *Journal of Learning Disabilities.* 16, 219-232.

Americans with Disabilities Act of 1990, 42 U.S.C.A. 12101 et seq. (West 1993).

American Psychiatric Association. (1994). *Diagnostic and Statistical Manual of Mental Disorders – 4th Edition.* Washington D. C.: Author

Cantwell, D. P. & Baker, L. (1991). Association between attention deficit-hyperactivity disorder and learning disorders. *Journal of Learning Disabilities.* 24(2), 88-95.

Holland, J. L. (1985). *The Self Directed Search.* Odessa, FL: Psychological Assessment Resources, Inc.

Hooper, S. R. & Olley, J. G. (1996). Psychological comorbidity in adults with learningdisabilities. In N. Gregg, C. Hoy & A. Gay. *Adults with learning disabilities: Theoretical and practical perspectives.* New York: Gilford Press.

Levinson, E. M. (1993). *Transdisciplinary vocational assessment: Issues in school based programs.* Brandon, Vermont: Clinical Psychology Publishing Co., Inc.

Krieg, F.J., Brown, P. & Ballard, J. (1995). *Transition: School to work.* Bethesda MD: National Association of School Psychologists.

Rehabilitation Act of 1973. Public Law 93-112, 87 Stat. 355 91973).

Robin, A. L. Attention Deficit Hyperactivity Disorder in adults: Assessment and management. Professional Advancement Seminars. Unpublished Manuscript.

Smith, J.O. (1992). Falling through the cracks: Rehabilitation services for adults with learning disabilities. *Exceptional Children.* March 451-460.

United States Depatment of Defense. (1984). *Test manual for the Armed Services Vocational Aptitude Battery.* North Chicago, IL: United States Military Entrance Processing Command.

United States Department of Labor. (1982). *Occupational Outlook Handbook.* Washington, DC: U.S. Department of Labor.

United States Employment Service. (1981). *Dictionary of occupational titles.* Washington, DC: U.S. Employment Service.

Weiss, L. (1992). *Attention deficit disorder in adults.* Dallas, Texas: Taylor Publishing Co.

College and University Students with AD/HD

by Mary McDonald Richard

An increasing number of students with AD/HD are entering colleges and universities and requesting academic accommodations related to their disability. Others more recently diagnosed with ADD are becoming aware of its impact on their progress and learning to use compensation strategies to cope with this disability. For these students the diagnosis and treatment of AD/HD has enabled them to achieve a measure of insight and control over a disorder that often interferes with performance in higher education.

College students with AD/HD and those who are working with them should be aware that the rights of students with disabilities in postsecondary education are protected by law. The opportunity for students with disabilities to fully participate in and benefit from the programs of a institution is required by Section 504 of the Rehabilitation Act of 1973 and more recently, the Americans With Disabilities Act (ADA). These statutes protect students who are qualified to participate academically and who meet other essential requirements for the program. Institutions must provide appropriate assistance to qualified students who disclose their disabilities and request accommodations such as reduced course loads, extra time for exams, and priority registration for classes, as long as such modifications do not fundamentally alter the program or impose an undue administrative or financial burden on the institution. Both the request for accommodations and their provision should be timely. The U.S. Department of Education regulations for Section 504, while not specifically mentioning the provision of auxiliary aids and services, have been interpreted by the courts as requiring them.

COLLEGE SUPPORT SERVICES

The use of appropriate academic accommodations and support services improves the academic progress and personal adjustment of many students with AD/HD. Each institution has its own method of delivering programs and services to students with disabilities.

Although most offer assistance through a designated office, staff sizes and qualifications as well as philosophy and practices may differ widely among institutions. Frequently, services for students with AD/HD are an outgrowth of programs originally established to serve students with specific learning disabilities. Students and those working with them can obtain specific information from several catalogs that list the names of two and four year colleges as well as universities that offer services for students with learning disabilities, and profile their program information.

Just as there is no universal model for postsecondary support services for students with AD/HD, neither is there a typical student with the disorder. Those served by support programs have diverse profiles of strengths and areas of need for improvement; they may have morbid conditions such as learning disabilities. Thus, accommodations for students must be arranged on a case-by-case basis in order to meet specific individual needs. In order to verify a disability, students are asked to release a copy of their diagnosis and treatment summary to the college's office of student disability services or designated service provider. Clinicians can facilitate the process of determining eligibility for accommodations by offering recommendations for appropriate measures in the reports written for college-bound and college students, or for adults who are planning to return to an educational setting.

The following brief descriptions detail components of a postsecondary student services program designed to support and assist students with AD/HD:

(1) **Support Staff and Disability Services.** The availability of an office of student disability services (SDS) and staff who are well informed about AD/HD and experienced in assisting students with the disability is key to the success of many students.

(2) **Faculty and Staff Awareness.** Faculty and staff who have had some training about AD/HD as a disability and are aware of the protections for students with disabilities mandated by law are important to the provision of campus-wide accommodations.

(3) **Student Involvement.** Students should seek involvement in programs of residence life, academic advising, and other campus activities. If they work, a part-time (10 hours/week) job on campus is preferable to one in the private community. Volunteering in a campus service learning program may also increase student commitment to staying in college.

(4) **Advocacy and Self-advocacy.** SDS counselors may work with staff and/or faculty in a variety of ways to advocate appropriate accommodations for students with AD/HD, including campus committees and staff development. Counselors may also instruct or coach students in the use of self-advocacy skills.

(5) **Degree Requirement Substitutions.** When a student's disability prevents him or her from completing a degree requirement in such areas as mathematics or foreign language, the SDS office may assist the student in obtaining permission to substitute approved courses.

(6) **Alternative Examinations.** Alternative examination accommodations are frequently requested by postsecondary students with AD/HD. Based on their individual needs and abilities, students may be able to take exams in a private or semi-private room, have extended time limits, and/or be assisted by a reader and/or scribe. Other assistive devices which some students may be eligible to use include use of a calculator, speller's dictionary, proofreader, and/or word processing.

(7) **Note taking services.** Some students with AD/HD may qualify for the use of note taking services. These services are facilitated in a number of ways including supplying the students with instructors' notes, making copies of another student's notes by formal arrangement, and provision of notes supplied by a paid note taker.

(8) **Recorded Reading Materials.** Students who have co-existing print disabilities may be eligible to receive their textbooks and reading assignments recorded on to audiocassette tapes.

(9) **Technological Tools and Auxiliary Aids.** Students with AD/HD may benefit from the use of a number of technological tools that are available, including electronic spellers and personal organizers, calculators, and tape player/recorders, and computers with word-processing, spread sheet, database, and time management software.

(10) **Tutorial and Learning Assistance Programs.** Institutions vary in their arrangements for providing content-based tutorial services for students with AD/HD.

(11) **Self-Management Instruction.** Interviews with college graduates with AD/HD indicate they have used a number of cognitive strategies for regulating attention and productivity. They frequently mentioned that "self-talk," note taking systems and time management tools were helpful.

(12) **Support Groups.** Support groups meet the needs of students who process information well through discussion and are validated by group support.

(13) **Individual Counseling.** Students with AD/HD may have more concerns about college and career than other students. Coping with a disability requires a good deal of effort and this may detract from resources needed by students to put toward achieving their goals. Individual sessions with a counselor who is knowledgeable about AD/HD can assist students to overcome feelings of frustration and being "stuck," as well as aid in identifying strengths, resources, and opportunities.

(14) **Strategic Schedule-Building.** Most institutions offer priority enrollment for students with disabilities. This assists students by allowing them access to enrollment in classes during the initial period of registration when more classes and sections are open at more times.

(15) **Reduced Course Load.** Students with AD/HD entering college are often advised to schedule no more than twelve to thirteen hours of credit per semester. If a student's grades are good after a semester or two, and the student believes they can be maintained, he or she may consider enrolling in an additional course.

(16) **Mentorship and "Anchoring".** The presence of a positive role-model or mentor may serve as an "anchor" for college students with AD/HD. Having a mentor available can greatly encourage students who are working to master the personal and academic challenges of college life.

(17) **Assistance with educational and vocational choices.** Students with AD/HD often benefit from programs that inform, guide, and support students who are choosing majors and considering related careers. Strategies may include counseling, the use of self or clinical assessment tools, workshops, classes for credit, as well as internships.

THE SUCCESSFUL STUDENT WITH ADD

Students with AD/HD who are successful in academic programs have learned that "the buck stops" with them, and have taken responsibility for their own lives. This indicates they are moving forward and using strategies and services that aid them in living with and compensating for their disability. They are not looking for a quick fix to their difficulties, but rather have learned that what lies between them and their aspirations consists of dedication and work. They have learned not to fear making mistakes and to manage their impulses to the extent that they do not entirely live "on the edge."

Critical to success for many students is the recognition of need to continue treatment for AD/HD, which may include medication and counseling, in addition to the accommodations and supports available through the SDS office. If a student needs accommodations or other assistance, it is important to seek help promptly and not wait until problems threaten academic progress.

STUDENTS WITH AD/HD AND HIGHER EDUCATION

Today's colleges and universities often describe the importance of diversity in their student bodies. Students with differences such as AD/HD can contribute to the richness of human educational experience in campus life and many have much to offer academic communities. The presence of successful students with AD/HD on campus is a tribute to individuals who are facing and beating the odds presented by their disability. They are taking charge of their lives and are bringing their abilities to bear on their education and future careers. In summary, they have developed the insight, coping strategies, work ethic, and resourcefulness that will help them to achieve their personal best.

Organizations that Provide Higher Education Resources

HEATH Resource Center operates the National Clearinghouse on Postsecondary Education for Handicapped Individuals. HEATH Resource Center can be reached at: One Dupont Circle, Suite 670, Washington, D.C. 20036-1193. In the Washington, D.C. metropolitan area, it may be reached at 202/939-9320; outside that area, call toll-free 800/54-HEATH.

AHEAD is a national, nonprofit organization of persons from all fifty states, Canada, and other countries committed to promoting the full participation of individuals with disabilities in college life. AHEAD is an acronym for Association for Higher Education and Disabilities, and can be contacted at: P.O. Box 21192, Columbus, Ohio 43221, 614/488-4972.

Reprinted with permission of ADHD Report, 2(6), (1994) by Guildford Publications, Inc., New York, NY.

Mary McDonald Richard is Coordinator of Services for Students with Learning Disabilities at the Office of Student Disability Services at The University of Iowa. In this position she directs a program of counseling and academic services for undergraduate, graduate, and professional school students who have attention, learning, and/or psychological disabilities. Her professional experience includes classroom teaching, counseling, and consulting positions in schools, education agencies, in- and out-patient psychiatry clinics, and substance abuse treatment settings. Ms. Richard has served as the executive editor of CH.A.D.D.er Box and as the chair of several committees. She has conducted research and published a variety of articles, professional materials, and book chapters on college students with ADD and other disabilities.

PRINT RESOURCES

The K & W Guide to Colleges for the Learning Disabled. Marybeth Kravets and Imy F. Wax. The third edition is available from Educators Publishing Service, Inc., 31 Smith Place, Cambridge, MA 02138-1000

A Comprehensive Guide to Attention Deficit Disorders in Adults: Research, Diagnosis, and Treatment. Ed. Kathleen Nadeau, Brunner/Mazel, Publishers, 19 Union Square W., New York, New York 10003. 800/825-3089.

The College Student with ADD, Ed. Patricia O. Quinn. Magination Press. 19 Union Square W., New York, New York 10003. 800/825-3089.

A Survival Guide for High School and College Students with ADD. Kathleen Nadeau. Magination Press, 19 Union Square W., New York, New York 10003. 800/825-3089.

Attention Deficit Disorder and the Law. Peter S. Latham and Patricia H. Latham. JKL Communications, P.O. Box 40157, Washington, D.C. 20016. 202/223-5097.

Higher Education Services for Students with Learning Disabilities and ADD: A Legal Guide. National Center for Law and Learning Disabilities. P.O. Box 368, Cabin John, MD 20818. 202/223-5097.

Succeeding in the Workplace
with ADD

by Patricia H. Latham, J.D. and Peter S. Latham, J.D.

A *recent* Wall Street Journal *article explored the world of contract workers. The article, entitled "High-Tech Nomads Write a New Program for the Future of Work," points out that, increasingly, work in America is project-oriented and that projects promote a blend of traditional employees and contract workers. This trend away from traditional jobs has many implications — decreased emphasis on job security and increased focus on one's own mastery of the field. The article quotes a software engineer, who recently left the corporate world for life as an independent contractor, as saying that now "I'm really independent . . . I'm attached only to what I know" (*Wall Street Journal, August 19, 1996, page 1).*

This evolving workplace may offer young adults with ADD greater opportunities for success. Trends giving more options as to work arrangements and greater control to the worker may have appeal to many persons with ADD. Similarly, greater flexibility in where and at what times work will be performed may prove beneficial to those persons with ADD who have difficulty with time management, relationships with supervisors, and social interactions in the workplace.

The workplace, as it is now and as it may become, offers greater opportunities to many adults with ADD than they have known before. A key advantage to the workplace, and difference from school, is choice. In the world of education, there are few choices and many demands in the early years. As we advance into secondary and post-secondary education, we have more choices but by no means the range of choice available in the workplace.

What choices do ADD adults have in the workplace? They may choose a career (type of work), a particular job or work arrangement, a change in position, a career change, or perhaps, even starting a business. The type of work should play to the strengths of the individual and not impact heavily on the weak areas. With a good job match, traits that have caused problems in the past may prove to be assets.

Individuals with ADD may also have legal rights to accommodations in the workplace that may prove helpful in the quest for success. Statistics released by the U.S. Equal Opportunity Employment Commission (EEOC) indicate that disability related discrimination charges are increasing. The most often alleged act of employment discrimination is discharge. The EEOC enforces the ADA as well as various other Acts which prohibit discrimination.

Let's review in greater depth legal rights, accommodations, and strategies to promote success.

LEGAL RIGHTS

Adults with ADD that substantially limits a major life activity such as learning or working are considered individuals with disabilities (for purposes of legal protection) and enjoy the right to be free from discrimination in the workplace. The bar against discrimination applies to: recruitment, advertising and job application procedures, hiring, upgrading, promotion, award of tenure, discharge, demotion, transfer, layoff, rehiring, compensation, leave, and various benefits. The right to be free from discrimination in the workplace is provided under two important federal laws: The Americans with Disabilities Act (ADA) and the Rehabilitation Act of 1973 (RA).

To invoke the protection of these federal statutes, the individual must establish that the statute applies and that he or she (1) is an individual with a disability, (2) is otherwise qualified with or without reasonable accommodation for the job, promotion, employment benefit, or privilege being sought, and (3) was denied it by reason of the disability.

Note that to obtain these protections, one must disclose that he or she has a disability. The individual may decide if and when to disclose. Where accommodations in the applications and entry testing process are not needed, many individuals will disclose at some time after they have commenced employment and have determined that they do need work accommodations.

When an individual discloses and requests accommodations, he or she must be prepared to submit professional documentation of the disability. Ordinarily, this documentation should set forth a diagnosis, evaluation of impact of ADD on the individual's functioning, and recommended accommodations.

When do the ADA and RA apply? Both prohibit discrimination against individuals with disabilities in employment, but the ADA has broader application. The RA basically follows federal dollars. It applies to the federal government, federal government contractors, and federal grant recipients. The ADA applies to virtually all employers except those with fewer than fifteen employees.

Who is an individual with a disability? Any individual who has a physical or mental impairment which substantially limits one or more major life activities qualifies as an individual with a disability. Learning disabilities are expressly recognized under regulations as impairments. ADD has been recognized in cases, letters of findings, and U.S. Department of Education memoranda. Note that, in order to qualify as a disability, the impairment must substantially limit a major life activity.

Major life activities include learning and working. In 1995, the EEOC recognized as major life activities concentrating, thinking, and interacting with others. Recognition of these specific processes may be helpful to individuals with ADD.

When is an individual "otherwise qualified"? One is "otherwise qualified" for a job when he or she can perform the essential functions of the job with or without reasonable accommodations. A reasonable accommodation is one that does not create an "undue hardship" for the employer. An accommodation that alters the essential nature of the job or results in significant difficulty or expense to the employer would create an undue hardship.

A few examples may be helpful in understanding reasonableness. A waiter with a vision impairment that makes it difficult for him to see in dim lighting may not compel a nightclub to accommodate him by providing bright lighting throughout its dining and lounge areas, as this would change the nature of the club and harm its trade. In another case, a school district that required that its teachers take turns driving school buses did have to restructure its job requirements to allow the hiring of a qualified teacher who had a disability that prevented him from driving. Bus driving is not an essential part of a teaching job.

When is the discharge (or other act giving rise to a complaint) by reason of the disability? The disability must be the reason for the employer's act. In one case, a surgeon with narcolepsy (controlled by medication) had her hospital privileges terminated by a hospital. The termination was held lawful because the surgeon had verbally abused staff members for years, and there was no evidence that this behavior was related to the disability.

ACCOMMODATIONS

Individuals with ADD who meet the tests described above are entitled to reasonable accommodations in the workplace.

What accommodations may be helpful to persons with ADD? The answer depends on the individual case. ADD does not present in exactly the same way in each individual. For example, hyperactivity may be an issue for some and not for others. Also, many persons with ADD have co-existing learning disabilities and/or other disabilities. Recognizing that an accommodation plan is an individual matter, we have listed below accommodations that may be helpful to many persons with ADD.

- Reduce distractions in the work area.
- Give instructions orally and in writing.
- Break tasks down into manageable parts.
- Give frequent and specific feedback
- Provide training course accommodations
- Provide test accommodations (e.g., extra time, quiet room)
- Provide job restructuring
- Allow job reassignment

STRATEGIES TO PROMOTE SUCCESS

The process of achieving success in the workplace involves the efforts of the employer in providing needed reasonable accommodations and of the individual with ADD in using strategies that will promote success. Like accommodations, strategies should be tailored to the needs of the individual, taking into account how ADD presents in the particular case and any co-existing learning disabilities or other disabilities. We will explore below some strategies that may be helpful to many persons with ADD.

Know Yourself and ADD

The individual with ADD must seek to know his or her strengths and weaknesses and to understand ADD and any co-existing learning disabilities and other disabilities. Reading books concerning ADD and obtaining information from disability organizations, such as CH.A.D.D., is most helpful. Evaluations and recommendations from medical, educational, psychological, and/or career counseling professionals may further promote understanding, facilitate coping with the disability, and assist self advocacy efforts.

Select a Good Job Match

Basically, the type of work should play to the strengths of the adult with ADD and not impact heavily on the weak areas. It's usually best to avoid work with: high paperwork and record keeping requirements, considerable supervisory or monitoring responsibilities, high stress, demands for rapid performance, and expectation for rapid learning especially in large group situations.

Certain career areas seem to work well for some individuals with ADD: the media, the arts, trades, sales, law enforcement, and fire safety. Many individuals will be most comfortable with an expertise in a particular area so that expectations are clear, and there are few surprises. A career that allows a high degree of autonomy may be better than one that will involve close and constant personal supervision. A high degree of structure is a must for some individuals with ADD.

Some young adults with ADD wish to consider the military. Possible advantages include: structure, clarity of expectations, and training opportunities. The presence of ADD does not itself preclude military service, but the current use of medication for academic skills disorders (e.g. methyphenidate) is disqualifying.

The positive side to ADD may open up possibilities. For example, the intensity about interests that may have led earlier to a seeming obsession about toy cars or music tapes may be channeled in adult life to yield great success. One adult turned an interest in antique cars into several successful businesses he owns and operates.

Remember, there are many paths to success — some traditional and others not so traditional. The adult with ADD must consider a range of options and discover what works best. For some individuals with ADD, one job may prove boring, so they may change jobs frequently or hold several part-time jobs simultaneously. Some may return to school in connection with a new career interest. Remember, some adults with ADD do better than ever before in the educational arena with added maturity, courses that are in their area of interest, and increased accommodations in post-secondary education. A number of individuals with ADD have observed that they enjoyed more success as adults in courses with specific career related objectives and clear expectations.

Use Aids

Today, more than ever, there are aids that promote success in the workplace. A few of these are:

- tape recorder to record meetings, conferences, training courses, etc.
- day planner (plan book, electronic scheduler or voice organizer) to keep track of work deadlines, meetings, appointments, and other obligations
- computer and software (e.g., spell check and grammar check)
- calculator or talking calculator.

Sometimes such aids may be provided by employers as workplace accommodations. Consider a case in which a special computer and software were provided by an employer to a research scientist with ADD to accommodate his disability and increase his writing productivity. This arrangement allowed the scientist to dictate to the computer and see the dictated material in print on the computer screen. The research scientist, a Ph.D. in Chemistry, had struggled for years with the research report writing part of his job. After initially getting little response to his request for accommodations and finding himself on the verge of being fired, he filed a complaint with his agency's Equal Employment Opportunity office and, as the result of a mediation process, obtained the requested accommodations.

Use Compensatory Techniques

There are various compensatory techniques for specific deficits. A few are explored below.

- If chronic lateness is a problem, leave fifteen minutes early for work, appointments and interviews. Do not become diverted unless there is an emergency.
- If hyperactivity is a problem, use breaks and the lunch period to get physical movement and exercise to refresh yourself
- If impulsive statements and loss of temper are problems, listen to others and take time before responding, especially if angry or negative feelings are present. If necessary, take time out to cool down and focus on what is important.

An example of a compensatory technique improving work performance involves a police officer. He had struggled with ADD through his school years and then found law enforcement to be the career for him. Soon, a problem emerged. He was often late to work — usually by just a few minutes. Why was he late? In part because he would become easily diverted, but also because early arrival would mean waiting to go on duty and feeling bored. The solution that worked for him: leaving fifteen minutes early and bringing along one of his many electronic gadgets so that he could enjoy using it while waiting.

In conclusion, young adults with ADD should seek to know themselves and their disabilities, inform themselves concerning their legal rights in the workplace, find an appropriate job match, use helpful strategies, and request reasonable accommodations, if needed. With all of this in place, they will be well positioned to move forward with enthusiasm to make contributions and reap rewards in the workplace. If, despite the best efforts, there is a setback, remember that succeeding in the workplace does not mean succeeding in every job but rather succeeding overall. What is learned from a disappointing experience may help focus in on what will work better in the future.

Patricia H. Latham, J.D. and Peter S. Latham, J.D. are partners in the Washington, DC law firm Latham & Latham, Directors of JKL Communications and Founders and Directors of the National Center for Law and Learning Disabilities (NCLLD). They have authored five books, contributed chapters to six additional books, and written numerous articles on ADD and learning disabilities.

Making It All ADD Up!

by Michael Ginsberg with Jay Sartain

Just before I sat down to type out this article, my mom was giving me the same encouragement that I often give to other adolescents with AD/HD. I often speak to others about how difficult it is for students with AD/HD to start a task, but once they are going, it is easy to keep going. I frequently use the analogy of driving a stick-shift car; getting from zero to five miles per hour is the hard part, but from there on, it's simple.

If we are to continue this metaphor, one might say that I just stalled. After finishing the first paragraph, I decided to get up and find my shoes because my feet were freezing. Now, the thing about shoes (or jackets, car keys, important papers, etc.) belonging to students with AD/HD is that those items are "possessed." They love to play games like "hide-and-seek." I am sure that my AD/HD mind projects a biological field around the shoes that makes them come alive and run from me. It does not seem to happen to kids that don't have AD/HD. Eventually, I found my shoes downstairs next to the pile of sheets that I left on the couch last night when I decided to sleep there because my bed was not comfortable enough for me. (This is another AD/HD trait: beds belonging to kids with AD/HD develop lumps in random spots that last for random amounts of time.) I decided to take the sheets back upstairs and make my bed. I then grabbed a drink of water and came back in here to the computer. Now, imagine what it is like when I'm not taking my medication.

My name is Mike Ginsberg. I am a senior at Bloomfield Hills Andover High School. I exchanged ideas about this article with Jay Sartain, a senior at Midway High School in Waco, Texas. When I heard that I would be working on this article with another student with AD/HD who was my age, I groaned; when two kids with AD/HD work together, they tend to work twice as slowly as one. But actually, we managed to get a great deal accomplished on the phone. We worked out a pretty efficient system; whenever he would start rambling, I would say something like, "Anyway, Jay, we were talking about …" and Jay would do the same for me when I got off track. Unfortunately, when we both got off the subject, MCI had a party and my Dad had a fit!

Jay and I had long time to write this article, but we acted like typical adolescents with AD/HD; we waited until the deadline. I had taken notes from our conversations on my computer, but we never got a chance to actually write the article together. The deadline rolled around and Jay suddenly had a change of family plans and could not be on the phone with me to write the article, so I decided to do it myself at the last minute from the outline we had put together. This is what it is like to be a person with AD/HD. We try, delay, try again, procrastinate, and finally get it right. We are in a constant fight with the universe, but somehow we manage. Jay and I have won many battles, and we intend to help other kids win their own.

Jay had one of his first major clashes with the universe in seventh grade. During a classroom discussion, Jay was idly tapping his pencil on his desk, just like any other student with AD/HD might. Suddenly, his teacher stopped in mid-sentence and stared directly at him.

"Jay, could I see you in the hall for a moment?"

Jay rose solemnly and shuffled into the hall after his teacher.

"Do you realize," she hissed, "that your constant tapping is distracting to others?"

"I'm sorry, ma'am," stammered Jay, "but I didn't even realize that I was tapping my pencil. I'll stop."

She sighed, "Look, I know you're . . . retarded or something, but . . ." Jay does not even remember the rest of the statement. All he remembers is the flash of anger, shame, and sadness brought on by his teacher's matter-of-fact remark. The pain haunted Jay for several years, but he says that he decided to become an advocate for other children with AD/HD on that day.

I, myself, remember being different from the other kids well before I was diagnosed with AD/HD. Throughout grade school, I experienced some rough times; kids picked on me and my self-esteem was pretty low. After I was diagnosed at the end of third grade, I was prescribed medication, which proved to be a big help and continues to help me today.

Middle school was a difficult time for me as well. So many different classes, different teaching styles, and more complex assignments made my AD/HD stand out. My teachers had more students than my elementary teachers had in their self-contained classes, so there were many new rules to follow and new expectations of assuming responsibilities in adolescence. It was a tough adjustment. It wasn't that the work was too difficult; I always completed my homework and school assignments, but I left them on my desk, at my computer, on the bus, in my locker, or dropped them in the hall. They got lost in the folders in my "Trapper Keeper" and they didn't surface fast enough for me to turn them in during class. I became a collector of zeros — no credit because the assignments were late or my name and date were missing. There was no safety net and my teachers just didn't understand. There was no flexibility in their thinking. They were measuring me on my disability rather than on the quality of my work.

I've found that AD/HD tends to manifest itself most strongly in school. I've also found that a good teacher knows how to help the student with AD/HD overcome the disorder, whereas a poor teacher allows the student to demonstrate his weaknesses. Jay and I have had our share of poor teachers and we know what makes an effective one. From my experiences, an effective teacher for students with AD/HD is one who can make learning fun and interesting. Teachers I consider effective put energy into their lectures, move around the room, use their hands to talk, vary their voice tone, and make jokes. They also write key points on the board or on an overhead projector. For example, I had an Advanced Placement Biology teacher who basically gave us notes to copy from the overhead while he lectured. He was one of the finest — and most effective — teachers I have ever had. Other important qualities possessed by effective teachers include not assigning more homework than absolutely necessary, giving students an opportunity to start on homework in class so they can ask questions, and grading group projects on an individual basis rather than as a whole. Essentially, a good teacher inspires his students to learn without forcing information down their throats.

Becoming certified under Section 504 proved extremely helpful to me in school; my case manager, who is wonderful, helped select teachers with a learning style that fit with my AD/HD, and my grades improved. Because I achieved, I know that other kids can too. I have decided to dedicate myself to helping other students with AD/HD in the hopes that they will have an easier time than I did.

In addition to impacting my school experience, my AD/HD has also affected my ability to drive a car. Articles have been written about the high incidence of auto accidents for drivers with AD/HD. Because of that, my parents worried tremendously about my attention span and distractibility during driving instruction. We drew up a "driving contract," which stated that I was to take my medication before driving the family car and would not have more than two other passengers in the car. One of my friends with AD/HD has a family rule that he is not allowed to listen to tapes or the radio while driving.

As far as my social relationships are concerned, I don't feel AD/HD has had an effect on dating (I have dates and girl friends like many other guys my age); however, it has impacted my friendships. I am not as physically hyperactive as I am verbally hyperactive. In other words, I frequently run off at the mouth. My ability to ramble on about nothing caused a very tolerant friend of mine to call me "the master of small-talk." Others were not so tolerant and got annoyed with me. My mouth gets me into a lot of trouble. Whenever I am told a really good secret, I feel like I need to scream it to the world. I usually end up writing it down and burning the paper or screaming it into my pillow.

Though the wounds from being teased in elementary school have healed, the scars remain, and I am still very suspicious of others. I remember when kids would pretend to be my friend, then suddenly turn on me as a joke. I guess that on a subconscious level, I am still afraid of that happening. My caution makes me seem cold to some people, and I am very selective about whom I call a friend, but I am learning to be warmer and more open, and I am making new friends in the process. I do sit with a table of friends at lunch. During my junior year, I was amazed to find out that every person (male and female) at our table had AD/HD and was taking medication. We had self-selected!

Impulsivity is another problem associated with AD/HD. It seems like I always leap, then look to see if it was a good idea later. Often, my mouth will do the leaping, and I will end up in a giant heap of trouble. It is not as frequent as before, but I used to say and do a lot of things that I later regretted. However, one particularly stupid impulsive move that I made two years ago still haunts me today.

As a high school swimmer, I train with weights. One day, while I was working out with my swim team in the weight room, the hormonal sixteen-year-old in me decided to prove that I was a man. I piled some three hundred pounds onto the leg-press machine and proceeded to lift it up. The next day, I had a sore back, which blossomed over a period of a couple of months to a crippling ailment. An MRI scan revealed a herniated disk in my lower back. I still wake up each morning in terrible pain, and I rely on ibuprofen to allow me to start the day. If I had not acted so impulsively, I would not have gotten this problem in the first place.

Jay and I have had a rough time growing up, and our experiences have certainly hardened us. We possess a psychological resilience that allows us to handle adversity with a certain practiced ease. Don't get me wrong — not every challenge that is thrown our way is a cakewalk. We handle the smaller crises that come our way with more ease than our friends without AD/HD. On the other hand, when the big problems rear their ugly heads, we get stressed out — and I mean really stressed out! Personally, I can panic with the best of them when

I get on overload. Still, I manage to solve the problem at hand.

I do not consider AD/HD an invader into my life. AD/HD is a part of me and it helps shape who I am. I think my attitude towards AD/HD has helped me the most. Some kids feel that AD/HD is a license to stop trying because they feel that their efforts will be fruitless. Other kids take medication and feel that the medication will do all the work for them. AD/HD is not a license and methylphenidate is not a wonder drug. To a kid with AD/HD, life is like a car with its parking brake on; no matter how hard you push, you do not get anywhere.

Ritalin merely removes the brake. You still have to push just as hard, but your efforts will be rewarded. AD/HD is not an excuse for failure — with medicine, discipline, and hard work, AD/HD can be overcome. The secret is to never give up, but to keep on trying and never blame your mistakes on AD/HD. Remember, AD/HD is a part of you, and you are responsible for what you mess up because of it. AD/HD is a challenge, and challenges can be a lot of fun.

This article first appeared in the Winter 1996 ATTENTION!

Where There's A Will, There's A Way

by Nichole Payne

"Nichole Anjanette Payne, Bachelor of Arts degree in Interdepartmental Studies — Counseling and Psychology, with Honors Recognition," the Commencement speaker announced from the podium as I walked across the stage to receive my diploma from the University of Iowa. I don't think I had ever been so proud of hearing my name being announced. Despite all of the hard work that I had put forth over the years, it was hard to believe that my dream had actually become a reality, especially considering that three years prior to this graduation celebration, I had flirted with the idea of giving up my pursuit of a college degree.

During my third semester of college, I was almost ready to quit. I was failing Spanish despite long hours of studying and I didn't know what the problem was. But then, I never seemed to know what the problem was when it came to succeeding in an academic setting. Since kindergarten, I could remember spending recesses inside because I didn't complete my work on time or was being punished for socializing with other students. My talent for making conversation was rarely appreciated by teachers. As a result of my behavior, the academic arena was not my strong suit. I wanted to do well in school, but it was always such a struggle, and my failing grade in Spanish was a reminder that my academic pursuits would not be any easier at the college level.

Recognizing my constant struggles in school, a colleague suggested that I might have a learning disability, and she suggested that I get tested. I'm glad I took her advice. After hours of verbal and written testing, the psychologist testing me gave me a preliminary diagnosis of Attention Deficit Hyperactivity Disorder (AD/HD), but noted that she would need information about my childhood to confirm the diagnosis. I had never heard of AD/HD, but I did as the psychologist requested and asked my parents about my childhood behaviors. Once they had an open invitation to discuss my childhood, they began to enlighten me on the many adventures I had taken them on. I was overwhelmed by all of the stories they had to tell.

One of their favorite stories, which is still used as a threat to embarrass me, involves late night refrigerator raids. I hadn't been hungry when my parents had found me at two a.m. in the kitchen. Instead, my excessive energy and creativity had led me to produce unique artwork with large amounts of food. Unfortunately, because my parents were not art connoisseurs, they didn't exactly appreciate waking up consecutive nights to find me standing in the middle of my "masterpiece." To stifle my creative juices, my parents decided to secure the refrigerator doors with chains and a pad lock. Although my parents could now laugh at this and the many other childhood escapades I had led them on, my behavior as a child confirmed the psychologist's suspicions; my hyperactivity, inattentiveness, and distractibility were evidence that I had AD/HD.

I remember feeling numb as I read over the literature on AD/HD that I had received from the psychologist at my final session. I had always known that there was a reason for my struggles in school, but it was a bit unnerving to find out that an actual disorder had been the cause. I still wondered how receiving an "official" diagnosis would help me academically. I was relieved to find that there was an office on campus designated to assist college students with AD/HD. This made all the difference in the world. The staff were supportive and helped teach me how to study more effectively and perform better on tests; they were patient and willing to teach me how to accept and work with my AD/HD instead of beating myself up because school wasn't easy for me, as I had perceived it to be for all of my fellow classmates.

Despite their efforts, there were certain areas even they could not help me with. I had to endure many painful and difficult times throughout my college career. One time in particular comes to mind. During exams one semester, I found myself in an uncomfortable situation. My university had allocated a number of accommodations for students with ADD, including Alternative Testing Services, which provided extended testing time and testing rooms free of distractions. It is mandatory for educational institutions to provide accommodations for students in need of assistance, and professors are obligated to comply with these accommodations. A particular professor had agreed to bring a copy of the exam in a sealed envelope to the testing services center, but failed to show up. I knew I would have to go to him and I was not looking forward to it because of the embarrassing incident I had with him earlier in the semester.

In the beginning of the year, the professor had said that no food consumption was allowed in the auditorium while he lectured, even though the class met during the lunch hour. Unfortunately, I had totally forgotten about his warning one afternoon as I finished eating a rather crispy apple. I was quickly reminded, however, as I heard the professor bellowing at me from his podium. It is amazing how quiet a room full of 300-plus students can become when a professor is singling out one of his students. I was humiliated, not to mention angry with myself for not taking my morning medication, which would have helped me to think more clearly.

I was thinking of that incident as I approached the auditorium where my professor was administering the test he forgot to deliver to me. I had a horrible feeling that he would react negatively once again. Although I realized that I was making the ordeal worse than it was by focusing on the incident, I couldn't help but feel as though I was Daniel walking into the den of a merciless lion. I was thankful that a staff member from the student accommodation office had accompanied me to the "Lion's Den," especially since my fears would indeed be confirmed. The professor showed his disapproval with a raised voice and distinct posture as the staff member inquired as to the whereabouts of my exam. To say that I was embarrassed would be a gross understatement; I was extremely uncomfortable as I looked around the room to see many of my fellow classmates peering at me, wondering why I was not taking the test with them. Fortunately, once the professor realized that the error was on his part, he gave a copy of the exam to the staff member and we quickly exited the auditorium. It was pleasantly ironic to receive an A in that class, despite the many obstacles I had experienced with the professor.

Along with the knowledge I gained during college, I learned many valuable lessons. Most importantly, I learned that by accepting my differences and finding ways to accommodate myself, I was able to find great freedom. Accepting myself enabled me to explore the gifts that I have. For example, I uncovered an intensity in myself that gives me a strong sense of creativity and the ability to complete tasks with passion and enthusiasm. My creativity has enabled me to successfully complete a senior honors research project, "Romancing the Inattentive," which explores the romantic relationships of couples in which one of the partners has ADD. In addition, as a result of my newly acquired study skills and my persistence, I was able to greatly improve my grade point average, so much so that I was able to graduate with honors and get accepted into graduate school, where I am currently working towards a Master's Degree in Clinical Psychology.

While I have endured many challenges throughout my academic career as a result of my AD/HD, I have been able to achieve success. I must admit, victory in the academic arena is truly sweet. My recollections of the obstacles I've encountered along the way are not meant to discourage individuals with ADD; rather, my hope is to paint a realistic picture of the challenges that may lie ahead. The key is to remember that challenges are merely potholes, not road blocks. Consider the challenges I have had to overcome. Who would have guessed that after my struggles in school, I would graduate with Honors from the University of Iowa? Who would have guessed that I would actually get accepted into graduate school? Who would have guessed that as my parents gazed at the chains that barricaded their daughter from creating havoc with the refrigerator over twenty years ago, that someday, it would all be worth it when they were able to sit proudly in the audience and watch their "holy terror" walk across the stage to receive her college degree? Take it from me; persistence does pay off — I'm living proof.

This article first appeared in the Spring 1996 ATTENTION!

CHAPTER 7

ONGOING CHALLENGES

An Introduction by Kevin Murphy, Ph.D.

University of Massachusetts Medical Center

Chief, Adult AD/HD Clinic

Assistant Professor, Department of Psychiatry

Adolescents with ADD and comorbid conduct problems and substance abuse are often the most difficult group to treat successfully. They present special and enormously difficult challenges and frustrations to parents, educators, and professionals. Some of the common issues these teenagers face include lack of understanding and denial of their disability, fear of being stigmatized and not being accepted, low self-esteem, treatment compliance issues regarding medication and counseling, acceptance of their disability and learning not to devalue themselves because of it, peer group influences, problems with the law, and the continual struggle between their drive for autonomy, independence, and freedom versus their parents' reluctance to grant it.

Although research studies suggest that the outcomes for this group are generally not as positive as for teens with ADD who do not have conduct or substance abuse problems, it is essential that all of us — parents, teachers and professionals — do not give up on them. Scientific studies report findings based on **group** data; not on any one individual. It is important to remember that group data does not dictate the outcome of any one individual. It is therefore critical that we identify and assist those with ADD/CD/substance abuse because underneath their problems they are so often skilled, capable, unique, and valuable people who could be significant contributors to society if properly treated.

We must help these adolescents learn ways to overcome their problems, instill hope, reduce discouragement and demoralization, and foster a belief that they can succeed in school and in life. They need to under-

stand they have a treatable condition and that they have some power, control, and responsibility in how effectively they learn to manage it. By addressing their needs in creative and effective ways, we can help remove the roadblocks to progress and help many of them reach their true potential.

Mental health professionals can play a powerful role by educating these adolescents and promoting understanding of their attentional and behavior problems, in teaching compensatory strategies and skills to overcome their difficulties, by instilling hope and empowering them to believe they can succeed in spite of their problems, in helping to chart a vocational path that "fits" for them, and in helping them become effective self-advocates so they can help others to better understand them. Professionals can assist in identifying and reinforcing strengths, aptitudes, interests, and special skills that can be marketable in the real world. These adolescents need to believe they *can* have a productive and satisfying future, *if* they take responsibility and do their part. In short, mental health professionals can help these individuals reframe their problems into something that is understandable, treatable, and manageable.

How can parents cope and assist their troubled teenager? Anyone who has experienced living with such a teen knows how challenging and at times demoralizing it can be. There are obviously no easy answers. Nevertheless, some general principles that seem important to keep in mind include the following. First, try not to lose sight of the larger picture. The more important goal for this group of adolescents is to become a reasonably well adjusted individual in life; not to get A's and B's in school. Second, try to continually offer encouragement, positive reinforcement, patience, and a belief you are behind your child and value their unique gifts. Third, try to keep a disability perspective. This means trying to maintain psychological distance from your adolescent's disruptive behavior, trying not to lose your cool, and remembering you are dealing with a person with a disability who cannot always help behaving as he or she does. It is important to hold adolescents responsible for their behavior, but it is also important for parents to let go of the anger, resentment, disap-

pointment, and other negative emotions that arise when certain behavior occurs. Finally, forgive yourself for your own mistakes in dealing with your adolescent's behavior and resolve to do better tomorrow.

Despite the generally poorer outcomes of the group with comorbid ADD, conduct disorder, and substance abuse, some of these adolescents do go on to achieve satisfactory outcomes. We need to better understand the variables that are correlated with positive outcome and continually work at bringing those about. The following articles offer some valuable data, insights, and suggestions towards this goal.

Some Relationships Between AD/HD, Substance Abuse, and Crime

by Harry K. Wexler, Ph.D. and Megan McClelland, B.A.

A growing body of research has shown that a relationship between AD/HD and disorders such as substance abuse may contribute to juvenile delinquency and adult criminal behavior. Childhood rates of AD/HD range from 2.2 percent to 12.6 percent and adult rates of AD/HD are 2 to 3 percent. Retrospective studies suggest that children with AD/HD often have a range of psychiatric problems extending into adulthood such as conduct disorders, depression, and antisocial personality (Wilens, 1995; Loeber et al., 1995). Similarly, prospective studies show that 40 to 50 percent of children with AD/HD may continue to have symptoms of AD/HD into adolescence and adulthood and 10 to 20 percent have persistent symptomatology with significant disability (Gittleman et al., 1985, Hechtman, 1985; Barkely et al., 1990; Weiss, 1992; Mannuzza et al., 1993). The purpose of this article is to explore how AD/HD is related to substance abuse and conduct disorders, and how the combination can affect criminal behavior in adolescents and adults. In addition, brief discussions of treatment interventions, protective and risk factors, and tips for parents are included.

Current research suggests that AD/HD may be a risk factor for substance abuse. Many of those treated for substance abuse also have AD/HD. One study reported that one-fourth of adolescents in substance abuse treatment had AD/HD (DeMilio et al., 1989). Another found that 20 to 30 percent of adults with AD/HD had substance abuse problems (Weiss, 1992). These studies suggest that impulsive individuals may be more likely to experiment with illicit drugs and impulsively relapse when in stressful situations. In addition, aggressive individuals with poor interpersonal and/or occupational functioning (which may be AD/HD-related) are at greater risk for substance abuse.

In family studies of children with AD/HD, elevated rates of alcoholism were found in 20 percent of fathers and 5 percent of mothers (Morrison & Stewart, 1971). In addition, having both AD/HD and conduct disorders was found to be strongly related to alcoholism in a familial nature (Stewart et al., 1980).

Children with AD/HD are often more difficult to control and discipline and may elicit negative behavior from parents. Negative parenting styles used by parents to deal with their child who has AD/HD can, in turn, contribute to the development of conduct disorders at an earlier age and an increase in the severity of problems later including substance abuse and criminal behavior (Loeber et al., 1995).

Research on AD/HD and substance abuse demonstrates that children with AD/HD may be more likely to develop conduct disorders. Conduct disorders are defined by a persistent behavior pattern "in which the basic rights of others or major age-appropriate societal norms or rules are violated" and is characterized by a repeated pattern of physically harming others and destroying property (DSM-IV, American Psychiatric Association, 1994). According to Patterson, conduct disorders are more likely to develop when children are taught to use coercion and aggression instead of negotiation to resolve conflict. These children are taught to resolve conflict through a "fight or surrender" method. The parents of these children are often permissive and do not monitor their children. When children reach adolescence, peer groups become influential and can contribute to the development of conduct disorders, which can lead to juvenile delinquency and later criminal behavior as adults.

The presence of AD/HD is considered a risk factor for the development of conduct disorders, substance abuse, and criminal behavior (Barkely et al., 1990). When AD/HD is found with early aggressive behavior, the likelihood of later substance abuse and criminality increase substantially. In a study by Loeber et al., (1995), the development of conduct disorders in boys aged 8 to 17 was significantly predicted by AD/HD. Over a period of six years, boys with AD/HD were five times more likely than boys without AD/HD to be diagnosed with conduct disorders before the age of twelve. Thus, having AD/HD was related to an earlier development of conduct disorders and also early crime convictions as juveniles and adults. However, there are many adolescents with conduct disorders who do not have AD/HD.

The comorbidity of AD/HD and conduct disorders significantly increases the probability of later substance abuse. Those adolescents who have conduct disorders co-occurring with AD/HD (10-20 percent of adolescents) have the poorest outcome. This group is more likely to become substance abusers and develop criminal behavior. An important consideration is that substance abuse is relatively common in adolescents and while the majority of criminals are substance abusers, most substance abusers, especially adolescents, are not criminals. Thus, having AD/HD and abusing substances in adolescence does not necessarily mean that a person will develop conduct disorders or criminal behavior.

TREATMENT STRATEGIES

Pharmacological treatment strategies for children and adolescents with AD/HD and substance abuse include psychostimulants such as methylphenidate and pemoline. These medications have been widely used with children and were found to be useful in reducing hyperactivity and increasing a likelihood to pay attention. Work has begun with adults to study the effects of psychostimulants.

Non-pharmacological interventions include psychotherapy and counseling designed to improve social skills and competence. Other helpful strategies are psychoeducational groups, family intervention, contingency management, and cognitive-behavioral therapies. By treating one disorder, beneficial effects may result in the course of another disorder. Using a multi-modal therapy approach is important and is stressed in literature on both substance abuse and AD/HD.

Although AD/HD is highly prevalent among juvenile and adult offenders, criminal justice professionals are generally unaware of AD/HD. Recent studies have found an incidence of AD/HD as high as 70 percent among juvenile offenders and 40 percent among adult prison inmates (Wexler, 1994). Working with offenders who have AD/HD requires the development of specialized interventions. A promising direction is to build on self-help and therapeutic community approaches, which have been demonstrated to be effective with substance abusing offenders (Wexler, 1995). AD/HD screening needs to be introduced into all criminal justice programs. Criminal justice professionals, mental health workers, and others who work with AD/HD need to collaborate and develop appropriate interventions.

PROTECTIVE AND RISK FACTORS, AND TIPS FOR PARENTS

Protective Factors

Hechtman (1991) has identified childhood factors that are related to positive AD/HD outcomes in adulthood. These factors are important in the prevention of the AD/HD, conduct disorder, and substance abuse combination that can lead to criminal behavior. Good health during pregnancy, birth, and infancy is a preventive beginning. Children who are active, adaptable, and socially responsive will elicit more positive responses from others. A reflective (vs. impulsive) cognitive style is beneficial and a higher IQ has also been related to more positive outcomes. Children who have higher self-esteem, positive coping skills, good social skills, and an achievement orientation will have better outcomes with their AD/HD. In addition, a warm, cohesive, affectionate, and supportive family with open communication is important. Parents who set clear rules and roles in the family and provide a high level of supervision create a secure and comfortable environment for the child with AD/HD. If parents set clear and realistic expectations for the child with AD/HD, they are contributing to the development of a confident, well-adjusted child who will be less likely to have negative outcomes in adulthood.

Risk Factors

Identifying significant risk factors for crime is important when evaluating the relationship between AD/HD, conduct disorder, and substance abuse. Researchers have identified a number of factors that are significantly related to the development of criminal behavior (Andrews, 1989; Andrews, Leschied & Hoge, 1992). Parents with children with AD/HD should carefully consider the following risk factors and actively seek help when they are present.

Family Of Origin

- Long-term reliance on public assistance (as opposed to occasional use of such services).
- Criminality in family of origin (parents, siblings, other relatives).
- Multiple psychological handicaps (low verbal intelligence, emotional instability, alcoholism, parenting skill deficits).
- Antisocial attitudes.

Personal Temperament, Aptitude, and Early Behavioral History

- Restlessly energetic, impulsive, adventurous pleasure-seeking, a taste for risk.
- Below-average verbal intelligence.
- Response to frustration more likely to involve resentment and anger rather than composure or anxiety/guilt/depression.
- Lack of conscientiousness.
- Egocentrism (below age-based norm for moral thinking).
- Poor problem-solving/coping skills.
- If diagnosed as a child, more likely to be diagnosed externalizing (conduct disorder) than internalizing (neurotic/depressive/withdrawn).
- Early and generalized misconduct (lying, stealing, aggression, and early experimentation with sex and drugs, including tobacco).

Early And Continuing Family Conditions

- Low levels of affection/cohesiveness within home.
- Low levels of supervision and poor discipline within home.
- Neglect/abuse.

School-Based Risk Factors

- Below-average effort.
- Lack of interest/being bored.
- Not worrying about occupational future.
- Conduct problems (truancy).
- Poor schools.

Interpersonal Relationships

- Generalized indifference to opinion of others.
- Rejected/rejecting.

Social Support For Crime

- Association with antisocial others.
- Isolation from noncriminal others.

Personal Attitudes/Values/Beliefs Supportive Of Crime

- High tolerance for deviance in general.
- Rejection of the validity of the law in particular.
- Applies rationalizations for law violations to a wide variety of acts and circumstances.
- Interprets a wide range of stimuli as reasons for anger.
- Thinking style and content is generally antisocial.

Behavioral History

- Criminal history, juvenile and adult (look for an uninterrupted history, beginning at a young age, including a variety of different types of offenses, and violations that continue even while under sentence).
- Alcohol and drug abuse.
- Aimless use of leisure time.
- Disorganized lifestyle.

Psychopathology

- High scores on measures of "antisocial personality/psychopathy." Many forms of emotional/behavioral disturbance when combined with a history of antisocial behavior (e.g., conduct problems plus shyness).

TIPS FOR PARENTS

When a significant number of risk factors are present, parents need to take action. Parents may need to either take preventative steps or find ways to respond when children get into trouble with the law. The following tips suggest steps parents can take to help their children who have AD/HD and are either demonstrating risk signs or having legal problems.

(1) Obtain Early Assessment
(2) Develop an Intervention Plan
(3) Learn and Apply Protective Factors
(4) Work Closely with Teachers, Counselors, and Other Helpers
(5) Provide Appropriate Supervision and Consequences
(6) Join Support Groups
(7) Learn to Let Go and Have Children Take Appropriate Responsibility
(8) Work With Criminal Justice Authorities and Inform Them About AD/HD

This article first appeared in the Winter 1996 ATTENTION!

Harry K. Wexler, Ph.D. is the Executive Director of the Psychology Center in Laguna Beach, California and a Principal Investigator for the Center for Therapeutic Communities at the National Development Research Institute in New York.

Megan McClelland worked as a Research Assistant for Dr. Wexler at the Psychology Center.

REFERENCES

American Psychiatric Association (1994), *Diagnostic and Statistical Manual of Mental Disorders. 4th edition.* Washington D.C.: American Psychiatric Association.

Barkely RA, Fischer M, Edelbrock CS, Smallish L (1990), The adolescent outcome of hyperactive children diagnosed by research criteria: An 8-year prospective follow-up study. *J Am Acad Child Adolesc Psychiatry,* 29, 546-557.

DeMilio L (1989), Psychiatric syndromes in adolescent substance abusers. *American Journal of Psychiatry,* 146, 1212-1214.

Gittleman R, Mannuzza S, Shenkar R, & Bonagura, N (1985), Hyperactive boys almost grown up: I. Psychiatric status. *Archives of General Psychiatry,* 42, 937-947.

Hechtman LT (1985), Adolescent outcome of hyperactive children treated with stimulants in childhood: A review. *Psychopharmacology Bulletin,* 21, 178-191.

Hechtman L (1991), Resilience and vulnerability in long term outcome of attention deficit hyperactive disorder. *Canadian Journal of Psychiatry,* 36, 415-421.

Loeber R, Green SM, Keenan K, Lahey BB (1995), Which boys will fare worse? Early predictors of the onset of conduct disorder in a six-year longitudinal study. *J Am Acad Child Adolesc Psychiatry,* 34, 499-509.

Mannuzza S, Klein RG, Bessler A, Malloy P, & LaPadula M (1993), Adult outcome of hyperactive boys. *Archives of General Psychiatry,* 50, 565-576.

Morrison JR & Stewart MA (1971), A family study of the hyperactive child syndrome. *Biological Psychiatry,* 3, 189-195.

Stewart MA, de Blois CS, & Cummings C (1980), Psychiatric disorder in the parents of hyperactive boys and those with conduct disorder. *Journal of Child Psychology and Psychiatry,* 21, 283-292.

Weiss G (1992), *Attention-Deficit Hyperactivity Disorder.* Philadelphia: W.B. Saunders Company.

Wexler HK (1994), "Crime, Punishment, Responsibility, and ADD," Children with Attention Deficit Disorder National Conference (CH.A.D.D.), New York, October.

Wexler HK (1995), The success of therapeutic communities for substance abusers in American prisons. *Journal of Psychoactive Drugs,* 27, 57-66.

Wilens TE, Lineham CE (1995) ADD and substance abuse: An intoxicating combination. *ATTENTION!,* 3, 24-31.

ADD and Delinquency: Myths, Pathways, and Advice for Parents

Keith McBurnett, Ph.D.

Are children with ADD likely to become delinquent? Are there warning signs that parents can watch out for? What can be done about the young person with ADD who is beginning to get into trouble with the law? These and countless related questions are being asked by parents concerned about their children with ADD. Good information on criminal offending and ADD hasn't been easy to find. This article begins by dispelling some of the myths about ADD and delinquency, and continues with how children become delinquent, and what parents can do to lessen the risk.

Myth #1: Parents don't punish their children enough, and they don't spank enough. If they did, their children wouldn't become delinquent.

Fact: A fairly consistent research finding is that serious delinquents often have been punished harshly and severely by their parents for their misbehavior (Wilson & Hernstein, 1985).

Myth #2: Children who become delinquent don't get enough love and acceptance. If the rest of us learned to give them more love and encouragement, they wouldn't become delinquent.

Fact: Antisocial youth, through their own behavior, elicit negative reactions and rejection from parents, teachers, and peers. The best way to increase the positive regard and acceptance that they receive from others is to improve their behavior.

Myth #3: "Get tough" programs like Scared Straight and boot camps are the best way to reduce delinquency.

Fact: Scared Straight and boot camp programs are ineffective in reducing delinquency, and sometimes even make delinquents worse in the long run (Lipsey, 1992). The best treatment programs seem to be those that take an intensive, comprehensive, and individualized approach (e.g., Henggeler, Melton, & Smith, 1992). The best prevention approaches focus on reducing aggression and noncompliance in early childhood and include specialized parent training.

Myth #4: ADD is just an excuse used by delinquents who got caught.

Fact: ADD is a disorder that can be reliably diagnosed, and one which is clearly linked to academic and social impairment (Lahey et al., 1994). If a delinquent has ADD, it does not excuse the youth for his or her offenses. It indicates that an important consideration for preventing future offending is getting treatment for ADD.

Myth #5: Regardless of whether they truly have ADD, delinquents shouldn't be given medications like methylphenidate because they will only wind up abusing these drugs.

Fact: It's true that antisocial adolescents and adults are at increased risk of drug abuse. However, this does not constitute a reason to withhold a treatment that is effective in reducing inattention, impulsivity, aggression, and hyperactivity associated with ADD. If there is a risk of abuse, stimulant administration should be supervised, but not curtailed.

Myth #6: ADD leads to criminality.

Fact: ADD appears to increase the risk of delinquent behavior, but the fact is, most young people with ADD do not become career criminals. The greatest risk is faced by children who have both ADD and aggressive Conduct Disorder early in life (beginning by age ten).

DEVELOPMENTAL PATHWAYS: ROUTES TO DELINQUENCY

Long-range research is beginning to trace different paths that young people take into delinquent behavior (Loeber, 1991; Moffit, 1993; etc.). It turns out that the greatest number of youth who become delinquent do so in adolescence, without showing much in the way of warning signs during childhood. So many young people, females as well as males, dabble in delinquent lifestyles during adolescence, it is almost a normal stage. In fact, estimates of the percentage of teens who engage in delinquent behavior range as high as 50 to 87 percent. Delinquents who take this "adolescent onset" route tend to commit mostly covert offenses (stealing, shoplifting, forgery, drug experimentation, etc.) and status offenses (behaviors that would not be illegal if done by an adult, such as drinking, truancy, curfew violation, running away, etc.). These youth also tend to stop their delinquent behavior on their own, whether or not they are caught and punished, by the time of late adolescence or early adulthood. Some in this group have ADD without having had Conduct Disorder as children, but the majority do not have ADD.

In contrast, youth who have the greatest risk for chronic, long-term delinquent and criminal lifestyles are those who show clear warning signs as young children. Many, if not most, of the young people in this group have ADD as toddlers and develop Conduct Disorder before their tenth birthday (Moffit, 1990). Males in this group far outnumber females. A typical path of development is that of a young male preschooler with a difficult temperament — quite stubborn and oppositional — and who will test the limits of defying and disobeying his parents. In some situations, his oppositional behavior may be punished. Other times he will "wear down" his parents or otherwise succeed in resisting efforts to control him, and thus be rewarded for arguing or "tantrumming" (Patterson, Reid, & Dishion, 1992). Parents learn to avoid certain confrontations, yielding an inappropriate amount of control and power to the child. They learn to issue many repetitive commands without expecting that the child will comply, and they find themselves getting involved in long, unproductive arguments about rules, rights, and commands. They often feel very conflicted about the child, and they find it difficult to find positive things to say to the child when there is so much to criticize in the child's behavior.

As the child begins interacting with peers, he uses this same pattern of coercion and rapid escalation of temper to the point of physical fighting. In the short term, this behavior "wins" the battles, but it loses the war because other children start to avoid and reject the aggressive child. The result is lost opportunities to learn sharing, turn-taking, and other reciprocal "nice" behavior in peer groups. The child may feel isolated, lonely, resentful, and angry. Often, the only children who will play with the aggressive hyperactive child are other rejected, aggressive children. This clustering of antisocial children fosters the formation of an antisocial view of the world. On top of these problems, the child typically is not doing well in school. After experiencing conflict, failure, and rejection at home, in the classroom, at recess, and after school, the aggressive hyperactive child with low self-esteem may be desperate to find some way to feel important and successful. This is accomplished by winning the admiration of the other rejected peers and of the nonrejected peers who are starting to be fascinated with delinquent behavior by such means as acting out dares; recounting real or imaginary antisocial feats; acquiring forbidden objects (cigarettes, minor weapons, drug paraphernalia, pornography, etc.); and displaying symbols of gangs, rebellion, drug culture, the supernatural, etc. Aggressive hyperactive children find that antisocial behavior is something they can be good at — something in which they can be leaders. Within the deviant peer group, there is active teaching of antisocial values and skills, peer pressure to escalate antisocial behavior, social reinforcement (approval) for deviant acts, and disdain for following the rules. Continued participation in this lifestyle brings contact with more deviant and dangerous peers in middle school, and increases the versatility (repertoire of overt and covert antisocial behaviors) of the aggressive hyperactive child. Before long, other problems develop, including school dropout, contact with the juvenile justice system, and substance abuse. By the time young people who take this longer route into delinquency get arrested for a crime, their self-identity is built around antisocial values, and their means of obtaining things they want and resolving conflict are antisocial behaviors. These adolescents are notoriously resistant to change and are highly likely to continue offending. This group is thought to be no more than 5 to 8 percent of offenders, but this small percentage of offenders commits over 50 percent of reported crimes.

What can parents of children with ADD do to reduce the chances of delinquency? If your child has made it into adolescence without much fighting, stealing, cruelty, or destructiveness, be grateful. Even if he or she gets into trouble with the law as a teenager, the odds are good that he or she can be helped to avoid repeating those mistakes. If your child appears to have taken the "early starter" route, the outlook is more sobering, but there is hope. As difficult as it may be, I recommend that you do everything you can to support your child and discourage antisocial behavior, while at the same time looking out for your own well-being by not letting you or your family be victimized, and by developing the ability to emotionally detach yourself from your child if and when you need to. Some specific recommendations:

- Have clear rules about what's allowed and what's not allowed. One rule in your family should be "No Aggression," and this rule should apply to threats, feigned aggression, and "accidental" aggression, not just intentional physical aggression. Don't allow children to "weasel out" of trouble — consider a "bent" rule to be a broken rule, and don't listen to "lawyering." And don't be overly concerned about being fair — if your child didn't realize he would be punished for bending the rules, he'll know the next time.

- Enforce the rules with a method of mild punishment that you can deliver consistently and without anger when rules are broken, as often as needed — even if that's twenty times a day some days! For children, this usually can be a brief "Time Out." If "Time Out" doesn't work, consult a professional.

- Don't allow yourself to be dragged into arguments. Don't respond at all to protests, guilt trips, and manipulations (e. g., "Why do I have to do this?" "You don't love me," "I hate you," etc.).
- Know what your child is doing, and with whom. Do not allow your child to associate with peers who are getting into a lot of trouble. Be firm about this, no matter how old your child is. Establish and enforce what you think is a reasonable curfew. If you keep weapons, cigarettes, or alcohol at home, keep them out of your child's hands.
- If you suspect your child of stealing, lying, cheating, or using drugs, don't be afraid to confront him or her in a calm way, even if you don't have evidence. If these kinds of covert conduct problems are going on, increase your level of supervision and restriction of your child's activities to the point that you can be reasonably sure that your child can't engage in them. Then, require your child to earn back his or her freedom (and your trust) in small steps by demonstrating the ability to handle freedom responsibly.
- Work on self-esteem by helping your child find activities that he or she can enjoy and do at least as well as others. Find something to praise in your child's behavior at least once a day. Spend a few minutes of quality time alone with your child every day, doing whatever he or she wants to do (within reason, of course).
- Try to find ways that your child can acquire basic skills needed for success in academics and sports. An approach that is usually successful is repetitive drill and practice of the basics, if it can be done in a way that is fun and enjoyable (there are teachers, tutors, and coaches who know how to do this!).
- Get treatment for your child's ADD. This can include parent training, behavior modification in the classroom, and/or medication. Realize that treatment is something your child will need for

years. If your child is at risk for delinquency, try to find a professional with specialized expertise with problem behavior — someone who's known to be helpful in working with families who have difficult children.

- Get help, direction, and support from others. Talk to other parents, teachers, school administrators, police officers, etc. They can help you in ways you probably aren't aware of.

This article first appeared in the Winter 1996 ATTENTION!

Keith McBurnett, Ph.D. is with the Department of Psychiatry at the University of Chicago.

REFERENCES

Lahey, B.B., Applegate, B., McBurnett, K., Biederman, J., Greenhill, L., Hynd, G.W., Barkley, R.A., Newcorn, J., Jensen, P., Richters, J., Garfinkel, B., Kerdyk, L., Frick, P. J., Ollendick., T., Perez, D., Hart, E. L., Waldman, I., & Shaffer, D. (1994). DSM-IV Field Trials for Attention Deficit/Hyperactivity Disorder in children and adolescents. *American Journal of Psychiatry,* 151, 1673-85.

Loeber, R. (1991). Questions and advances in the study of developmental pathways. In D. Cicchetti & S. L. Toth, Eds., *Rochester Symposium on Developmental Psychopathology,* Vol. 3: Models and integrations (pp. 97-116). Rochester, NY: University of Rochester Press.

Moffitt, T.E. (1993). Adolescence-limited and life-course-persistent antisocial behavior: A developmental taxonomy. *Psychological Review,* 100, 674-701.

Moffitt, T.E. (1990). Juvenile delinquency and Attention Deficit Disorder: Boy's developmental trajectories from age 3 to age 15. *Child Development,* 61, 893-910.

Patterson, G.R., Reid, J.B., & Dishion, T.J. (1992). Antisocial boys. Eugene, OR: Castalia.

Wilson, J.Q., & Hernstein, R.J. (1985). *Crime and human nature.* New York: Simon & Schuster.

Research: A Discussion with Russell A. Barkley, Ph.D.,

the University of Massachusetts Medical Center

Here at the Medical Center, there are five avenues of research that we are pursuing at the moment — four of which are federally-funded initiatives and a fifth, for which we are not receiving funding.

The first and the longest running project is taking place in Milwaukee, Wisconsin, but is coordinated through the University of Massachusetts. This study has been going on for several years. Mariellen Fischer, of the Medical College of Wisconsin, and I have been following a large group of hyperactive children and a comparison group of children. We have been tracking these individuals since I first saw them, when they were between five and nine years of age. They are now in their mid-twenties. We recently finished bringing them back in for their young adult evaluation. We bring them back for evaluations roughly every five years.

Much of the information we have learned so far corroborates other follow-up studies, showing higher risks for educational problems, higher risks for conduct problems, and some delinquency. Difficulties with education, employment, and interpersonal functions are the three areas that seem to show widespread similarities with other findings. This study has also uncovered some additional risks that other studies really had not focused on.

One, for example, is in the area of medical risks, which I alluded to in my CH.A.D.D. presentation last year. This area explores the lifestyles that these individuals are leading — their lack of concern for health-related behavior, such as diet, exercise and so forth; and the fact that they are smoking and drinking more than our control group. These factors lead us to believe that they are placing themselves at greater risk for cardiovascular disease as they get into later life. Also, their general risk-taking behavior puts them at greater risk for accidents. We have established higher incidence of motor vehicle accidents, speeding, and other areas as being linked to this group.

A second area of the medical risk category that we studied is the rather heedless sexual conduct of our subjects that leads them to have more partners than our control group has had. Though the rates of intercourse are actually the same for the AD/HD group and the control group, those in the AD/HD group have more partners and have significantly more unprotected sexual relations. As a result, over half of the AD/HD group have had themselves tested for HIV. Fortunately, none of them have tested positive. About 25 to 30 percent of them, however, have already had a sexually-transmitted disease for which they have sought treatment.

Also indicating this rather high-risk sexual lifestyle is the fact that, out of forty-two births that occurred in the two groups, forty-one were born to the AD/HD group. While the control group is behaving like the general U.S. population and are waiting to have their children until their later twenties or even early thirties, individuals in the AD/HD group are conceiving children while they are still quite young — in their late teens to early twenties — which is about six years ahead of the control group. About 54 percent of the AD/HD group who have had children do not have custody of their children.

A second project we are involved in is studying the driving ability of young adults with AD/HD. We are using a variety of tactics to measure driving ability — reviewing driving records; interviewing the individuals regarding their driving history; obtaining rating scales on their safety and driving behavior from parents and others who have driven with them; and conducting computer-generated driving simulations. So far, we are corroborating our earlier findings, which were that the individuals with AD/HD are in a high-risk category. They speed more and pay attention and obey the laws less; they are more erratic in their steering and braking; and they are not able to operate the motor vehicle as consistently as individuals who do not have AD/HD. Generally, those with AD/HD are not very good drivers. It has nothing to do with knowledge — they know how to drive a car and they know the rules — they simply do not know how to apply these rules when they get out there. By conducting studies like this one, we may be able to identify these high-risk drivers early, get them help, and forewarn their families.

The third project is one that we have been working on for five years and will be concluding later this year. As part of an early intervention program, during the last four and a half years, we have been screening young preschool children who are entering the Worcester, Massachusetts public school system's kindergarten program, for behaviors that indicate a high-risk for AD/HD, aggressiveness, and/or opposition. Once we have identified those children who are at high-risk, they receive a full evaluation. Then they are assigned to one of several different kindergarten programs, one of which we have designed ourselves and operate here. These children receive a year's worth of treatment in one of the kindergarten programs — some of them get parent training, and some of them come to our kindergarten.

What that gives us is a comparison of children who get the standard kindergarten, children who get the standard kindergarten plus parent training, children who get our kindergarten program but no parent training, and a group of children who received both of our treatments. The program lasts for one year. Then we follow the children for two years after they leave the program to determine whether the program has reduced their educational and/or social risks. This process has not been completed, so the results are not yet available.

A fourth project we are involved with tests different family therapies for families with teenagers who have AD/HD in which there is a great deal of conflict. We are actually testing two different family programs: one is a program designed by Dr. Arthur Robin that focuses on problem-solving, communication skills, and changing belief systems; and the other combines Dr. Robin's program with behavior modification training for parents.

Finally, we are conducting some studies on my theory of AD/HD, particularly with regard to sense of time. To conduct these studies, we are using some very simple tests of time estimation and time production. What we are finding so far is that individuals with AD/HD overestimate the time interval and under-produce it, which tells us that they are perceiving time as moving more slowly than it really does. There are at least two predictions that can be made as a result of these findings. The first is that individuals with AD/HD are always going to be late. For example, if a teacher gives a child twenty minutes to finish his assignment in class, he won't finish it on time because to him, twenty minutes is moving more slowly than it actually is — he thinks he has more time than he does. Therefore, not being punctual, not meeting deadlines, and that sort of thing all would be predicted for someone whose sense of time is not parallel to real time.

The second prediction is that individuals with AD/HD will get very impatient if they are asked to wait because they will sense that the waiting period lasts longer than it actually does. It can be expected, then, that adults with AD/HD may run red lights and drive on the shoulder of the road to get around a delay in traffic and children with AD/HD may elbow their way to the front of the lunch line and yammer at their teacher, "I'm hungry — let's get out of here," in an effort to terminate the waiting interval.

I believe the field of ADD research is moving toward several areas. The first of those areas is neuro-imaging and other studies of brain function. As the technology has leap-frogged ahead here to allow us to look at the brain and brain function, I think that we are going to start seeing more studies like Dr. Judy Rapoport's brain imaging study and studies that not only show us the structure of the brain in very fine-grained detail, but also the function of the brain, much like Dr. Alan Zametkin's early studies have done. I believe we will see more sophisticated measures, such as this new functional MRI procedure, which is as good or better than PET scans and does not carry some of the risks that the PET does. I think these will help us to more clearly document the neuro-behavioral nature of AD/HD.

The second area is behavioral genetics. We have seen, just in the last year, three separate reports of possible genes linked to AD/HD. I see this doing several things. The first is that it would certainly allow us to quickly develop a genetic test for the disorder. That would help for diagnostic purposes. We would no longer just be relying on behavior, but would actually have a genetic marker that would help us. Secondly, it may also help us break down the disorder into more homogeneous subgroups; right now, we treat AD/HD as one large group. Third, I think, if we can identify the gene or the genes, we can learn what those genes do in the brain. If we could determine what gene is involved with AD/HD, we could actually develop medications that would very explicitly target that function in the nerve cells. We also will be able to learn much more about which combinations of treatments do and do not benefit individuals with AD/HD. It will be nice to know which of these treatments are really worthwhile, and which are not.

Finally, research has led to the development of several theories on AD/HD. It is encouraging to see this development as it marks a sign of scientific progress. A mature science is a theory-driven science.

This article first appeared in the Summer 1996 ATTENTION!

Russell Barkley, Ph.D. is Director of Psychology and Professor of Psychiatry and Neurology at the University of Massachusetts Medical Center. He is a clinical practitioner, scientist, and educator who has authored four books and co-edited two others. He has also created four professional videotapes on AD/HD, two of which won the 1992 Golden Apple Award for educational videos.

The Search

by Karenne Bloomgarden

For practically all of my life I searched: I searched for the reasons why I felt so different from everyone; why I couldn't seem to fit in anywhere; what was wrong with me. Unfortunately, during my search I often chose the wrong places and relied upon the wrong people. I just wanted to find acceptance, understanding, and love, but the roads I chose to travel always seemed to lead me to dead ends. It wasn't until just five years ago, after a lifetime spent following the wrong path and making many poor choices, that I finally found the answer I had been desperately looking for, and my life has never been the same.

Even as a little girl I knew I was different from other children. I can remember sitting in class — fidgeting, squirming, my mind racing to a million places — while my classmates listened carefully as the teacher gave the class directions for assignments. By the time the teacher was through, I was either out of my seat or on a totally different subject. I just could not pay attention, and I certainly couldn't focus on my teacher's words long enough to follow directions. As a result, my grades were very poor. I did succeed, however, in being extremely loud and rambunctious. I was constantly clowning around and trying to make people laugh. Since I didn't have many friends, I suppose humor was just about the only thing that connected me to my peers. Unfortunately, my teachers and family members didn't usually find my antics so funny, as was evidenced in their insistent pleas for me to "Quiet down!", "Stop that!", "Pay attention!", and "Try harder!".

I'm sure my parents were looking for an answer of their own during this time — namely, a way to calm me down! They tried a variety of tactics, none of which worked. At one point, they thought ballet and piano lessons were the answer, believing that if I had something to take pride in, I might become better disciplined. Of course, that was merely wishful thinking on their part. I hated both and didn't take either seriously. In fact, all I did during class was joke around. The only thing I did enjoy doing was watching television, which I did as much as I possibly could. Because my grades were so poor, however, my parents thought limiting my TV time was appropriate. It was a pretty miserable time for me.

As I got older, the problems only worsened. During my teenage years, I felt even more alone and rejected. My grades were still bad and I was still acting out. Only now, my quest for acceptance and love led me to do everything in excess. One of the first areas my excessive behavior manifested itself in was my eating habits. I went through a period where I was constantly sneaking food into my room so that no one would know how much I was eating. Because I was eating so much, though, my problem eventually became impossible to hide, as I had gained noticeable weight.

During this stage of my life, I felt that the only attention I received from my parents was negative, so "negative" behavior became my primary focus. I started chasing boys, hanging out with the wrong crowd, experimenting with drugs, and acting out sexually. The people I was with were older than I was and thought drugs were "cool," so taking drugs made me feel accepted, and acceptance was something I had lacked until that time. Throughout my teen years I screamed for help and reached out in any way I knew how to find love and attention. On several occasions, my pursuit even led me to attempt suicide. I enjoyed staying in the hospital because of all the attention I received — it made me feel cared for, at least for a while — but it certainly never provided me with any answers for why I was feeling and behaving the way I was.

Despite my poor grades throughout school, I was able to make it into college. I suppose by this point I had learned how to manipulate the system. I had become such a crafty manipulator, in fact, that I was able to cheat in school on a regular basis without getting caught. While my grades remained poor overall, my peers and superiors constantly told me how intelligent I was. Because I was so determined to please people, I had somehow managed to give teachers and administrators the answers they wanted, but I was never able to retain the information I needed.

During college, my search continued to lead me down the wrong path — I was still hanging out with the wrong crowd and seeking attention from men the only way I knew how. I also continued to use drugs as a tool for acceptance. While I was not addicted, I had begun to use more powerful drugs by this time. Even though I had "friends" and "boyfriends," I couldn't have felt more alone, more dejected, more misunderstood. I was so busy trying to please others so they would like and accept me that I never took the time to figure out what it was that I needed. My behavior and attitude were not doing anything but fueling my insecurities and lack of self-esteem.

For years following college, I continued to blame myself for everything that went wrong in my life — and guilt becomes more and more difficult to carry around after decades of not confronting it — so my self-esteem continued to be low. On some level, I knew that I truly couldn't control my impulsive behavior as hard as I had tried, but a large part of me could not stop blaming myself for my problems. What stuck in my mind was all of the hurtful things people said about me, all the crazy stunts I had pulled to get attention, and all of the times I just wanted to die because it seemed I would never get better. The guilt continued to pile on.

Throughout all of the difficulties, there was one bright spot in my life: children. For some reason, I'd always been loved and accepted by children, and I felt safe enough with them to give them my unconditional love. One of the best choices I made in my life was to become a physical education teacher. I began working with children and spending my summers directing children's camps. My energy was finally getting channeled into something positive and I was enjoying every minute of the time I spent with "my kids." I was finally a success at something in my life. At last, I had found what I had been searching for — or so I thought.

Although I had carved a niche for myself and found a career that was suitable for me and that I was good at, I had never identified the reasons for my destructive behavior. As a result, it continued. Through my involvement with the summer camp industry, I became executive director of the American Camping Association in New York. As an executive, I had a 9-5 office job — this was the first time I had no direct interaction with children. Extremely unhappy shuffling papers and working with many bosses, I once again started down that same, dark road that I had traveled so many times before. The road led me deeper into drug use, only this time, I became addicted. I was no longer in control and it was becoming apparent to others. If it weren't for Morry Stein, a dear friend who convinced me that I needed help, I never would have survived. Thankfully, I did get help (I've been sober ever since), but I still hadn't uncovered the reason for my impulsive, often destructive, behavior.

Then, after nearly forty years of searching, I finally found that answer I had been looking for. As I impatiently awaited my turn to speak to a CH.A.D.D. meeting in New York on the subject, "How to prepare your child and select a summer camp," a man named Dr. A. Wachtel addressed the audience. I, of course, was listening to the traffic outside, thinking about what I had to do, and constantly looking at my watch, wondering when I would be able to speak. Then, Dr. Wachtel said something that grabbed my attention. My attention! He was telling a story about a teenage boy with AD/HD. He described the boy's symptoms and behavior. Then it all started to click. Maybe my excessive behavior hadn't been caused by me — as I had always assumed — after all. Maybe there really was a legitimate reason for my inability to control my inattention, hyperactivity, and impulsive behavior. It all began to make sense — I had all the symptoms Dr. Wachtel described.

I was, indeed, diagnosed with AD/HD and now take medication to control my impulsivity and hyperactivity. Thanks to Dr. Wachtel and CH.A.D.D., my search was finally complete and the answers became known. Understanding what having AD/HD has meant in my life and learning how to effectively deal with the symptoms has made a dramatic difference in my life. Today, I am a special education and physical education teacher, a teacher trainer, and a successful entrepreneur. I teach children ages four to thirteen-years-old who have various neurological and/or physical disabilities. Having AD/HD, myself, allows me to communicate better with my students and be a much more effective teacher. In addition, I founded my own camp referral service, KB Camp Service, and am now in my twelfth successful year in business. I've actually become an expert of sorts on children's camps and have appeared on national television programs and in publications. I have to admit, I do still enjoy the attention, but at least now, it comes from a positive source.

Indeed my search was filled with many obstacles and many trials, and although my life is not perfect today, I am no longer following that destructive path that I once thought would provide me with acceptance. I know that there's only one person that I should seek acceptance from, and that's me. Understanding that AD/HD has had an impact on many of the decisions I've made in my life and learning to manage my behavior, I've been able to accept myself for who I am. I used to say that I had to slow down so people could catch up — now I go at my own speed and try to surround myself with people who move at my pace. The energy I have as a result of my AD/HD has helped me to achieve success; recognition and effective management of my AD/HD has helped me to maintain it.

This article first appeared in the Spring 1996 ATTENTION!

CH.A.D.D. Membership Form

✓ *Yes, I want to succeed with CH.A.D.D.*

Please provide the following contact information:

Name _____

Organization (if organizational membership) _____

Occupation _____

Address _____

City _____ State _____ Zip _____

Telephone (daytime) _____/_____ Telephone (evening) _____/_____

FAX number _____/_____ Chapter Affiliation _____

Is this a new membership or a renewal? ❐ **NEW MEMBER** ❐ **RENEWAL**

Please indicate type of membership: ❐ **REGULAR** (SPECIFY BELOW)

    ❐ $35 Family or Educator
    ❐ $65 Health Care Professional
    ❐ $100 Individual International Membership
       (outside of the U.S. and Canada)

❐ **ORGANIZATIONAL** (SPECIFY BELOW)

    ❐ $200 Organizational Membership
    ❐ $400 International Organizational Membership
       (outside of the U.S. and Canada)

PAYMENT (SPECIFY BELOW)
❐ Check Enclosed   ❐ VISA
                  ❐ MasterCard
                  ❐ American Express

Name on card _____

Card # _____

Expiration Date _____

Signature _____

Detach & mail or FAX *to:*

**CHILDREN AND ADULTS WITH
ATTENTION DEFICIT DISORDERS
499 N.W. 70TH AVENUE
SUITE 101
PLANTATION, FL 33317
FAX # 954.587.4599**

Or join by e-mail:
http://www.chadd.org/

*For further information,
contact CH.A.D.D. at
954.587.3700.*

Shipping and handling included in all membership fees; all funds submitted must be in U.S. dollars.

ADD *and Adolescence:*
Strategies for Success from CH.A.D.D.

✓ *Please process the following order:*

Please provide complete shipping and payment information:

Name _____

Mailing Address _____

City _____ State _____ Zip _____

Telephone _____/_____ FAX number _____/_____

CHECK ALL THAT APPLY:

❏ Parent of child with ADD   ❏ Educator   ❏ Health Care Professional   ❏ Other

---

$15.00 PER BOOK + $2.75 SHIPPING AND HANDLING
BULK PRICING: $260.00 (CASE OF 20) + $15.00 SHIPPING AND HANDLING

PLEASE SEND THE FOLLOWING:

_____ Copies @ $17^{75} ea.
         (includes shipping) $_____.___

_____ Cases @ $275^{00} case
         (includes shipping) $_____.___

Florida residents
add 6% sales tax $_____.___

TOTAL $ _____.___

PAYMENT (SPECIFY BELOW)

❏ Check Enclosed   ❏ VISA
                           ❏ MasterCard
                           ❏ American Express

Name on card _____

Card # _____

Expiration Date _____

Signature _____

All funds must be in U.S. dollars.

Please return this form with your remittance to:

CHILDREN AND ADULTS WITH ATTENTION DEFICIT DISORDERS
499 N.W. 70TH AVENUE, SUITE 101, PLANTATION, FL 33317

phone 954.587.3700   •   fax 954.587.4599